Dalit Society and the Challenge of Development

Dalit Society and the Challenge of Development

Om Prakash Sangwan

Commonwealth

Dalit Society and the Challenge of Development

Edition : 2020

ISBN 81-7169-368-7

Published by :-
COMMONWEALTH PUBLISHERS (P) LTD.
4831/24, Govind Lane,
Ansari Road, Darya Ganj,
New Delhi - 110002
Ph. : 23272541, 23242541
e-mail : commonwealthpublishers2016@gmail.com

Distributed by :
ARJUN PUBLISHING HOUSE
4831/24, Govind Lane,
Ansari Road, Darya Ganj,
New Delhi - 110002
Ph. : 23272541, 23242541
e-mail : arjunbooks2001@gmail.com

Laser Typesetting by :
Dimple Computers
Delhi

Printed at :
Milan Enterprises
Delhi

Preface

The Supreme Court of India, in its famous judgement upholding the implementation of the Mandal Commission Report, had laid down the following principles in respect of reservations: Reservation for socially and educationally backward classes other than Scheduled Castes and Scheduled Tribes is constitutionally valid; reservation should not cross the maximum limit of 50 per cent, except in those areas where an extraordinary situation prevails; the creamy layer among the Other Backward Classes (OBCs) should be excluded from the reservation pool, and it implicitly recognised the principle of dereservation of those castes that cross the threshold of backwardness. The moot question is: What is backwardness?

Recent years have seen a great upsurge of Dalit sentiment and determination in India. The upsurge is interpreted as an awakening and is as such welcome in a country where more than 70 per cent of the population lives in the rural, including backward, areas, and also where over 60 per cent of the population lives on or below the poverty line. The collective consciousness of the Scheduled Castes, Scheduled Tribes and Other Backward Classes represents the consciousness of the larger part of India. However, the political implications are diverse and the political diversity of India is tied up inextricably with its social and regional realities. As with other movements, the Dalits constitute a vocal and decisive segment of the population of the country. They are a force to be reckoned with.

The following collection of articles, papers, excerpts and documentary notes has been put together with the intention of providing the social scientist, scholar and researcher basic structured material which will constitute valuable reading as supplementary text in the related courses of study and research. It covers the social structure including the dynamics of the caste system, the evolution of the system, the law and its interpretations, the present status and the hopes and aspirations of the dalit communities in terms of social and economic betterment.

EDITOR

Contents

PREFACE v

1. Social Structure and the Evolution of Classes 1
2. Dalits: Past and Present Constitutional Reality 23
3. Depressed Classes: A Socio-Economic Profile 61
4. Dalit in the Modern World: Search for Identity 75
5. Constitution and Politics of Reservations 100
6. Bonded Labour in India 127
7. Educational Development Among Scheduled Castes 149
8. Scheduled Tribes: Educational Perspective 191
9. Dalit Struggle for Liberation: A Prospective 224
10. Dalit Self-Reliance: Two Studies 251
11. Awakening Dalit Tribals 290

APPENDIX I: Eight Plan Approach to Welfare and Development of SCs and STs 321

1

Social Structure and the Evolution of Classes

Introduction

The origin of Varna and Jati is usually associated with the advent of Aryans on the Indian soil. There is no research finding that they existed prior to that or within the Dravidian society. This probably explains antagonism to Brahminism as representing conquering Aryans and the claim of some groups to the designation of Adi-Dravidas in Tamil Nadu.

As social institutions, Varna and jati have undergone changes but have shown the rarest of resilience to survive. They have survived the major political upheavals, invasions by Alexander, Genghiz Khan, Timur, Ghazanavi and Nadir Shah. They have withstood the onslaught of anticaste religions—Buddhism, Jainism, Christianity, Islam and Sikhism. Neither the Upanishadic metaphysics nor the Advaita Bhakti Philosophy preached by saints all over India had any serious impact on them. The reformist movement of the 19th century, such as Brahmo Samaj, Arya Samaj or Prarthana Samaj have not made any appreciable dent on them.

Western ideas of liberal democracy and equality or the principles of social justice (of socialist creed) could hardly push them into background. Mahatma Gandhi's message of love, tolerance and conversion of heart has hardly motivated anybody to come out of caste barriers. Conversions to Christianity or Islam and even conversion of Dr. B.R. Ambedkar (and his followers) to Buddhism, did not make the caste system irrelevant. It only created a new caste—neo-Buddhists.

Prohibition of discrimination on the ground of caste imposed by Articles 14, 15 and 16 of the Constitution and its enforcement for the last 30 years has hardly led to the establishment of a casteless society or to any significant step in that direction. In spite of abolition of untouchability by Article 17, the dragon is still at large. In fact, atrocities on the Harijans are on the increase.

Except for family (which is a natural institution), no other institution known to human civilization has shown such a strong instinct to survive and dominate. The Caste system, in true sense of the term, is sui generis.

Ancient Hindu society, ordered on the model of Manu's dictum showed complete subservience of law to the caste system. Law not only helped to maintain the status quo of the caste divisions but contributed to their further creation, consolidation and efficacy.

Constitutional Implications

The Constitution, on the other hand, aims at establishment of a more equal and just social order. The Constitution has established (at least theoretically) the supremacy of law. It is itself a fundamental law. The social order is what the organic law preserves. It prohibits continuation of certain institutions and practices, which are contrary to establishment of a just and equitable social order. All agencies of State, including courts, are to translate the basic plan of the Constitution in concrete measures. There are long-term measures and short—term actions. The notorious tenacity of caste-system (in dominating the social life) has rendered the problems of social engineering too tardy and difficult.

How to reconcile organised caste claims for political domination with the long-term goal of a casteless society? How to achieve equality when the ringing cry is for equalisation? How to break narrow caste considerations in personal matters such as marriages? What is the formula for making public, opportunities for education and for public service available to those, who were denied the same for ages? But a more fundamental question is how to resolve these controversies peacefully within the framework of law and by known legal methods of resolving disputes? How to stop extra-constitutional and extra-legal eruptions into caste riots and atrocities? They threaten the very existence of a constitutional and legal order.

These problems are socio-legal problems. We may, therefore, note how the sociologists analyse them.

"Varnas" and Castes

The main features of varna are:

1. There are only four varnas—Brahmin, Kshatriya Vaish and Sudra. If Harijans who are literally beyond the "pale of caste", are included, they are five;
2. There is a single all-India hierarchy, without any variation between one region and another;
3. The hierarchy is clear; and
4. It is immutable. This hierarchical pattern is a hall mark of caste system also.

According to one theory, the various castes are created by marriages between two varnas of different hierarchical order. Whatever its original theory, castes are hereditary, that is, by birth. They are endogamous groups. That is, the marriages take place in the same castes. Each of these groups has a traditional association with one or two occupations. Everywhere there are priests, peasants, artisans, trading and serving castes and untouchables. In its fundamental characteristics, caste is undoubtedly an all-India phenomenon. The origin of varna and, therefore, of castes is traced to the sacred religious books like the Vedas and the Gita. Certain Hindu theological ideas, such as samsara, karma and dharma are woven into the caste system.

According to the varna model, the Harijans or untouchables are outside the caste system and contact with Harijans pollutes members of the other four varnas. But if economic, social and even ritual relations between the castes of a region are taken into account, Harijans are an integral part of the caste system. They perform certain essential economic tasks in agriculture; they are often village servants, messengers and sweepers; and they beat the drum at village festivals and remove the leaves on which people have dined at community dinners. In fact, the relations between various castes are invariably expressed in terms of this idea of pollution and purity (M.N. Srinivas, Social Change in Modern India).

Untouchability

The phenomenon of untouchability in India underwent a long and gradual process. Its emergence is an obscure area in the sense that not much work has been done on it to date. Compared to that, there are more studies on the contemporary situation of the untouchables, and measures adopted for their betterment are all based on these studies. But upliftment of the untouchables or measures to induct them into the mainstream of Indian life will not be effective unless the reasons for the emergence of untouchability in society are ascertained definitely. The urgency of the situation may be better realized if it is put in figures. The Scheduled Castes comprise at present more than twenty million people who constitute nearly ninety per cent of the 200 millions living below the subsistence level (Statesman, 7 December 1976, Calcutta, p. 12). Not all of the

Scheduled Castes are untouchables. The untouchables are estimated to comprise one-sixth of India's total population of 68,38,10,000.

Obviously, this number was not so staggering before. But, in spite of their relatively small number at the beginning, the reason for their being untouchables did not go unnoticed. It is, therefore, incorrect to assume that until very recently there has never been any criticism about untouchability or of the varna system for that matter. Looking back, one could almost assert that, from about the time when society was divided into four varnas, questions had been raised not so much about the justification of ordering the society into such segments as to their subsequent immutability. Admittedly, the critical attitude toward this division in society often assumed the form of religious movements which questioned the Brahmanical supremacy and preached equality of all men before God.

Thus, not only the ideological content of these movements should be analysed but their human component also, *i.e.* the varnas involved in them, should be examined. Otherwise, the character and the real purpose of the movement may not be ascertained. But the two aspects of the problem in content and form, ideological and human, become difficult to ascertain, because almost all treatises reflect the viewpoints of their Brahmanical authors who occupied a dominant position in society both intellectually and otherwise. Nevertheless, from fragmentary evidences, often inadequate and indirect, it is not altogether impossible to present an account of the origin and development of untouchability in India. From the description of different aspects of life of peoples and of society it is seen that there were social groups besides the four varnas, and that their social position underwent changes over time. The alignment kept on shifting all the time. Ultimately, some from these groups were reduced to the category of the untouchables.

Untouchability occupies the extreme and the lowest position in the hierarchical division of Hindu society. From early times the peoples were not unaware of the injustice done to the untouchables. It is true that dissent seldom assumed the character of direct protest against the varna system, probably because that was too strong an institution to go against. Moreover, the varna division was sacrosanct and was strengthened by the Vedas, which imparted sanctity to the mythical origin of the four varnas. Proceeding therefrom, other groups not only explained their emergence but also their respective location in social hierarchy in relation to these four varnas. Carvaka, an early materialist philosopher, had the temerity to question the very basis of this elaborate superstructure and openly defy the authority of the Vedas. Supposedly, Brihaspati stated: 'The three authors of the Vedas were buffoons, knaves and demons' (SDS. 1961: 10). Other religious sects like those of the Jainas, Ajivakas and Buddhists, did not accept the Brahmanical orthodoxy, and recognized the rights of the Sudras and slaves, among whom there were presumably untouchables too. Tradition has it that the Buddha took a robe from a Pukkusa Mallaputta (Dutt 1971: 131), and that his last meal of pork or truffles was taken from a cunda, supposedly a blacksmith (or candala?); the candalas and pigs were generally associated with each other. The Buddha died of food poisoning thereafter (Rhys Davids 1932: 260, n. 1).

However, none of these religious sects or reform movements, which appeared intermittently and continued up to the early part of the twentieth century and later came to be known as bhakti movements, openly condemned the caste system. The views of their leaders found expression mainly through a humanitarian standpoint. They treated the Brahmanas and the untouchables alike insofar as their religious rights were concerned. The earlier movements, like the one led by the Buddha especially, seriously questioned the hereditary supremacy of the Brahmanas. According to the Jain and Buddhist doctrines, specific virtues and not birth made one a Brahmana.

Significantly, some of the leaders of the bhakti movements like Ravi Das, Kabir, etc. themselves came from the untouchable castes. But even they did not openly violate the caste rules or oppose the system. Ultimately, the followers of these religious leaders ended up by forming new castes of their own (Briggs 1920: 206, 210 and c.) while remaining at the same time within the broad category of the untouchables. Therefore. the untouchables and similar social groups did not cease to exist in India. On the contrary, their ranks swelled numerically as time went on, when job specialization led to further fragmentation, each new group forming a new caste.

The problem of the untouchables, however, became a national concern when in recent times a political dimension was added to it. In order to examine untouchability, we have to look back in history. As mentioned earlier, the untouchables belonged to the lowest rung in the varna hierarchy, and they were always there. From time to time in history we come across one or other of these groups, in one context or another. One such group was that of the forest-dwellers (*i.e.*, the atavikas) who received King Asoka's attention. But other groups beyond the varna social structure did not require a political intervention, at least we do not have evidence of that. Instead, from about the later part of the eighteenth century we notice that the problem of some of these people had become acute enough to require prompt action on the part of the British Administration.[1]

One should, therefore, start with the emergence of the Scheduled Castes and Tribes a broad category under which the untouchables are also included. We find the issue of the Scheduled Castes and Tribes becoming a live problem along with:

1. The gradual deterioration of the tribes and 'low' castes resulting in intermittent rebellions and calling for measures adopted by the British Administration;
2. The opinions and demands of the Scheduled Castes and Tribes as spelled out by their leader and spokesman Dr. B.R. Ambedbar; and
3. The attitude and standpoint of the Indian National Congress as voiced by Mr. M.K. Gandhi.

A spurt of rebellions broke out, in which the armed uprisings of the Mundas in 1789, 1797, 1812, 1819-20 and the Santal Rebellion of 1855 (Ghurye 1963: 46, 40) were of more serious nature than others. Apparently, gradual encroachment on their land and their increasing dependence on moneylenders drove them to desperation and sparked off the conflicts. Since the tribes lost their lands mostly to the Hindus who were also moneylenders, the relation between the tribes and Hindus was neither friendly nor happy (*ibid.*, 25, 45).

In order to 'protect' the tribes and their interests, separate tracts of land were created for them under the Scheduled Districts Act of 1874. The Santals were settled in one part of the Santal Parganas; and under Section 52-A (2) of the Government of India Act of 1919, any other territory could be declared as a 'backward tract' (*ibid.*, 39, 91). The culmination of all the struggles, manoeuvres and bargaining gave birth to the Government of India (Scheduled Castes) Order of 1936, First Schedule to the Government of India Act of 1935.

Along with the measures taken by the British Government by categorizing the Scheduled Castes and Tribes, the problem of the untouchables drew the attention of the nationalist leaders like Ambedkar and Gandhi. Gandhi could sense the growing animosity between the caste Hindus and those listed under the Scheduled Castes and Tribes, but it did not assume a serious dimension until the policy of 'Protective Discrimination' in the form of separate electorate was proposed by the government. Thereafter, it formed an essential part of the national question, and Gandhi and Ambedkar took up their cause in right earnest. In the course of time, the question of untouchables and untouchability, and of similar other groups, took the form of 'caste struggle' as Ambedkar put it.

Both Gandhi and Ambedkar made attempts to understand and explain the phenomenon of untouchability in society. Its evil effects on Indian life did not escape their attention, and they viewed the phenomenon with growing concern. They completely agreed that the practice of untouchability should not be allowed to continue, and that the untouchables should have their rightful place in Indian society. While Gandhi held the firm view that the untouchables were Hindus, Ambedkar maintained an ambivalent attitude. This difference in attitude not only explains their respective approach toward untouchability and the methods suggested for its eradication but also Ambedkar's later acceptance of neo-Buddhism as a way out. To Gandhi the problem of the untouchables was one of the many evils the Hindu society was beset with; with Ambedkar it was virtually the only concern. Probably because of this difference in their approach. Ambedkar took his stand on historical facts and made exhaustive studies on the untouchables, while Gandhi was concerned with the contemporary situation and, primarily, with the removal of untouchability from Hindu society. Ambedkar, himself an untouchable, viewed the problem as an insider, so to speak. He took up the cause of his own caste(s), and was out to prove that there was nothing inherently evil or impure concerning the untouchables. Gandhi, on the other hand, was a caste Hindu (a Vaisya), and by his own admission 'miscalled superior class or caste Hindu' (Sitaramayya 1946: I, 548). He assessed the problem from above and as an outsider, so to speak. To him the issue of untouchability was mainly a question of 'bettering' the lot of the downtrodden people placed in the lowest rung of social hierarchy. The respective caste ideology of Gandhi and Ambedkar may have influenced their outlook on the question of untouchability and its eventual removal from society.

Ambedkar made attempts to find out how untouchability emerged in India and also to examine some of the current theories in this context. His contention was that there was no agreed opinion on the definition of untouchability or precise reason(s) for its emergence; nor was there an expressed condemnation of untouchability till about the fourth century A.D. Ambedkar concluded that it was based purely on political and religious grounds.

As to who were the untouchables, Ambedkar started with the specific term antyavasayin, because this term happened to be connected quite often with the untouchables alone. The literal meaning of this term is one living at the end, outside or beyond (the boundary wall of a village/town/human settlement). His argument was that it was not true that the untouchables had once lived within the village before they became untouchable (Ambedkar 1969: 33-34; 42-43). Because nothing about their expulsion from the village had ever been mentioned any where, nor was it feasible to evict fercibly such a vast community and settle it outside the village boundary (see also Sharma 1980: 144).

What happened, in his opinion, was that the bulk of these people were from the conquered tribes who, when separated from their own tribes, were at a loose end and occupied a place outside the village boundary. Ambedkar called them 'Broken Men'. They comprised a band of so-called 'watch and ward' people who, in return of their services rendered to the village, received food and shelter from the villagers. In support of this hypothesis, he cited the case of untouchables in Maharashtra who even today demand their right to maintenance from the 'touchable' Hindu villagers, as it is one of fifty-two rights granted to them apparently by the Muslim kings (Ambedkar 1969, 43-44).

The rank of the outskirt-dwellers further swelled, Ambedkar continues, with the Buddhists joining them. When Brahmanism regained its lost ground and Buddhism was on the decline, the Brahmanas became powerful again. As a retaliatory measure, the Buddhists were treated with contempt and were allowed to live on sufference. But not all of them were reduced to this plight. Men from every walk of life embraced Buddhism, and those belonging to higher castes and/or having wealth remained unaffected. But others, probably those without any means of influence, were forced by the Brahmanas to live outside the village. Still, none of them was untouchable yet (*ibid.*, 97-99).

Now, Ambedkar comes to the crucial point, *i.e.*, the reason(s) for untouchability. In this context, he first discusses some of the current hypotheses about untouchables and points out their fallacies. Reasons offered for the rise of untouchability are mainly two: racial and occupational. Ambedkar discounted the racial theory with the help of physical anthropology, and proved that so far as physical characteristics were concerned with there was hardly any difference between the Brahmanas and untouchables belonging to the same region (*ibid.*, 76-80). Next, he examined the occupational aspect of untouchability because of the oft-repeated purity-pollution theory held by many, and concluded, by quoting from the Narada Smrti, that even when household slaves were engaged in sweeping the road, gateway, privy, etc. they were not treated as untouchables (*ibid.*, 83-84.).

According to him, religion played an important part in this respect. From about the fourth century A.D. Brahmanical orthodoxy took a firm stand on the society, and killing of cows became a punishable offence. Before that, at the time of Asoka or in the lawbook of Manu, killing of cows was not a serious offence but a minor one (upapataka in the M.S.). Gradually, however, excessive veneration for cows and cow-worship was advocated, possibly, as a reaction to Buddhism, and the Brahmanas, therefore, promulgated the law against cow slaughter. It was no half-way measure. From killing of cows the Brahmanas went a step further; they went against eating beef, although they ate it previously (*ibid.*, 114-22). Cows were now held sacred, and beef-eating was considered profane. Consequently, those who did eat beef came to be regarded with scorn in society (*ibid.*, 146-47). Ambedkar thinks that hatred for Buddhism coupled with contempt for beef-eating were the main reasons for making these people untouchables.

One may raise the question: 'why did not the untouchables accept the ban on cow slaughter or stop eating beef for that matter?' The point to note in this context is that, over time, the untouchable castes have tried to emulate caste Hindu manners and customs, thinking—erroneously though—that such imitation will raise their social status. In the opinion of Ambedkar, since the untouchables did not kill the cows themselves for eating their flesh but ate only dead cows' meat (possibly killed by others or those dying a natural death), the ban was not applicable to them (*ibid.*, 162-63).

Gandhi did not treat the topic of the origin of untouchability so elaborately as Ambedkar did, and, therefore, not so coherent an account is found in his writings. Yet, from the twenties onward, he often discussed the subject in public meetings, and wrote articles in papers from which one can form an idea of how he considered the problem. To him it was terrifying reality 'imposed by custom' (emphasis added), and he agreed that the untouchables led an animal-like existence (Gandhi 1339; 29, 58, 107, 19). It was, indeed, a shame that downtrodden people (*i.e.*, the untouchables) had to live outside a village or a town (*ibid.*, 19).

Personally, he looked at the issue principally from moral and religious angles—predominantly a religious one (Sitaramayya 1946: I. 540). Untouchability, according to him, was the greatest stigma on Hinduism but was never a part of it. Nevertheless, Hinduism committed a sin by supporting it (*ibid.*, 29, 32). Therefore, with the removal of untouchability Hinduism will be free from that blemish (*ibid.*, 65). In his own words: 'In attacking untouchability I have gone to the very root of the matter, and therefore, it is an issue of transcendental value' (Sitaramayya 1946: I. 552).

Since untouchability was linked up with the varna and the jati divisions of Indian society. Gandhi frequently expressed his views on it. According to him, the varna division, as and when created by god, was justified but not in its present form (*ibid.*, 1, 89, 101), and the jati division should be abolished (*ibid.*, 82).[2] Since the varna system was a divine institution, hereditary occupation should be followed by all (*ibid.*, 79). There should be no grading of 'high' or 'low' status in occupations or any ill-feeling among people following different occupations. Every occupation was important, however 'noble' or 'lowly' it may be, and its followers should be respected by all. Untouchability arose out of aberration of the varna dharma, for all men were born equal (*ibid.*, 104, 89, 75).

Gandhi expressed his sentiments by agreeing to call the untouchables 'Harijan', the people or children of the Hindu God Hari.[3] The main responsibility for removing untouchability, according to him, lay with the caste Hindus. It was their duty to serve and help the untouchables through personal contacts. This should be done with love and with a spirit of self-dedication (to the cause of the untouchables), justice and righteousness (*ibid*,, 58-59; Sitaramaryya 1946: I. 52, 226, 332). There should not be any discrimination against the untouchables. Temples, schools, colleges and jobs must be open to them (Gandhi 1339: 43, 75).

Addressing the untouchables, Gandhi asked them to observe cleanliness in order to counteract the argument that they lived in squalor and filth, to abstain from drinking alcohol and not to eat left-over food from others' plates (*ibid.*, 34-35). For the improvement of their lot, they should not seek redress from the government. If they did, that would spell a greater disaster for them. Change of their religion or resort to violence would also not solve their problem (*ibid.*, 47-48). Here one would point out that the 'untouchables' had been trying from very early times to free themselves from upper-caste domination by becoming Jainas. Buddhists, Muslims, Christians, and recently, neo-Buddhists, but with very little effect. Gandhi suggested that, instead of seeking redress through change of religion, they should be self-reliant and independent as self-purification alone would help them (*ibid.*, 44). They should be tolerant and patiently wait for the Hindus to change their own heart (*ibid.*, 43).

While discussing the topic of beef-eating, a fact very much held against the untouchables, he asserted that protection of cows was more important to the Hindus than the varna dharma (*ibid.*, 3). Hindus made those leave their society who ate cows' flesh, and it was then a justified step but not now. However, cows should be protected, because among all animals only cows had all along been and still are beneficial to mankind. By protecting them men protect the entire mute animal world (*ibid.*, 6).

In reply to a friend, Gandhi described his plan for a future society in broad outline (Gandhi 1927). There were four areas of activities in human society, namely, education, defence, production of wealth and jobs entailing physical labour (*ibid.*, 95). Let all men first turn into Sudras, the lowest of the four varnas, who supposedly performed the bulk of domestic and other types of manual and menial services. Gradually, the other three varnas would emerge out of them. Very few would be really learned to become Brahmanas, the spiritual and educational guardians, still less Ksatriyas who would be the trustees of the people and give up their life serving the nation. The Sudras would be the smallest in number, as no personal services would be required from them. The largest member, however, would be the Vaisyas, because they would include traders, artisans, and peasants (*ibid.*, 91).

Apparently, the exchange of views regarding untouchability was not confined to written propaganda. The issue was taken up officially by the Indian National Congress, and, since Gandhi was an important figure, he influenced the organization to include the cause of the untouchables in its programme.

As early as in 1885, W.C. Bonnerjee had suggested in the first session of the Indian National Congress 'the eradication, by direct friendly personal intercourse, of all possible race, creed, or provincial prejudices' (Gupta 1985:151). However, it was in 1917 that the National Congress addressed itself to its members to remove untouchability 'imposed by custom upon the depressed classes' or suppressed classes so called at that time (Sitramayya 1946: I. 52). In the course of time as the problem crystallized, so were the resolutions and programmes of the Congress. For instance, in 1921 and 1928, it was decided that every Hindu Congressman should try to remove untouchability and better the conditions of the untouchables by personal contact and by rendering services to them. Furthermore, Congressmen were urged to do all they could, and help the untouchables in every possible way (Sitaramayya 1946: I. 226, 332).

When the proposal of separate electorate for the depressed classes was suggested by the Government in 1932, Gandhi reacted vehemently against it in the following words (*ibid.*, 495):

> One word more as to the so-called 'untouchables'. I can understand the claims advanced on behalf of other communities, but the claims advanced on behalf of the 'untouchables' are to me the unkindest out of all. It means a perpetual bar sinister. We do not want the 'untouchables' to be classified as a separate class. Sikhs may remain such in perpetuity, so may Muslims and Christians. Will the untouchables remain untouchables in perpetuity? I would far rather the Hinduism died than that untouchability lived. Those who speak of the political rights of untouchables do not know India and do not know how Indian society is constructed. Therefore, I want to say with all the emphasis I can command that if I was the only person to resist this thing, I will resist it with my life.

Gandhi repeated his arguments against what he thought the dismemberment of 'untouchables' from the Hindu fold (*ibid.*, 509). In fact, even when backward areas were created by the British for the so-called aborigines, politicians saw in the attempt to keep India further divided within herself (Ghurye 1963: 129). According to Gandhi, separate electorate was not the way to remove this 'bar sinister' (Sitaramayya 1946: I. 538).

Now, Congress mustered its forces against untouchability and in 1932 unanimously passed the following resolution (*ibid.*, 536):

> The Conference resolves that, henceforth, amongst Hindus no one shall be regarded as an untouchable by reason of his birth and that those who have been so regarded hitherto will have the same right as other Hindus in regard to the use of public wells, public schools, public roads and all other public institutions. This right shall have statutory recognition at the first opportunity and shall be one of the

earliest Acts of the Swaraj Parliament, if it shall not have received such recognition before that time.

It is further agreed that it shall be the duty of all Hindu leaders to secure, by every legitimate and peaceful means, an early removal of all social disabilities now imposed by custom upon the so-called untouchable classes, including the bar in respect of admission to temples.

On the eve of passing the bill on 'separate electorate' for the depressed classes, Gandhi decided to 'fast unto death'. He declared (*ibid.*, 551): 'What I want, what I am living for, and what I should delight in dying for, is the eradication of untouchability root and branch.... It is in order to achieve this, the dream of my life for past fifty years.'

Such an adamant attitude, both of Gandhi and the British Government, created a deadlock. Desperate attempts were made to solve this impasse by the leaders of the caste Hindus and the Scheduled Castes. A solution was found in the statutory reservation of seats, through primary election (Gupta 1985: 290-99).

However, all these attempts for the removal of untouchability were not much effective. One, therefore, cannot blame Ambedkar who, disillusioned mainly by the moral overtone of Gandhi and the National Congress toward untouchability, summed up the moves of the Congress initiated by Gandhi for the removal of untouchability as 'Congress's Plan to kill by Kindness'.

It is a sad commentary on the approaches of both Ambedkar and Gandhi that, even after several decades and in spite of time-bound constitutional safeguards, the problem, instead of abating, is gaining an impossibe proportion today. Despite Gandhi's 'dream of life' to remove 'this bar sinister', untouchability is as live a problem now as it was then. The issue is a sensitive one, and it generates heat from both sides.

In order to gauze the depth, intensity, magnitude and infectiveness of the problem, as systematic study of every facet of the life of untouchable castes should be undertaken.

It is only from the beginning of the twentieth century that serious attempts are being made to study scientifically the position of the untouchables. While some readily came forward to study their contemporary position (to name only a few like Bailey, Bose, Briggs, Cohn, Freedman, Fuchs, Mencher, Moffat, etc.),[4] some amount of hesitation and reluctance is noticed among Indologists and historians to study the past history of the untouchables. It seems as if the volume and magnitude of the task acts as a deterrent to a systematic study of the issues involved. Yet without a proper understanding of the genesis and development of this phenomenon, no measure or propaganda would be successful for the eradication of this pernicious evil.

With this view in mind, the present study attempts at tracing the origin and development of untouchability in Hindu society. This obviously limits or inquiry, so far as the time dimension is concerned, to ca. tenth century A.D.. by which time the issues involved generated the problem faced in contemporary history.

As to who became the untouchables, there are several hypotheses. The most popular one is that some of them were of tribal origin, which is supported by Oppert, Fick, Bose, Sharma and also by Ambedkar who called them 'Broken Men'. This is probably due to the fact that at least one group of untouchables, the candalas, which exists in India even now, is identified with the kandaloi, whom Ptolemy referred as a tribe besides others such as bhills, pulinda, etc. (Bose 1942: I. 436; Fick 1920: 204-06; Oppert 1972: 155, 22, 80; Sharma 1980: 71, n. 3, 139).

Another hypothesis is that the untouchables originated from the family and village slaves (Ruben 1957: 98). This is based on the fact that within a family there were domestic slaves who did all the 'unclean' jobs, although they all lived within the same household. To begin with, in spite of the 'impure' nature of their work, the family slaves were not considered untouchables. But at the same time they were not allowed to cook food for the family (*ibid.*, 98-99).

The third hypothesis, which has been raised to the status of a theory, is ancient and indigenous, advanced by the Brahmana legists of India. According to them, the untouchables were born of miscegenation among four varnas, the Sanskrit term for such children being varna-samkara, *i.e.* born out of mixture of four varnas. Children born of hypergamous marriages (known as pratiloma) were worse than those born of hypogamous unions (known as anuloma), and the pratiloma children belonged to the category of the untouchables.

Three sets of hypotheses as regards the physical origin of the untouchables are thus available to us for our examination of the problem. While all of them need to be examined separately, for each may be valid to some extent, none of them alone can explain the origin of untouchability satisfactorily. Like the oftquoted Indian parable of seven blind men and the elephant, these hypotheses deal with parts only and not with the whole. An elephant is to be seen to be believed. So may be the study of untouchability.

The reason, put forward as to why these particular groups of people become untouchable, is usually that of ritual purity and pollution (Haimendorf VIII in Fuch's book). The untouchables are ritually impure, because they follow unclean profession or vice versa. But did the voluntarily choose such loathsome occupations? Moreover, why those who are engaged in such occupations as basket-making, weaving, oil-pressing, etc. should be considered untouchables? Therefore, this hypothesis needs a close scrutiny, because the purity-pollution factor may well be the effect and not the cause of untouchability.[5]

In continuity with the trend of argument in the same theory, it is proposed by some that untouchability is essentially of urban origin, as the kind of services rendered by the untouchables is required in towns and cities only (*ibid.*). This, however, does not necessarily explain their presence in villages today, or for that matter in the past. There are jobs requiring the services of scavengers and sweepers even in villages such as removing animal carcasses, cleaning streets, attending to cremation rites, etc. besides cleaning latrines which may be connected with urban settlements only.[6]

Since the present study deals with the phenomenon of untouchability in history, it is better to state at the outset how untouchability has been defined in it. Obviously, the primary attribute of the untouchables is that they are asprsyas to the caste Hindus, and the secondary relevant attributes are their segregation into distinct hamlets, non-commensality and non-connubiality with the caste Hindus. The term 'untouchability', however, is somewhat confusing as it may be temporary or permanent. For the present study, untouchability has been treated as a permanent phenomenon and as legally defined by the High Court. In the words of the First High Court which considered the question, it (*i.e.*, untouchability) includes only practices directed at 'those regarded as "untouchables" in the course of historic development', that is, those relegated 'beyond the pale of the caste system on grounds of birth in a particular class' (Galanter 1963: 551 in Lynch 1974: 27).

The present study begins with the Rgveda, the earliest written Sanskrit document available. In order to denote those people who either composed the hymns themselves in the Rgveda or those who plaped the dominant role, I have used the word 'RV people', or their self-styled name, the 'Aryas' (vide, Kosambi 1956: 75). I have deliberately avoided the word 'Aryan' because of its unhappy connotation in the recent past.

As untouchability makes sense only when it is juxtaposed against touchability of caste Hindus, the materials are collected mainly from the Brahmanical (or Hindu?) sources, covering a period of about 2,500 years. Apart from those texts which are primarily sacred in character, greater reliance is placed on the evidence obtained from lexicons, Nirukta, grammars of Panini and Patanjali, the Arthasastra of Kautilya, accounts of Greek travellers and epigraphical materials.

I have left out the consideration of the Puranas but have consulted the epics to some extent. The former type of literature, although of immense historical importance, may prove too much to cope with at this stage of my study. Moreover, the main purpose of the study is to trace the origin of untouchability. This one can discern from the literature consulted, which clearly shows the main features and contours of this phenomenon as it emerged and took shape.

The task undertaken was not only a time-consuming one but often frustrating too. It was like sailing on an uncharted sea without a life-line. After a long and tedious wandering through the labyrinth of innumerable texts, one may find a word or a line about people not liked by that particular author. And even when the relevant material is found, one has to ask the question: 'Who writes for whom?' Furthermore, it is always uncertain whether the texts portrayed the 'ideal' or the 'real' situation existing in society. Nevertheless, one can probably draw a valid inference regarding the real situation by accepting the 'ideal' situation as maximizing the trend of a particular phenomenon the author had in mind. The limit thus indicated may refer to the positive or the negative aspect of the phenomenon.

What, however, is not easy while studying these texts for describing the emergence of untouchability is to arrange the available information under suitable chapters with well-demarcated phases. Often the types of literature cut across the accepted chronology of those texts. Because of the uncertain dating of those texts primarily, it is rather difficult to define clearly and demarcate these phases. The boundary lines are soft, and there will be frequent chronological overlappings from one phase to another.

What I have done, therefore, is to arrange the texts according to the landmarks in the account of the untouchables as recorded in these texts. Then the materials have been placed under relevant chapters. This might have ignored, in some places, the accepted chronology of certain texts. It was unavoidable. Instead of entering into the controversy at this stage as to their relative dates, I have thought it better to collect as much materials as are available and to rely more on the recorded development of untouchables than otherwise.

Admittedly, in view of segmentation of society into numerous groups and subgroups, we should probe further than look into the Sanskrit literature alone. I have, therefore, made limited use of the Jaina and Buddhist sources. The Buddhist ideology was a serious challenge and posed a greater threat than the Jaina ideology to the Brahmanical viewpoint. I have also had recourse to some archaeological findings validating the bibliographical materials, and to certain travellers' accounts. For instance, the (archaeological) remains of the Indus Valley, indicating the level of material.

NOTES AND REFERENCES

1. Surveys on castes and tribes in different parts of India were first initiated by the British probably in 1869 (Memoire of the Races of the North Western Provinces of India, 2 Vols., Sir H.M. Elliot). From 1891 (Risley, Tribes and Castes of Bengal) systematic data on castes and tribes were collected for helping the British in administering India. These were mainly ethnographical studies which even today serve as bed-rock for researches on castes and tribes in India.

2. The two terms, varna and jati are often confused probably because of the blanket term 'caste' which is indiscriminately used both for varna as well as for jati. In order to avoid this confusion, I have refrained from using the word 'caste', unless absolutely necessary. If at all, 'caste' will be used only in the sense of jati. (In this context, see Mukherjee, 1957: 62-66).

3. At the time when it was used by Gandhi in the early thirties, although the term was first suggested by a poet-saint of Gujarat

(Gupta 1985: 30), it appeared that he gave an honourable name to the untouchables by calling them 'Harijan'. It was even sincerely believed that at last here is the identity which they have been searching for. But now very few make use of this term. 'They feel it connoted the idea of being a bastard and also brought to mind patronising upper caste benevolence' (Lynch 1969: 31).

4. After World War II, however, the field is increasingly crowded by American anthropologists and sociologists. Untouchability in India is probably somewhat parallel to the Black problem in the USA. To quote Lynch: 'Untouchability in India, like discrimination in the United States, has become a pejorative term; one must avoid publicly practising either' (*Ibid.*, p. 210).

5. It was a happy coincidence to find the same opinions expressed by Lynch and Sharma. 'Socially constituted differences among men are the source and origin of the fundamental belief, underlying purity and pollution' (Lynch 1978: 120; see also Mukherjee 1982: 187-90 on Sharma 1980: 146. n. 4).

6. That only urban settlement requires the services of such people is not disputed. But who cleaned the soak-pits, drains, etc. in Mohanjodaro and Harappa? Since that time to that of the Arthasastra, we do not find any evidence of them. That Kautilya forbids a pledged slave to touch dead bodies remove human excreta, etc. shows that there were others doing such jobs. Who were they? (*See also* Ambedkar 1969: 84; AS. III. 13).

2

Dalits: Past and Present Constitutional Reality

This nation, with all its boasts and all its hopes, can never really be free till all its citizens are free—free socially and economically as well as politically. Ambedkar, that militant Mahar,[1] had this as his life's message that sans social democracy, even benignantly ameliorative political exercises would sound hollow. If every fourth or fifth man is a social leper that society is leprous. But to overcome such a deeply entrenched and pan-Indian caste-based, cultural resistance movement what should be the attack tactic? Can law do it alone? Can social reform movements deliver the goods? Should politics arrogate to itself the monopoly right of deliverance? Is a comprehensive ideology, visualising a combination of cultural social forces, on the larger stage and in the wider connotation, essential if law and politics, in happy alliance, are to wage and win the war for social democracy?

The basic, materialist solution for the problem of utter social backwardness is socialism—the Nehru marg[2] (which incidentally, has cured Cuba of the malady of 'coloureds'). The half-religious Gandhian recipe is the equalised incorporation of Panchamas[3] into the Hindu fellowship. The indignant

Ambedkar insistence is on better representation in Administration and in Legislatures through reservation and abolition of social vices and inequities through constitutional legal provisions and administrative measures. The final Indian answer is all this, plus spiritual—a supremely concentrated pace of evolutionary swiftness, by long strides of society to surpass the sins of centuries and, by conscious struggle, to scale the walls of the Past to reach the secret principle of cosmic unity of being and, by an inward march, to discover the Universal Soul and be united in consciousness with all existence —the Aurobindo Veedhi.[4] This higher social evolution through human collaboration is the enduring remedy for the divisive, disparate, down-fallen state of the many by a mental-moral and, inevitably, material transmutation, radical in every sense, of the intolerable Ignorance into ineffable Knowledge. From Rabindranath and Vivekananda to the mystic roots of our Vedic[5] culture this lasting spiritual testament has been striving for expression of full liberation of man and mind. 'Into that heaven of Freedom, my Father, let my country awake!' is the song form of this goal. "A sarvodaya[6] cult, indigenous to the soil, to wipe out the tears from every eye, in a feeling of communal oneness'. is the Vinoba verdict.[7] These synthetic notes are at once materialist and transcendental, socialist and spiritual. These views may look bizarre, these proposals irrelevant, these approaches supra-mental; but (in the Mark Twain strain) is not irreverence the champion of liberty and its only sure defence? Should not time-barred orthodox materialism rise to the scientific higher reaches of the spirit? In ultimate terms, the Harijan-Girijan[8] uplift issue is one of human dignity and development, outlawing the forced cultural sterility of the lower masses, of the emergence of free and equal nationhood and, towards that end, of exploding the apartheid-brand bigotries, stalking from the cemeteries! That is the fulfilment of our social tryst with destiny.

Now back to the world of living actualities and practical remedies. The miasmic Past—the feudal Past, acerbated by the colonial ethos—is too much with us in the shape of socio-economic backwardness. What was the Old Order, how far have we ushered in the New?

The Constitution takes cognizance of our social realities and sets the great goals for the future. What did prevail as the rule of life on Indian earth, in pre-Independence days, for those below the 'civilized' line? What was the Indian agrestic order like? Before we glimpse the focal forces of the past, it is but right to concede the powerful point made by Dr. Ambedkar that the sine qua non of a meaningful, stable democracy is an egalitarian ethos. He argues:

> "My definition of democracy is 'A form and method of Government whereby revolutionary changes in the economic and social life of the people are brought about without bloodshed'. . . . If democracy can enable those who are running it to bring about fundamental changes in the social and economic life of the people and the people accept those changes without resorting to bloodshed, then I say that there is democracy. . ."
>
> The first condition which I think is a condition precedent for the successful working of democracy is that there must be no glaring inequalities in the society. There must not be an oppressed class. There must not be a class which has got all the privileges and a class which has got all the burden to carry. Such a thing, such a division, such an organisation of society has within itself the germs of a bloody revolution, and perhaps it would be impossible for the democracy to cure them . . . the deep cleavages between class and class are going to be one of the greatest hindrances in the success of democracy . . . if the privileged few will not willingly and voluntarily surrender their privileges, then the distance between them and the lower orders will destroy democracy and bring into existence something quite different. There is, therefore, no doubt in my mind that if you examine the history of democracy in various parts of the world, you will find that one of the causes for the breakdown of democracy is the existence of these social conditions."[9]

The Nehru analysis, impeccable in its social dialectic, stresses the socialist rather than the social facet of the solution. He argues, his faith:

> "I am convinced that the only key to the solution of the world's problems and of India's problems lies in socialism, and when I use this word I do so not in a vague humanitarian way but in the scientific, economic sense. Socialism is, however, something even more than an economic doctrine; it is a philosophy of life and as such also it appeals to me. I see no way of ending the poverty, the vast unemployment, the degradation and the subjection of the Indian people except through socialism. That involves vast and revolutionary changes in land and industry, as well as the feudal and autocratic Indian states system. That means the ending of private property, except in a restricted sense, and the replacement of the present profit system by a higher ideal of cooperative service. It means ultimately a change in our instincts and habits and desires. In short, it means a new civilization, radically different from the present capitalist order" . . .
>
> "Socialism is thus for me not merely an economic doctrine which I favour; it is a vital creed which I hold with all my head and heart. I work for Indian Independence because the nationalist in me cannot tolerate alien domination; I work for it even more because for me it is the inevitable step to social and economic change".
>
> "The problem of untouchability and the Harijans again can be approached in different ways. For a socialist it presents no difficulty, for under socialism there can be no such differentiation or victimization. Economically speaking, the Harijans have constituted the landless proletariat, and are economic solution removes the social barriers that custom and tradition have raised."[10]

Gandhiji quietly challenged the evil of social suppression, not by hortative exercises nor by ideological analysis, but by living in the Bhangi[11] colony, by feeling his way to a new freedom. Live and solve, was his way, by the brotherhood of the upper and the lower classes, by grant of temple entry, abolition of untouchability and allied inflictions, and equalisation in social, economic and political life. The first President of India, he once ventured, may be a Harijan and his fasts for Harijan causes had a quaint but volcanic primitivity.

The great social reformers, spiritual in their magnetic methodology, have, from cyclonic Vivekananda to quiet Sree Narayana, struck down the unspiritual and asuric adharma[12] of serfdom. The great saint Ramanuja, a few centuries back, converted Panchamas wholesale into Brahmins! Sree Narayana urged that there was but one caste, one religion, one god for man—Vivekananda called the caste-ridden society a lunatic asylum.

We have thus many humane engineering programmes for attaining the goal, not the least of which is the very process called the rule of law—the forward-looking social justice-inspired dharma. The operation of the legal system steered by activist administrators and aware judges, will promote a caste-less society, given luscent legislative support. A secular revolution through the law is a potent means of social justice. The legal projects for social justice have a cosmic hue?

The Upanishads[13] have proclaimed:

> "Law is the king of kings, far more rigid and powerful than they; there is nothing higher than law; by its prowess as by that of the highest monarch, the weak shall prevail over the strong."[14]

This dynamic egalitarian potential of law cries for fuller exploitation in our unequal times.

Before entering these areas of search for solutions, we may look at life in the raw in Harijan India. After all, not abstractions but empirical insights prescribe the strategy for the break-through. The Past serves to tell us the genetic damage done and suggests how the environmental factors can be manipulated to shape the present and the future. Sociology and history teach us that man masters society not by force but by understanding. And understanding the roots—the social DNA and RNA—is necessary to read the programmed growth of the tree. A dialectical analysis of the thesis and the antithesis is necessary before we direct the social forces towards a new synthesis. And so, to the erstwhile lot of the Panchama proletariat—a flight into the Past and a peep into the struggle for human rights.

The social story of our holy land is replete with godly inhumanity. Large numbers have been condemned to nearslave situations and to unspeakable chores. They were chattel and attached to land, sold as lands passed hands. They could not, with social legitimacy, cover their bodies with decent clothes, especially their women! They had no right to walk along public streets, own lands or worship in public shrines. Segregated into ghettos, eating carcasses and doing menial labour, slaving for their masters, illiterate, fed on sub-culture and condemned to untouchability and even unapproachability, this derelict bunch of communities was banished from the civilized belt and the blessings of decency and dignity in life. These abominable communal cruelties were realities even as late as the early decades of our century and still do play hide and seek with democratic values in the feudal villages of many States where Harijan beating in happy sanctity is a living fact. If India 1975 felt, during Emergency, the urgency to abolish bonded labour and to give land to the landless by law—and victims of bonded labour and landless labour are 'Harijans' and 'Girijans'—there is here internal evidence that quasi-slavery is covertly prevalent in the darker hill features and twilit jungles and plains of our cultural geography!

Judical decisions may be relevant for sociological enquiries and, in that sense, I may begin by quoting a case in 1970 when the controversy was about the law governing inheritance to a tiny fragment of land left behind by a Harijan. In the course of the judgement, I had occasion to refer to the socio-legal destitution of these humble brethren:

> "To serve as background for this enquiry, counsel for the respondent drew my attention to the lurid facts of a decision reported in Korath Mammad v. Emperor (AIR 1918, Mad. 647) which related to Pulayas, more or less inhabiting the same region as Korumbi and They yon. That case reveals the tragic and unsavoury truth that as late as 1913 (the date of Ex. B. in that case) slave trade was occasionally occurring in Malabar and the 'rice salves' or Pulayas (see Gundert's Malayalam Dictionary) were the subject matter of sale by one jenmi to another jenmi. Napier J. refers to the number of salves in the various Taluks of Malabar and also to a letter from the Judge of Calicut in 1841 to the Sadar Adalat pointing out facts which had come judicially to his notice of sales of slaves. Mr Logan also mentions that in 1852 and 1855 the traffic in slaves still continued. He summed up the position in the year 1887:
>
> > 'There is reason to think that they (Cheramans) are still even now with their full consent bought and sold. . . . . .'
>
> In short, a flash-back will make us blush to see that Pulayas 'were treated more or less like salves' in and around Kurumbanad Taluk where Theyyon and Korumbi were born. I mention this because a community which has itself been treated as property to be bought and sold would be alien to property consciousness and could not have evolved any laws of inheritance and succession which postualte possession and ownership of properties on a large scale by the members of the community. If the Pulaya fold remained 'untouched' by the concept of landed property the task of crystallising the customary law relating to inheritance in that community turns into an obscure search."[15]

That such painful absurdities were part of our ugly antiquity is evident from many studies made by researchers and historians. A dialectical student of the demoniac darkness of agrestic Kerala, Dr. Saradamoni, has made a remarkable chronicle of the cruel chapter of the life of Pulayas, the most numerous of the Harijan multiplicity of castes on the West Coast of India. At this stage, I shall liberally quote from the study of Saradamoni which covers Kerala Pulayas and is surely illustrative of the lurid lot of their counterparts in the rest of the country. Our decade marks the socio-political watershed *vis-a-vis* the utterly backward people of India and it is frightening to notice that not long ago slavery of sorts afflicted rural India. Saradamoni writes—and I take you to over a Century ago:

> "Most of our information on slavery in those days, and especially of the conditions of the Pulayas is based on the census reports, the writings of Collectors, Special Commissioners and other British officials posted in Malabar, and individuals like Brown, an English estate owner in Malabar, whose estate was mainly cultivated by slaves. Interestingly Brown himself inherited the estates and the slaves along with it from his father, who was an overseer in the English Company's pioneering plantations in the Wynad hill slopes. . . ."[16]

Baber who had served for several years in Malabar in various capacities and finally became judge and magistrate in South Malabar wrote:

> 'Of agrestic predial slavery, the origin is of very remote antiquity: the general term given for this description of slavery is 'adima', or literally, as I understand the term, serf, aboriginal or indigenous, being held previously under the same tenures and terms as the land itself, throughout, under some slight modifications, the Malabar coast.'[17]

"Walker agreed with what Buchanan had noted and observed in his report on the tenures of Malabars".

> 'The Chermas are absolute property; they are part of the livestock on an estate. I selling and buying land it is not

necessary that they should follow the soil; both kinds of property are equally disposable and may fall into different hands. The Chermas may be sold, leased or mortgaged, like the land itself, or like any cattle or thing.'[18]

"Pulayas in the beginning of the 19th century did not have a life of their own. They never worked or earned a living for themselves. Their entire life was dependant on the masters. They did not own even their children. They begetted children so that the masters could have a continuous supply of workers. Naturally they did not make decisions or plans either for themselves or for their children. 'Their time was wholly their master's, and they had no particular hours which they could call their own. Not a day in a week was granted them either for rest or for prayer".[19]

Great cruelties were also practised on the persons of the slaves. Major Walker pointed out that, by the ancient laws of Malabar, the proprietor of the slave was not accountable to any person for the life of his own Cherumas. He was the 'legal judge of their offences' and could punish them by death if they should appear to deserve it'. Vaughan learnt, from direct information he collected from various districts that barbarities like cutting off the nose was practised in olden days. But during his time, these severities had lessened to corporal punishment. Even if the severity of corporal punishment had lessened by 19th century, life was in no way less harsh to the slaves.[20]

'The rules of Malabar prescribed that a slave of the castes of Pulayan, Walooran and Parian shall remain seventy-two paces from a Brahmin and from a Nair, forty-eight from a Teean; a slave of Kunnukun caste sixty-four paces from a Brahmin and Nair and forty from a Teean; and the other castes generally forty-eight paces from a Brahmin and Nair and twenty-four from Teean'.[21]

'The lower servile classes, wherever they go, give notiee of their coming by uttering a particular cry at every four or five paces; if the cry be answered by another uttered in like manner by a superior, giving warning that he is approaching, the slave instantly quits the road and retires'.[22]

'If you have tears to shed them now', I urge, and add, if you have cheeks to blush and heads to hang, blush and hang at least now'. Nay, more. If you are capable of moral indignation, grow angry in divine wrath but fuelled by social justice. This immoral order had its inhuman play when the social system was organised on a hierarchical basis. The colonial rule had some ideological identity with making man a rural tool or urban cog worthy of amoral exploitation. Even so, western winds blew in more advanced ideas as industrialisation and capitalism crept in. The old order changeth.

Feudal tranquillity was slowly stired by the currents of western industralism and freedom. I go back to the Malabar story of the mlechchas.[23]

As early as 1822, Graeme Wrote:

"It is not requisite to make such an abrupt innovation upon established rights and customs as to declare the slaves to be free forthwith, but a proposal should be opened for the eventual but gradual emancipation and proprietors should be indemnified by the payment of a maximum price, which should be previously ascertained for each district and promulgated."

"At the beginning of the 19th Century when the English established their supremacy over Kerala, the Pulayas and Cherumas were living as slaves, in conditions of barbarity and cruelty which defies description".[24]

But social forces of change uprooted old dogmas, though the new values were not of socialism but of quasi-freedom which even colonialism brought about. Paradoxically, there is a progressive edge to exploitative systems to help exploit the better! The alien rulers reacted on this social basis:

> "The British administrators in Kerala had taken notice of slavery existing in the region quite early. In 1792, the year in which the East India Company's rule commenced in Malabar, the Joint Commissioners under whom the region was placed issued a proclamation prohibiting slave trade. 'This proclamation was, however, directed chiefly against the practice, then prevalent, of bands of robbers carrying off by force from their houses the children of the most useful inhabitants, the Tiyars and other cultivators."[25]
>
> All this happened in spite of the fact that "Slavery was legally abolished in Malabar by the Government of India Act. No. V of 1843."

To liberate the semi-slaves from the feudal hold for the labour market was the focal point of British conscience and British business! We need not dilate upon the hesitant steps which led to the anti-slavery measures but may note that formal extinguishment of slavery in the eye of law took place when the Penal Code of 1862 made it an offense, sounding 'the death knell of a system which for many centuries was a prolific source of untold miseries for at least nine million of the inhabitants of the land'.

This proclamation was more law than life: for, "The Slavery Abolition Act" did not result in the immediate emancipation of the slaves. Benedicts Hjejle commented: "Having worked through all the consultations in the Legislative Council, I can say with certainty that Act V of 1843 was passed without any idea of the real extent and nature of slavery' and the Act had little to offer to the slave population'.

Without being too anti-romantic but all the same realistic, the thaw, one might state, had begun and law entered the field to produce social change and State action ignited Dalit[26] amelioration. I will illustrate this aspect of gradually burgeoning sense of social justice by quotes from "Kerala in Social Change":

"The demand for the abolition of agrestic slavery in Travancore began with a petition submitted to the Maharaja by the thirteen British missionaries through the British Resident on March 19, 1847.

"The missionaries 'ventured to submit' that the history of slavery showed that it was the most costly labour, that it degraded the owners as much as the slaves, and that its extinction greatly conduced to the wealth, intelligence and social comfort of man wherever it had been achieved."[27]

Medieval opposition, in its decadent resistance to change, is part of the conflict of historical forces before a new synthesis is established. Reflecting this factor is the reply of the Dewan of Travancore, a relatively progressive State, to the tepid suggestion of manumission of new-born Pulayas:

"The humane policy of ameliorating the conditions of the grown-up slave population is unquestionable, but with regard to declaring all children born of slaves free from a given date, the subject requires much consideration, as the adoption of the measure might prove a matter of grievance and much inconvenience both to the owner and the parents."[28]

The slow, steep ascent to Dalit liberation was aided by the progressive winds of change, religious, social and political. But the backward segments were chained to land which in many civilizations and countries has been the anchorage of Reaction. The hard core of reactionary values is entrenched in agrarian fortifications so that the main attack on the ramparts of social suppression must be with agrarian reform artillery. In any agrarian society socio-economic hierarchies are built on land relations and the older such agrestic infra-structures, the deeper their hold on the status quo ante. India, with its ancient caste system and rural-feudal organisation, is such a society. The blow must fall on the primitive land system if the social proletariat is to break off their shockinshackles. The tremendous significance of the twin projects of land reforms and bonded labour abolition, out of the twenty-point programme[29] of the Prime Minister, lies in its lancet thrust into the soft undeside of the beast of feudalism. Further, Harijan betterment cannot fall like manna[30] from heaven but perforce, has to be wrested by struggles. These militant uprisings have to be part of a total mutiny by an awakened people rather than sporadic bursts of ameliorative compassion, touching a particular class or moved by a charitable motive. Feudal economics has no heart and its grave-diggers cannot have any. Therefore, any massive assault on the citadels of social suppression must possess a larger perspective and relentless spirit. In this larger war, social and economic forces mingle and overlap. Degrees of backwardness shade off into each other and a united battle informed by an anti-exploitative ideology becomes essential for success. The hostile strengths in their serried ranks must be intelligently identified. They may range from cruel landlords and callous capitalists to temple traditions and pious souls and puritan practices and obscurantist bigotries, not to speak of a hundred other vicious social fall-outs from the caste-class tyranny.

The deplorable animal lot of the Panchama proletariat began to change gradually. A humanist stir did disturb the peace of the social graveyard. Going to Kerala as typical of the rest of the country—perhaps a little ahead of other States—we find the Cochin Census Report of 1931 recording thus:

> "The first decade for the 20th Century saw the community in its old dormant condition, content to take things lying down and meekly submitting to the social disabilities it was subjected to under the rigours of the Malayali caste system, which had branded it with an unapproachability of 36 degrees. Within two decades, they have been transformed into a well-organised community with their samajams and associations, successfully working for their social, moral and spiritual uplift, and waging war against social disabilities. They also had a religious reformation, removed pollution with reference to lower castes, opened temples where even the lower castes could come."[31]

Shrimati Saradamoni has forcefully portrayed the impact of the zeit geist on the untouchables of Kerala, with a sense of history and perception of social forces:

> "What was happening to the Pulayas and other lower castes during this period of flux and change in Kerala? While changes all around them could not leave them out for long, their problems and their remedies were fundamentally different to that of the Nayars, Nambudiris or even the Izhavas. The changes in land relations or the security of tenure for tenants did not affect them for they had practically no land. Neither was the change in inheritance laws relevant to them as they had no property. The opening of schools and creation of avenues for government employment also had no impact on them, as they were so low in the social ladder that they could not even dream of education and Government jobs.
>
> "The problem of adjusting to modern conditions did not confront them, as it confronted the other communities for they were still not far removed from slavery. Their struggle was to lift themselves up from the slough of extreme social degradation and abject poverty. There was not even a tiny segment among the Pulayas, who were economically or socially better off and could provide necessary leadership to the community as was in the case of Izhavas. The struggle of this poor illiterate, untouchable community for social equality and economic betterment was harder and their climb steeper. But the strong current of change that sweeping over Kerala had its impact on the Pulayas and impelled them to break out of their age-old submissiveness and helplessness. They launched a valiant struggle which, though not as spectacular as that of the Izhavas, put them on the long and hazarduous road of real social and economic emancipation. But this period showed that there is a sense of human dignity and a strong sense of protest against humiliations and discrimination even in the most oppressed and submissive people.

"There is no doubt that the movement launched by Sree Narayana Guru and the activities of the S.N.D.P. greatly helped to kindle new awareness and sense of self-respect among the other low and 'untouchable' castes. But the atmosphere of protest and change threw up their own leaders among the Pulayas and the tallest among them was Ayyankali (1863-1941) of Travancore who led the struggle of the community for over half a century. Ayyankali was born at Venganur, near Trivandrum. He did not have much education. It was with great difficulty that he could write his name in Malayalam. But this man who was barely literate, was deeply hurt at the degradation and misery that his community was subjected to. The struggles of the Izhavas and the preachings of Sree Narayana Guru inspired him. But he was more a contemporary of the Guru and not a follower. From the age of thirty he decided to dedicate his entire life for the betterment of his community. Ayyankali's vision and farsightedness was such that he anticipated many of the demands of the poor and socially backward sections that remain unsatisfied even today.[32]

There were heroes and heroic movements all over and their emergence was itself part of the nationalist awakening out of the dope of feudal-colonial life-style The Great Divide was provoking great struggles. In Kerala, the militancy was more than elsewhere perhaps, but, largely, it was the manifestation of the spirit of the masses to revolt against the classes. Saradamoni sums up for Kerala thus:

"The character of the movement also changed with the growing consciousness of the Pulayas. The early period of petitioning the government by individuals and groups gave way to more organised agitations. The formation of the Cochin Pulaya Mahajana Sabha in the early thirties was an important landmark in the progress of the community. The activities of the Sabha in its early years was confined to annual meetings presided over by high governmental officials. But with the emergence of the newly educated younger sections it became a militant organisation.

"The new leadership of the Pulayas realised that petitions and 'welfare measures' did not solve the problems of the low caste people. They concentrated their attention in organising struggles against untouchability, social oppression and economic exploitation. They believed that education was an important weapon for the emancipation of the community and carried on intensive campaigns among the Pulayas to send their children to school. Some of the leaders of this period, like K.K. Kunjan and Pmk. Chathan gave up their teaching jobs in the government service and devoted their entire time in the service of the community.

"The Pulaya Mahajana Sabha took up all cases of eviction, attacks on Pulayas etc. with the police and other authorities and functioned as the watchdog of the interests of these poor people with a high degree of success. At the same time, they worked among the masses, educating them against the evils of dirty and unhygienic living, alcoholism and about the benefits of sending their children to school. The awakening among the Pulayas that resulted, led to inevitable clashes with upper castes. The Pulaya Mahajana Sabha continued to be active till after independence. The last major struggle led by it was the famous Paliyam Satyagraha in early 1948, for the right of the former 'untouchables' to walk along the public road in the Paliyam estate, near Cochin."[33]

Then came the era of swaraj[34] politics which did not confine its self to mere political demands but took in its wings the economic upsurges of the peasantry and the working class and the social struggles of the utterly suppressed backward segments of society. Gandhi came and in his own simplistic, mystic style led a people's campaign with typically Indian tactics and ideology, at once progressive and traditional. Many movements, many leaders, each with a methodological individuality, arose but this panorama of uplift activities had one broad feature. They were all inspired by the aspirations of nationalism and imbued with the touch of socialism—not insular nobility nor singular social service.

The freedom movement acquired a new consciousness, a deeper dimension. Our nation became self-aware that Freedom was, integral—political, social and economic—that justice too had triune facets and social justice to the underdog was implied in the overthrow of imperialism. This larger synthesis became militantly clear with the plenitude of the Nehru leadership and the arrival of socialist and communist thought on our soil. Swadeshi[35] and socialist reconstruction of the nation implied, more and more importantly, the involvement and equal status of the human numbers. In this wider view, Dalit welfare, anti-untouchability, land distribution, Zamidari[36] abolition and land-to-the-tiller and workers' movements became parts of a whole—a politicization of social justice and a socialisation of politics and economics. The massive poor, as against the classy elite,—We, the People of India—came into their own. The Constitution was born under these stars of conscience and consciousness with a clear-eyed graze oncultural liberation and legal humanization.

This takes us on to a study of the militant best of that beautiful totality of the super-law of the Constitution. Its profound portent and affirmative import are worth a deeper probe from the point of view of activist legal processes and political projects to achieve social justice for the most disadvantaged. A constitution is not a sky of ideals but the terra firma of high values and pragmatic processes. It is the guide book of a nation's life and the directory of its match.

The law of the Constitution, in its majestic diction, has laid down fundamental national directives and set out fundamental personal rights, both converging towards societal egalite plus development of personality. The Constitution is not a self-working mechanism but has to be interpreted and operated by men. Thus the sociological vision and democratic passion of the legislative, judicative and executive branches of the State, together with the progressive stance of the personnel manning them, must be dynamically oriented on the dharma of the Constitution and spurred into positive action, if a favourable, result-based social justice report is to be possible.

The social urgency and temporal imperativeness of the problem and the vast under-privileged numbers involved in securing salvation, compel the construction of creative thought-ways—a forward-looking Harijan jurisprudence, a pro-backward administrative culture and socially energised legislative methodology, all of which call for novel constructs and adaptation to the complex needs of a banished but burgeoning huge segment of Indian brotherhood.

Court-centred constitutional law is of great significance in Indian system because Article 141 makes the Judges of the Supreme Court the final exponents of the command of law, even constitutional law. The cornerstone of the rising Harijan jurisprudence is the rule of equal protection enshrined in Articles 14, 15 and 16. We may, therefore, study, for a while, how the transforming principle of these Articles works in the context of a society of gross inequality and great poverty.

It is judicially customary to make equality mechanical and truncate its range of validity by construing it to be merely equal treatment for each among similarly situated persons. But the influence of Part IV upon Part III converts the latter into an activist agency of equalisation—a dynamic seed of change. This seminally affirmative aspect, in confrontation with the superficially attractive, formally equal, view of the law, came into sharp focus in the Indian Supreme Court in Kerala versus Thomas,[37] as it did in De Funis[38] in the American Supreme Court. The 42nd Amendment to the Constitution has now explicitly subordinated individual fundamental rights guaranteed by Part III to the collectivist catalyst in Part IV. The amended Article 31C would read:

> "Notwithstanding anything contained in Article 13, no law giving effect to the policy of the State towards securing all or any of the principles laid down in Part IV shall be

> deemed to be void on the ground that it is inconsistent with, or takes away or abridges any of the rights conferred by Article 14, Article 19 or Article 31, and no law containing a declaration that it is for giving effect to such policy shall be called in question in any court on the ground that it does not give effect to such policy:
>
> Provided that where such law is made by the Legislature of a State, the provisions of this article shall not apply thereto unless such law, having been reserved for the consideration of the President, has received his assent."[39]

The change is largely a legislature recognition of a judicially decocted role. The new message of the collective welfare dominating individual good is the contribution of Kerala versus Thomas. The potential for equalisation this ruling contains justifies the propriety of dealing with this landmark case and the ampler connotation of discrimination it expounds.

The concept of equality lies at the core of democracy. Where glaring disparities between large groups mar the stark social geography, affirmative state action by way of equalisation becomes obligatory to reach actual equality. The enrichment of the equal protection clause (Art. 14) by the promotional programme mandated by Article 46 makes noetic sense. Article 46 stipulates that "The State shall promote with special care the educational and economic interests of the weaker sections of the people, and, in particular, of the Scheduled Castes and Scheduled Tribes, and shall protect them from social injustice and all forms of exploitation."

'Protective discrimination', as a realistic necessity to attain preliminary equality, is a sine qua non for the play of 'equal protection', given a vast heterogeneous nation characterized by profound inequalities of caste and class. The Constitution is caste-blind, the goal being a casteless society. But 'benign discrimination' is a requirement of the larger conceptual Siamese twins of equalisation and equality.

A similar issue has arisen in America where concessions for coloureds have been castigated as 'reverse discrimination'. De Funis presented this constitutional question:

> "Whether race can be a constitutionally valid criterion for admission to state law school if the law school's purpose and the effect of its policy is not to stigmatize or segregate but partially to rectify and ameliorate the consequences of racial segregation by effectively affording equal educational opportunity to certain minority group members where previously it did not exist, notwithstanding the admitted detriment imposed on certain displaced non-minority group applicants."[40]

Although the U.S. Supreme Court declined to decide the case, the briefs submitted unfold my meaning:

> "Equal protection is the constitutional mandate, and this may indeed require, as the Courts have decreed, the recognition and use of racial classifications. On the same ground, the brief submitted by the American Bar Association concludes that 'preferential programmes enhancing minority access to the mainstream of American society are not 'invidious' discrimination since the goal of compensatory programmes is not the separation of races but the equalization of two cultures within one society'. In short, racial classifications are constitutionally permissible when utilised to eradicate the vestiges of a dual society."[41]

Of course, the quota system and reservation scheme cannot be perpetual. Then the end is defeated by the means. Professor Hardgrave of Texas raised this issue in a paper:

> "Advocates of preferential admission, like O'Neil, argue that such policies 'should remain in force as long as—but only as long as they are necessary to bring about equality of opportunity, access, and choice'. But at what point would such programmes' self-destruct'? When the percentage of admissions for minority groups corresponds to their

presence in the larger society? Or when proportionate representation is achieved within the profession?"[42]

The dilemma of protective discrimination—whether in India or the United States—is that by the very use of racial, and caste criteria these distinctions are perpetuated and endowed with a vested interest in their own survival.

This is the risk built into the special treatment policy, that the first part, the caste concessions, will become so deeply entrenched that the second part, the conditions of genuine integration and equal opportunity, can never come about.

The Indian courts have werstled with this legal sociological problem for long but Kerala versus Thomas marks the conscious enlargement of 'equal protetion' by extending it to validate unequal treatment to unequal classes in a pluralist society.

Beginning with Dorairajan,[43] through Balaji,[44] Rajendran[45] and others, the question of special discrimination in favour of the weaker sections climaxed in Kerala v. Thomas where a Bench of seven Judges upheld a rule affording an extended period to Harijans to pass qualifying tests for in-service promotion, as against other classes of citizens. In that leading case, several opinions were handed down. In his separate judgement, Ray, C.J., observed:

> "There is no denial of equality of opportunity unless the person who complains of discrimination is equally situated with the person or persons who are alleged to have been favoured."[46]

* * * *

> "The rule of parity is the equal treatment of equals in equal circumstances. The rule of differentiation is enacting laws differentiating between different persons or things in

different circumstances . . . ., but the role of differentiation is inherent in the concept of equality. Equality means parity of treatment under parity of conditions. Equality does not connote absolute equality."[47]

* * *

"Preferential treatment for members of backward classes with due regard to administrative efficiency alone can mean equality of opportunity for all citizens...... Equality of opportunity for unequals can only mean aggravation of inequality. Equality of opportunity admits discrimination with reason and prohibits discrimination without reason. Discrimination with reason means rational classification for differential treatment having nexus to the constitutionally permissible object....... Therefore, differential treatment in standards of selection are within the concept of equality."[48]

Mathew, J. justified compensatory State action to dissolve social disparity so as to make equal what the cruel force of circumstances had made unequal.

In a separate concurring judgement, I sought to explain the deeper philosophy and intelligent pragmatics behind just discrimination to raise to an equal level those considerable segments of the community whom the ancient injustice of an inherited sub-culture had monstrously condemned to a life below the civilized line.

I wrote in my opinion:

" . . . . . some memorable facts must be stated. The Father of the Nation adopted, as his fighting faith, the uplift of the Bhangi and his assimilation, on equal footing, into Hindu society, and the Constitution, whose principal architect was himself a militant Mahar, made social justice a founding faith and built into it humanist provisions to lift the level of the lowly scheduled castes and scheduled tribes to make democracy viable and equal for all. Studies in social anthropology tell us how cultural and material suppression has, over the ages, crippled their personality, and current demography says that nearly every fifth Indian is a Harijan and his social milieu is steeped in squalor."[49]

"The domination of a class generates, after a long night of sleep or stupor of the dominated, an angry awakening and protestant resistance and this conflict between thesis, *i.e.*, the status quo and anti-thesis *i.e.*, the hunger for happy equality, propels new forces of synthesis, *i.e.*, an equitable constitutional order or just society. Our founding fathers, possessed of spiritual insight and influenced by the materialist interpretation of history, forestalled such social pressures and pre-empted such economic upsurges and gave us a trinity of commitments—justice, social, economic and political. The 'equality Articles' are part of this scheme. My proposition is, given two alternative understandings of the relevant sub-articles (Articles 16 (a) and (2), the Court must so interpret the language as to remove that ugly 'inferiority' complex, which has done genetic demage to Indian polity and thereby suppress the malady and advance the remedy, informed by sociology and social anthropology. My touch-stone is that functional democracy postulates participation by all sections of the people and fair representation in administration is an index of such participation."[50]

"The core conclusion I seek to emphasize is that every step needed to achieve in action actual, equal, partneship for the Harijans, alone amounts to social justice—not enshrinement of great rights in Part III and good goals in Part IV. Otherwise, the solemn undertakings in Articles 14 to 16 read with Arts. 46 and 335 may be reduced to a 'teasing illusion or promise of unreality'. A clear vision of the true intendment of these provisions demands a deep understanding of the Indian spiritual-secular idea that divinity dwells in all and that ancient environmental pollution and social placement, which the State must extricate, account for the current socio-economic backwardness of the blacked-out human areas described euphemistically as Scheduled Castes and Scheduled Tribes. The roots of our constitutional ideas —at least some of them—can be traced to our ancient culture. The noble Upanishadic behest must evolve out of 'equality', if we are true to the subtle substance of our finer heritage."[51]

The progressive nidus of the humane jurisprudence and the jural postulates of post-Independence India is the Constitution. A carefully debated, cautiously visionary, creatively down-to-earth, socially radical super-document, it projects the paramount objective of establishing a just society. In a terribly unequal system, equal justice is impossible and absolutist arbitrariness inevtable without a dynamic rule of law. And where ugly social realities reveal gaping disparities, equal justice under the law is but pleasing legislative prattle unless a mighty effort at levelling up or equalisation through action-oriented legal processes is attempted. Where social stratification has become a fossilising fact of economic life, the technology of justice through jural uplift may have to break new legislative ground, adopt novel legal measures, inject potent statutory control systems and audit procedures so that distributive justice is actually delivered to the lowly in the social ladder. The broad basis and constant inspiration for these big changes can be found in the constitutional mandates. More particularly, our concern here is with social justice to the Scheduled Castes and Scheduled Tribes and generally to the backward human areas. A rapid resume of the relevant articles of the Constitution may therefore be apposite.

The keynote thought of the Constitution is social revolution; its juridical signature is social justice; its political motif is government by the people, for the people. Its conscience or inner voice speaks through Parts III and IV whose integral yoga[52] is the promise judges have sometimes missed but the latest constitutional amendments have stressed. A study of the relevant provisions discloses that unless a penetrating interpretation, informed by the spirit of Dalit advancement, were adopted, the thrust of Article 15(2) (a) (b) and (4) will be lost in courts. The assured equality may breach the dykes of protection of the weak by treating the big and the small alike. A disingenuous device to take the teeth out of Articles 14 to 16 vis-a-vis the backward-most sections of the people is to romanticise these equality clauses and render them sterile. The form of counter-attack is, as earlier pointed out, called 'reverse discrimination' in American juristic parlance. The coloureds—and women too—are sought to be rebuffed in their demand for approximate equalisation of glaringly unequal groups as precondition for and as part of the activist process of equal legal protection. To echo Nehru, where jutice is in peril, the nation is not non-aligned. Among unequals, equality is vicious neutrality in disguise, and cover perpetuation of current disparity. Equalise first: equality next—such is the strategy of justice. The argument in some of the opinions, vindicating this life-logic of 'equality' as inclusive of equalising measures, may be culled from Kerala versus Thomas to prove the conceptual soundness of this stand:

> "The basic question thus is one of social dynamics implied in Article 16(1). Let us go to the fundamentals and ignore the frills. In a spacious sense, 'equal opportunity' for members of a hierarchical society makes sense only if a strategy by which the underprivileged have environmental facilities for developing their full human potential. This consummation is accomplished only when the utterly depressed groups can claim a fair share in public life and economic activity, including employment under the State, or when the classless and casteless society blossoms as a result of positive State action. To help the lagging social segments, by special care, is a step towards and not against a large and stabler equality."[53]
>
> "My conclusion is that the genius of Articles 14 to 16 consists not in literal equality but in progressive elimination of pronounced inequality. Indeed, to treat sharply dissimilar persons equally is subtle injustice. Equal opportunity is a hope, not a menace."[54]

"If the Court has its listening posts on raw Indian earth, its assessment of 'equal opportunity' cannot remain legalistic or individualistic but should see the age-old inequality to mend which is also the means to real equality, a demanding command of our Constitution."[55]

"Jurisprudence, to be living law, must respond to the bhangi colony and the black ghetto intelligently enough to equalise opportunities within the social, political and economic orders, by making up for long spells of deprivation. Hence, if a court is convinced that the purpose of a measure using a suspect classification is truly benign, that is, that measure represents an effort to use the classification as part of a programme designed to achieve an equal position in society for all tribes and groups and communities, then it may be justified in permitting the State to choose the means for doing so, so long as the means chosen are reasonably related to achieving that end. The distinction would seem to be between handicaps imposed accidentally by nature and those resulting from societal arrangements such as caste structures and group suppression. Society being, in a broad sense, responsible for these latter conditions, it also has the duty to regard them as relevant differences among men and to compensate for them wherever they operate to prevent equal access to basic, minimal advantages enjoyed by other citizens. In a sense, the theory broadens the traditional concept of 'state action' to require government attention to those inequalities for which it is not directly responsible, but which nevertheless are concomitant features of the existence of the organized state."[56]

"Differences and disparties exist among men and things and they cannot be treated alike by the application of the same laws but the law has to come to terms with life and must be able to recognize the genuine differences and disparities that exist in human nature. Legislature has also to enact legislation to meet specific ends by making a reasonable and rational classification. In Morey v. Doud it was so aptly observed:

> "To recognise marked differences that exist in fact is living law; to disregard practical differences and concentrate on some abstract identities is lifeless logic."[57]

Thomas has cast new responsibilities on the State. After this Special Bench decision, the way is cleared for the State to take affirmative action at various levels to produce equality by discriminatory provisions, legislative, administrative and other. No longer is it possible to plead the alibi of judicial interdict. We, therefore, have to look forward to a dynamic era of new Harijan laws and executive projects which would be tested by what I have called the 'Harijan jurisprudence' and passed for their validity.

Recently I received a letter from a gentleman in Hyderabad where, after referring to Kerala v. Thomas, he asked me:

> "If the statistical data discloses the fact that the Scheduled Castes and Tribes are not adequately represented in the services under the State and that this inadequacy is due to the indifference or reluctance on the part of the Government to make adequate provision for reservation of appointments and posts in favour of Scheduled Castes and Scheduled Tribes, does it not amount to defiance of the constitutional mandate and breach of trust? If so, whether the exercise of the power can be enforced by Courts? As it will be a case of collective injustice to the community as a whole, can any member of the Scheduled Castes or Scheduled Tribes question it in a court of law? If the exercise of this power cannot be enforced by Courts can we hope that these down-trodden people, who have been held in social and economic thraldom for thousands of years with least possible resistance from their side, would exhibit their zeal to "seek hope in the streets?"[58]

The point raised has a challenging meaning to activists who believe in affirmative court action.

Let me re-commence on the theme of India's New Political-Jural Pilgrimage. The most historic handiwork of Ambedkar—the Indian Constitution—serves as a landmark. The national objective, expressed in Nehru diction, has been spelt out, with sunrise glow, in Articles 38 and 39 and the modus operandi to accomplish it has been set out with nascent verve and legal awareness in Article 34A. The intimate blend of legal programming with social welfare projects is true democracy through nomocracy. Prime Minister Indira Gandhi more than hinted at this joint strategy in a message to a lawyers' meet:

> "Several important measures to help the poorest segments of our society have been taken up in recent months. The abolition of bonded labour and various forms of rural debt, the provision of house sites, the distribution of land to the landless and arrangements for credit are among the items of the Twenty-point Economic Programme which are being pursued with vigour. However, vested interests try to block the implementation of every progressive measure. As regards legal remedies, there has been a long and unequal battle between the rich and the poor. I am greatly concerned with the question of enabling the under-privileged to get greater justice."[59]

Back to the constitutional pillars of the unfolding just society and the cornerstone of my Lectures:

> "The State shall strive to promote the welfare of the people by securing and protecting as effectively as it may a social order in which justice, social, economic and political, shall inform all the institutions of the national life."[60]

> "The state shall, in particular, direct its policy towards securing (a) that the citizens, men and women equally, have the right to an adequate means of livelihood."[61]

Collective justice as the ethos of society, equality as a principle in action and common striving for community welfare, have been the vedic exhortation and remain the constitutional quintessence distilled in Article 38. To see Valmiki[62] in every Harijan and divinity in every human is the jural core of our social order.

While social servitude is interlaced, in the Hindu cultural tapestry, with rural primitivism, the hierarchical life style has bred protean forms of bondage, and our founding fathers being realists have therefore felt the necessity for constitutionally forbidding traffic in human beings and forced labour. Article 23(1) contains a stern stricture and is worded thus:

> "Traffic in human beings and begar and other similar forms of forced labour are prohibited and any contravention of this provision shall be an offence punishable in accordance with law."[63]

Now to Article 29. When backwardness is exacerbated by minority complexes, the social resultant is helpless suffering. Article 29 is a protective mantle for minorities although its main beneficiaries today are the more noisy religious minorities. In a manner not fully explored, the scheduled castes and the tribals are cultural minorities.

The disturbd social conscience of the Constitution is writ large in the Directive Principles of State Policy set out in Part IV with the avowed object of creating "a social order in which justice—social, economic and political—shall inform all the institutions of the national life." The painful impact of Article 46 cannot be missed by any sociologist concerned with promotion of the educational and economic interests of Scheduled Castes, Scheduled Tribes and other weaker sections. The provision reads:

> "The State shall promote with special care the educational and economic interests of the weaker sections of the people, and, in particular, of the Scheduled Castes and the Scheduled Tribes, and shall protect them from social injustice and all forms of exploitation."[64]

There are yet other constitutional provisions regarding representation of the Scheduled classes in the Administration and in the Legislatures. These are Articles which obligate the

President to appoint Commissions and Commissioners and take other steps to brighten the kismet[65] of these down-trodden denizens of India.

This aerial survey of the constitutional complex of clauses is but a bookish exercise unless we venture into the marshy areas of pragmatics out of the gardens of legal romantics. Independence has given India a unique opportunity, and an awesome responsibility. It has given us a majestic legacy and a terrible heritage. Time, opportune for peaceful transformation, is winging away and impatience, explosive in its womb, is on its way. The politics and law of serious ideology and speedy execution mock at us. We will be punished if we tarry and toddle in actualising functional success.

"It is only in a Swaraj Constitution", observed Ambedkar, "that we stand any chance of getting the political power into our own hands, without which we cannot bring salvation to our people."[66] It is a gloomy Silver Jubilee Report to make that 27 years after the Constitution, we are dragging with the weight of iron in our feet representing the diehard ethos enshrining unjust values. Was Dr. Ambedkar a prophetic sociologist when long years before Freedom, he argued:

> "Where will the centre of political power be? Who will have it? Will the depressed classes be heirs of it? These are the questions that form their chief concern. The depressed classes feel that they will get no share of the power unless the political machinery for the new Constitution is of a special make. In the constitution of that machine certain hard facts of Indian social life must not be lost sight of. It must be recognised that Indian society is a gradation of castes forming an ascending scale of reverance and a descending scale of contempt—a system which gives no scope for the growth of that sentiment of equality and fraternity so essential for a democratic form of government. It must also be recognised that while the intelligentsia is a very necessary and a very important part of Indian society, it is drawn from its upper strata and, although it speaks

in the name of the country and leads the political movement, it has not shed the narrow particularism of the class from which it is drawn. In other words, what the depressed classes wish to urge is that the political mechanism must take account of and must have a definite relation to the psychology of the society for which it is devised. Otherwise you are likely to produce a Constitution which, however symmetrical, will be truncated one and a total misfit to the society for which it is designed."[67]

Verbal valour or paper radicalism cannot destroy the rural vastness and centuries-old roots of the varna[68] mores of a-rigidly stratified society. The Bhangi has still not a dog's chance of equality with the Brahmin beeause the hard core of the hierarchical apparatus survives intact. The agents of Dharma, politically speaking, are still the upper castes and so whatever the policies to breakdown the old social order their sharp edges will be blunted by a Government of higher castes. The bureaucracy which is the executing agency is still higher class and its sympathies for a socialist transformation involving social equalisation have a restricted operational range. Rarely ever a higher casts Marxist marries or allows his children to marry a Harijan! Most unjustly, a sinister issue of the American magazine 'Time' once pictorialized Jawaharlal Nehru as the biggest brahmin of India, I faintly recollect. None more secular, rationalist and truly casteless than he sat in power in India! And yet, the false change had a metaphorical sting. Political power is still varna conscious in India, which is a bad omen. A quantitative and qualitative census of scheduled castes in public offices will make tragic disclosures. An insignificant fraction of Indian untouchables manning a microscopic number of posts in the wider public sector, is a tribute to Ambedkar's cynicism and a tragic elegy on Gandhiji!

And Ambedkar had little hope from British India and much from Indian democracy:

"We must have a Government in which the men in power will give their undivided allegiance to the best interest of

> the country. We must have a Government in which men in power, knowing where obedience will end and resistance will begin, will not be afraid to amend the social and economic code of life which the dictates of justice and expediency so urgently call for. This role the British Government will never be able to play. It is only a government which is of the people, for the people and by the people that will make that possible."[69]

We, the people, did get power exercised through a Party and Parliament of mixed ideological colours and an executive machinery fabricated by the Raj for different, not dynamic, goals.

And so the greatness of Gandhiji faded ineffectually in producing Bhangi-Bramin oneness. The Mahatma's mission who to end Harijan inequality with his magnetic silence and stormy tranquillity.

Can any truth-telling politician deny Dr. Radhkrishnan when he writes:

> "Caste has ceased to be a social evil but has become a political and administrative evil. We want to get our votes and we set up candidates suited to the people who have to vote. If it is a Nadar Constituency we set up a Nadar. If it is a Harijan constituency we set up a Harijan. If it is a Kamma constituency we set up a Kamma. This is what we have been doing. It is therefore essential that politics should be as far as possible lifted out of this kind of morass."[70]?

The fashionable constitutional retort is the reservation and other privileges accorded to the backward classes, scheduled castes and scheduled tribes! But all these large lakes of benefit, educational, public-office-oriented and financial, are being denied to the truly deserving darker segments of Dalit society by the craze of semi-forward groups to 'backwardise' themselves to batten on the butter meant for the mlechcha. Prime Minister Indira Gandhi punctured the tendency when she said:

"We should be against making backwardness a vested interest. We thought the word 'backwardness' would gradually go out of our vocabulary but we find more and more people seeking to get listed as backward. It is being joked that at this rate the whole population would be listed as backward. This is a backward-looking approach."[71]

The double danger of half-hearted enforcement of the policy of the Constitution and the deceitful deprivation of the benefits by dilution of backwardness now faces the Dalit proletariat.

The implementation of the constitutional promise must pre-eminently be through the annihilation of the caste life-style. In a country where sanyasins and scientists have the subtle sense of caste and subconscious feeling of superstition, where politics preserves caste marks in its heart and public education nurtures elitist classification, where Gods themselves bear birth-marks and laws, in enforcement, reveal a varna complex. We have miles to go, many miles to go, to attain the constitutional goal.

The lesson of our history of success—there has been great success—and of our drama of defect—for, egalitarian India, even in social life, is a far cry—is simply that a cultural revolution is the principal means for bearing true faith and allegience to constitutional meanings! How we may strive in this direction, with sure symbiotic processes of law and politics, is the seminal chapter which our jurists and statesmen, in constructive collaboration, must write.

I may conclude by stressing the basics. Law occupies a position of crucial significance for a legal system and expresses in the most vivid and real way what a society stands for. It tells what is officially and publicly considered to be right, although what is officially and publicly considered and done may conflict with what is unofficially, secretly and extensively considered and done. If the latter situation arises, law becomes socially illegitimate or societal practices become illegal. We have to use law in its functional role as a messiah and maker of change to establish new socio-economic relations supported by its coercive sanction. It is an established verity that law is an instrument in the hands of the dominant classes in society. That is how in the past the State has been a machine for the oppression of one class by another, whether it be a slave-owning State or serf-owning State or a raw capitalist State. The essence of a class society has remained the same, holding fast to class-exploitation through State power. All history is filled with persistent attempts by the oppressed classes to cast off oppression. The old law of bondage sometimes takes new forms. People will not be deceived for long by the glitter of liberal laws, and so, in a feudal-capitalist State the new watchword of 'freedom for all' has to be received cautiously. Thus society, declaring its dominance to be based on freedom, really declares property free and not the people free. We have, therefore, to use law to fit into the new values and evolve a new technology of change through a new jurisprudence. We cannot stop there either. We must train up new cadres in the three great branches of government; for victory can be real and decisive only where we have competent cadres.

The conscience of the Constitution found adequate expression on this theme, in Dr. Ambedkar's words of caution and premonition in the Constituent Assembly:

> "We must begin by acknowledging first that there is complete absence of two things in Indian society. One of these is equality. On the social plane, we have in India a society based on privilege of graded inequality which means elevation for some and degradation of others. On the economic plane, we have a society in which there are some who have immense wealth as against the many who are living in abject poverty. On the 26th of January 1950, we are going to enter into a life of contradictions. In politics we will have equality and in social and economic life we will have inequality. . . . .We must remove this contradiction at the earliest moment or else those who suffer from inequality

will blow up the structure of political democracy wchich this Assembly has so laboriously built up."[72]

Judges may differ in constitutional construction but, without peril of distorting the substance, cannot discard the activism of the equal justice concept in the setting of deep concern for the weaker sections of the community. What I endeavour to emphasize is that equal justice is an aspect of social justice, the salvation of the very weak and down-trodden, and the methodology for levelling them up to a real, not formal, equality, being the accent.

On these ideological foundations we have to build up a legal-social system which will answer the expectations and invite the penalty for inaction spelt out by Ambedkar. Do or die is the crucid challenge to India.

NOTES AND REFERENCES

Lecture No. 2.

1. Mahar. See foot note No. 2 of Lecture 1.
2. Nehru Marg. Literally means the path of Nehru or Nehru doctrine Here refers to his conception of socialism.
3. Panchama. See foot No. 29 of Lecture 1.
4. Aurobindo Veedhi: Literally means way or method. Here it refers to the method pursued by Aurobindo.
5. Vedic: Pertaining to Vedas, the holy scripture of Hindus.
6. Sarvodaya. See foot note No. 4 of Lecture 1.
7. Vinoba Verdict. Vinoba Bhave, the greatest living disciple of Mahatma Gandhi and the leader of Sarvodaya movement, preaches for equal justice through 'Gam-Vibhag' that is equal sharing.
8. Harijan-Girijan. See foot note no. 3 of Lecture 1.
9. Ambedkar, B. R.—On Parliamentary Democracy, Honorary Secretary, Poona District Law Library, Poona, 1932.
10. Refers to Nehru Marg, (Nehru, J.—India and the World, George, Allen and Unwin, London, 1936).

11. Bhangi. The term used in North India refers to the group which occupies the lowest position in the Caste hierarchy. Their main occupation is scavenging.

12. Asuric Adharma. Adharma referststo deeds which are outside the 'duties', or something which is not prescribed. Asuric which literally means 'devilish' is used here as adjective.

13. Upanishads: Upanishads are the first recorded attempts of the Hindus at systematic philosophizing. These ancient documents constitute the earliest written presentation of their efforts to construe the world of experience as a rational whole.

14. Brihad-Aranyana Upanishad, Fourth Brahman, Stanza 14.

15. Justice V.K.K. Iyer, Supreme Court, 1970.

16. Saradamoni. "Kerala in Social Change' (Unpublished dissertation)".

17. *Ibid*.

18. *Ibid*.

19. *Ibid*.

20. *Ibid*.

21. *Ibid*.

22. *Ibid*.

23. Mlechchas. See foot note no. 7 of Lecture 1.

24. Graeme (1822)—quoted from Saradamoni, *op. cit*.

25. Government of India Act, No. V of 1843.

26. Dalit. See foot note no. 1 of Lecture 1.

27. Sarodamoni—*op. cit*.

28. Dewan of Travancore. —quoted from Sarodamoni, *op. cit*.

29. 20.point programme. The economic programme advocated during the period of Emergency (1975-1977) by the then Prime Minister Mrs. Indira Gandhi.

30. Manna. Refers to the food that was believed to be dropped by God to the Israelites when they ran short of food during their exodus from Egypt. The term is now used to refer to the Gift of Grace.

31. Cochin Census Report, Census of India, 1931.

32. Saradamoni, *op. cit*.

33. *Ibid*.

34. Swaraj. See foot note no. 60 of Lecture 1.

35. Swadeshi. Literally the term means indigenous. Gandhi advocated the consumption of indigenous products which led to what is popularly referred to as 'Swadeshi Movement'.

36. Zamindari. Means 'Landlordism'. The system was introduced by the British, where landlords used to get rights over land in return of payment of tax to the British Empire.

37. Kerala vs. Thomas. 1978—I.S.C.R., p. 906.

38. De Funis. De Funis vs. Odegaard: 416 U.S. 312—40 L.Ed. 2d 164, also 82 Washington 2d 11.

39. Article 31 C (Saving of laws giving effect to directive principles). 42nd amendment, Constitution of India.

40. De Funis. *op. cit.*

41. *Ibid.*

42. From the speech of Prof. Hardgrave of Texas. Commenting on the De Funis vs. Odegaard case, 1976 (Unpublished).

43. All India Reporter, 1951, S.C., p. 226.

44. All India Reporter, 1963, S.C., p. 643.

45. All India Reporter, 1968, S.C., p. 507.

46. From the judgement of A.N. Ray, Chief Justice of India, in Kerala vs. Thomas case, p. 928.

47. *Ibid.*, p. 929.

48. *Ibid.*, p. 933.

49. From the Judgement of 'Justice V.R.K. Iyer in Kerala vs. Thomas Case, p. 969.

50. *Ibid.*, p. 921.

51. *Ibid.*, p. 973.

52. Yoga. See foot note no. 5 of Lecture 1.

53. From the judgement of Justice Fazal Ali in Kerala vs. Thomas case, p. 979-980.

54. *Ibid.*, p. 981.

55. *Ibid.*, p. 983.

56. *Ibid.*, p. 981-982.

57. *Ibid.*, p. 100.

58. From a letter received by Justice V.R.K. Iyer, from a gentleman in Hyderabad, commenting on Kerala vs. Thomas Case.

59. From the message of India Gandhi to the All India Lawyers, Meet, 1976 (Unpublished).

60. Article 38. 'State to Secure a Social Order for the promotion of Welfare of the people', Constitution of India.

61. Article 39-A. 'Certain principles of policy to be followed by the State' Constitution of India.

62. Valmiki who wrote the epic Ramayana, was epic dacoit Ratnakar before being known as Valmiki. Ratnakar, the evil, became, Valmiki, the good after repentance. Here it refers to the divinity which is there within each and every individual.

63. Article 23 (1) Constitution of India.

64. Article 46. Constitution of India.

65. Kismet. The Urdu word for fate.

66. Keer D.—*op. cit.*, p. 142.

67. *Ibid.*

68. Varna. Literally means colour. Here it means the classes. Traditional Indian society was stratified into four varnas: Brahmin, Kshatriya, Vaisya and Sudra based on their occupations.

69. Ambedkar, B.R. 'On Parliamentary Democracy—Hon. Secretary, Poona, District Law Library, Poona, 1952.

70. Radhakrishnan, S. Bhavan's Journal, Bombay, May 13, 1962.

71. Statement by Mrs. Indira Gandhi—The Hindu, Madras, May 22, 1971.

72. Ambedkar, B.R. Constituent Assembly Debates, Vol. IX. pp. 962-970.

3

Depressed Classses: A Socio-Economic Profile

It has been estimated that nine-tenths of the small marginal cultivators households received an income of less than Rs. 2,600 (annual average), and half of the small cultivators' households less than Rs. 1,000/. The budget of the small cultivator household is, therefore, almost always unfavourable, the deficit ranging from 5 per cent to 27 per cent. Thus the large majority of the very small landholders are in perpetual debt. The average total assets of 'small cultivators' in India is Rs. 2,573 only. This puts his credit-worthiness at a very low level.

People from the Scheduled Castes (Untouchables) and Scheduled Tribes form a large proportion of these suppressed categories. The majority of the Scheduled Castes and Scheduled Tribes, who form about one-fourth of the total Indian population, subsist below the poverty line and besides face problems peculiar to them. Continuing to pursue traditional occupations they are unable to avail of the fruits of economic growth and participate fully in the process of modernization. The population of the Scheduled Castes in India is about 100 million. They have very few assets and are generally dependent upon agricultural labour, leather work and other low-income occupations.

Of the total working population of Scheduled Castes, 52 per cent are agricultural labourers and conversely 33 per cent of all of India's agricultural labourers are Scheduled Castes. The few cultivators amongst Scheduled Castes are sharecroppers or subsistance farmers. Others mostly pursue traditional occupations and are unable to avail themselves of the new employment opportunities. Their literacy level is only 14.7 per cent as compared to the all-India level of 33.80 per cent (excluding Scheduled Castes and Tribes). Female literacy among them is as low as 6.44 per cent against an all-India female literacy level of 22.5 per cent (excluding Scheduled Castes and Tribes). In spite of their adverse conditions, they contribute significantly to the sustenance and growth of the production system of the country. The practice of untouchability against Scheduled Castes creates a special handicap for them; even the few educated groups amongst them are unable to compete for various job opportunities. The Scheduled Tribes still remain largely outside the mainstream of development, mainly because of their relative isolation and their exploitation by outside agencies. A large portion of bonded labourers are also Scheduled Castes [SCs] and Scheduled Tribes [STs].

In the case of both SCs and STs, social and economic impoverishment are the main causes of their backwardness. In spite of constitutional directives and a number of legislative and executive measures by the government, their situation has not improved perceptibly owing to the lack of genuine support. Although special programmes were formulated in the five-year plans for the upliftment of weaker sections in general, the economic base of SCs and STs continues to be extremely weak.

While a number of special programmes aimed at ameliorating the conditions of the weaker sections in general have been sponsored by the government, not a single agency has been created specifically for the economic development of the Scheduled Castes (Untouchables). Some of the special programmes implemented for weaker sections in general are: Intensive Agricultural Development Programme (IADP), Drought-Prone Areas Programmes (DRAP), Crash Scheme for Rural Employment, Small Farmers' Development Agency (SFDA), Marginal Farmers' and Agricultural Labourers' (MFAL) development agency, Integrated Rural Development Programme (IRDP), Regional Rural Banks (RRBs), Farmers' Service Societies (FSSs) Tribal Development Agencies, etc. of these programmes, SFDA and IRDP have been selected for detailed discussion in this paper, as they focus on rural weaker sections among whom SCs and STs are concentrated.

Small Farmers' Development Agency. The All-India Rural Credit Review Committee (1969), which tried to evaluate the progress of the Crop Loan Scheme and the Scheme of Outright Grants introduced for the benefit of small farmers on the recommendation of an earlier panel, namely the Committee on Co-operative Credit (1960), found that the performance was hardly inspiring despite a few noticeable bright spots. The flow of credit continued to be biased in favour of large and medium farmers; the weaker sections received very little support even from the co-operatives primarily meant for them. The committee, while emphasizing the need for speedy and complete restructuring, recommended the creation of special agencies for the first time in India for small and marginal farmers and agricultural labourers, namely Small Farmers' Development Agencies (SFDAs) and Marginal Farmers' and Agricultural Labourers' (MFALs). Eighty-seven projects of these two development schemes were operating for the benefit of the weaker sections in rural areas since 1971. On the recommendation of the National Committee on Agriculture (NCA) in 1973, two major changes were initiated during the Fifth Five-Year Plan period (1974-75 to 1978-79). First, the number of projects (agencies) was enhanced from 87 to 160 spread over 200 districts all over India. Secondly, the programmes for small farmers, marginal farmers and agricultural labourers were combined to make 160 composite SF/MFAL projects. These composite projects were called SFDAs; one was assigned to each selected district to reach a target of 50,000 beneficiaries with 5 years. A person holding land between one and two hectares was to be considered as a small farmer and one holding less than one hectare a marginal farmcr. Those benefiting under the category of agricultural labourers include persons earning a major part of their income by expending wage labour on farms. They include, apart from those having no other means of livelihood, marginal farmers and rural artisans such as carpenters, blacksmiths, cobblers, potters, etc.

The SFDAs were to be managed by the government officers of high rank, elected members of Parliament and State Legislative Assemblies and local bodies, and one or two members from small farmers and/or agricultural labourers. They were to be administered by the Deputy Collectors and a small team of technically suited officers.

Objectives of the SFDA scheme were to:

1. help increase the output of small farmers by enthusing and educating them for undertaking intensive cultivation and provide facilities such as supply of credit and other inputs and marketing of produce,

2. provide facilities for developing subsidiary occupations like animal husbandry, dairying, farm forestry for the target group,

3. supply credit, raw materials and service to the artisans and caftsman with a view to upgrading their skills and modernizing their trades, and

4. encourage production by artisans through the small village industries agency for sale within the rural community.

Critical Evaluation

Evaluation of the performance of SFDAs made by a number of expert panels reveals the following features:

1. Identification of Target Groups. The studies made by the Reserve Bank of India (RBI) and the Project Evaluation Organization (PEO) of the Planning Commission of India revealed that all the participants were not identified exclusively from the originally defined target group of small and marginal farmers, but also from larger farmers with holdings of 3.00 to 3.20 hectares (RBI on MFAL; and PEO on SF, MF and AL). Lands owned by these farmers in other villages were also not taken into account for judging their status (RBI on SFDA; and ASCI (Hyderabad) on SFDA of Hassan district). The findings of the PEO and Administrative Staff College of India (ASCI), Hyderabad, reveal that the Village Level Workers (VLWs) misused their discretionary powers under the powerful influence of big landlords. Tenants were excluded from the list in almost all the agencies. Even supervising officers who noticed the discrepancies appeared to be helpless in the matter. PEO observed that a substantial number of farmers were identified wrongly. Very little attention was paid to the identification of the agricultural labourers many of whom are Untouchables. In several projects, this group was not identified at all (RBI on SFDA). The factors responsible for slow progress of agencies and wrong indentification of target groups were certainly casteism, lack of sympathy for the poor, and influence and pressure of the caste Hindus and better-off sections on the officials of the agency.

2. Coverage of Beneficiaries. Up to the middle of 1980, a total of more than 168 lakh [168,000] families were identified in 168 SFDAs. This amounted to coverage of a little more than one lakh [100,000] families per agency. This was more than the targeted strength. Of these, nearly 73 lakhs (43.2% only) were enrolled as members of different co-operative societies. The study of MFALs of ten districts conducted by the RBI in 1973, revealed that no agricultural labourer (a category that would include large numbers of Untouchables) was enrolled as a member of any primary agricultural co-operative credit societies (PACs) in six out of the ten districts, though the MFAL was started there in 1969 for doing this job (RBI on MFAL, p. 210). The reasons for this were traced to sociological factors, conservative attitudes and to efforts to retain power balance. Most PACSs managed by the big land-lords felt that they would lose a source of cheap labour if these people became economically independent (*ibid*, p. 190) On the whole, no determined efforts were made to enrol agricultural labourers as members in PACs.

Out of the 168 lakhs of identified pontential beneficiaries, about 80.33 lakhs (47.8%) have so far been covered under one scheme or the other of the programme. Almost 62 lakhs (77% of identified and 77.5% of beneficiaries) were assisted in one way or the other in improving their agriculture. The next group includes those assisted under the schemes in the animal husbandry sector such as help in starting dairy, poultry, piggery, etc. Under these schemes a mere 9 lakh families (5.3% of the identified and 11.2% of the beneficiaries) have been assisted. Almost an equal number have been helped to improve or expand their irrigation facilities. Thus almost 99 per cent of the beneficiaries are from agricultural pursuits. Apart from the above three groups of schemes, assistance under other schemes have reached only a small number, *i.e.* 1 per cent only.

3. Expenditure on Programmes. Government assistance under these schemes has been devoted mainly towards the payments of subsidies and financial grants to organizations, besides administrative expenses. Total expenditure incurred on 87 agencies during a 5-year survey period, was to the tune of Rs. 4,153.48 lakhs, which comes to Rs. 47.74 lakhs per agency. Total expenditure after the end of the Fourth Plan up to June 1980 was of Rs. 19,198 lakhs on 161 agencies, which came to Rs. 114.27 lakhs per agency. The all-India average expenditure per beneficiary comes to about Rs. 290.

The major component of the above expenditure was in the form of subsidies to beneficiaries mostly linked with capital investment loans of medium and long term, extended by either co-operatives or commercial banks.

4. Disbursement of Loans. Since inception of the scheme to June 1980, a total amount of over Rs. 406 crores (4,060,000,000) have been disbursed as either medium or long-term loans. The per capita loan comes to Rs. 506. Since around 30 per cent of a term loan represents the subsidy, about Rs. 152 out of Rs. 290 (average expenditure per beneficiary) might have been utilized towards subsidy per borrower.

It is clearly seen from the disbursement of credit by the co-operatives and the commercial banks that there is a rising trend in the figures of disbursement of loans by both the agencies, after the Fourth Plan period. This was partly because of an increase in number of projects in the Fifth Plan and partly because of a real fillip to SFDA activities. However, one can observe that a gradual decline in this respect occurred. The decline is more in co-operatives than in commercial banks. This was due to the shortfall in the performance of co-operatives, which were specially meant for weaker sections. This was also due to the slow-down of the SFDA activities in general. The commercial banks have given a better performance than co-operatives at every level.

Thus one can see that on the whole the performance of SFDAs in respect of financial assistance is on the decline. This can be attributed partly to the exorbitant rate of interest charged to the borrowers and/or unsatisfactory terms regarding repayment. Overdues in co-operatives in rural areas are as high as 50 per cent. Owing to this unsatisfactory position, credit disbursement is declining.

5. Co-operativization of the Poor. The performance of the agencies in bringing the identified persons into the co-operative movement was not at all encouraging, though the co-operative movement was primarily meant for the poor. In nearly 50 per cent of the SFDAs, half of the identified persons were not members of co-operatives which were specially meant for them. The percentage varied from as low as 8 (ASCI, Hyderabad, on SFDA) to 98 (PEO on SFDAs). The RBI had revealed in its report that in more than one-third of the districts, less than 25 per cent of the identified persons were enrolled as members in co-operatives. Participation in co-operatives by the marginal farmers and agricultural labourers was the lowest.

The main reasons for low membership of the weaker sections were domination of co-operatives by better-off sections, casteism, lack of sympathy for the poor, low credit worthiness, indifference by the poor due to bad past experience, lack of adequate knowledge, etc.

6. *Response by the Co-operatives.* The performance of credit co-operative was not up to the level. The position was bad in most of the agencies. The RBI study reveals that in 50 per cent of the Central Co-operative Banks the amount of loans shared by the small farmers was below 20 per cent. It was less than 10 per cent in eleven Central Co-operative Banks out of nineteen. The financial assistance in the form of share capilal contribution, managerial subsidies, risk fund contribution, etc., by the agencies produced good results in only a few projects (RBI on SFDAs).

The main factors responsible for the poor performance in this respect by the co-operatives were the indequate funds with the co-operative banks and diversion of funds to the dominating better-off sections, besides low membership of weaker sections.

Various studies revealed that agricultural labourers, including the many Untouchables, were not in receipt of required credit. The PEO has observed that of the total loans invested in SFDAs and MFALs, the amount used to benefit the agricultural labourers was insignificant (1% only). Of the amount advanced, the share of co-operatives was negligible. In several project areas, agricultural labourers had absolutely no access to co-operative credit. Marginal farmers and agricultural labourers are mostly in need of consumption loans which are not extended by the PACSs in villages.

Performance in Respect of Individual Programmes

The SFDAs and MFALs had undertaken programmes such as intensive agriculture, minar irrigation, dairying, poultry, piggery, sheep-and goat-rearing and rural works programmes for the benefit of the target groups in rural areas. The role of agencies in these programmes is discussed below.

1. Intensive Agriculture. Owing to inadequate infrastructure facilities, the agency could not do much in this respect. A major shift in the cropping pattern in most of the project areas is not in evidence. Not enough efforts were extended by the agencies to prepare well-suited crop rotations and persuade farmers to adopt them. Nor were special efforts made for adoption of new techniques of cultivation and for multiple cropping.

2. Minor Irrigation. The achievements by the agencies varied considerably from below 10 per cent to above 80 per cent; the achievement of most of the agencies ranged between 26 and 75 per cent (PEO; RBI; and ASCI on SFDA and MFAL). The programmes did not make much headway due to fragmented and small holding and hilly topography.

3. Dairying. Though the programme of supply of milch cattle had been taken up by all the agencies, it was of significance in only a few project areas. As reported by several studies (PEO and RBI on SFDAs), most of the SFDAs achieved more than 50 per cent of their target, but the situation with MFAL programmes, whose potential beneficiaries were mostly Scheduled Castes and Tribes, was not encouraging. Thus the agencies took care only of farmers in supplying milch cattle and not the category of landless agricultural labourers in which Untouchables are concentrated.

Some of the problems often faced by the agencies were inadequate market facilities, high cost and non-availability of cattlefeed, absence of breeding facilities, unsatisfactory health coverage, non-availability of high yielding milch cattle, and lack of co-ordination with the programmes of government departments. In spite of these handicaps, dairying emerged as one of the relatively successful components of the programmes.

4. Poultry. Most of the agencies introduced poultry schemes, but only in a few agencies did it make satisfactory progress. The performance of SFDAs was relatively better than MFALs in this field also. Main factors for slow progress were high price of feed and low price of eggs, non-availability of breeds, inadequate marketing arrangements and lack of veterinary aid.

5. Piggery, Sheep-and Goat-Rearing. Only in a few projects were these schemes introduced. In these projects the beneficiaries were covered in very small numbers. In a few projects the piggery scheme failed due to the adverse attitude of participants to this occupation, high cost of feed and lack of good market. Sheep-rearing was quite popular in some areas due to availability of plenty of grazing fields and lower cost of maintenance. The performance was poor in the case of goat-rearing. Hervy casualties occurred due to improper health care and lack of veterinary facilities.

6. Rural Works Programme. The Rural Works Programme relates to the construction of godowns [storage sheds] and market yards, community wells and devices for lift irrigation, provision of custom services to the farmers and other rural works programmes designed to generate employment opportunities for marginal farmers and agricultural labourers during the slack season.

These programmes were undertaken by most agencies much later than the other above discussed schemes, and consequently the progress in this respect was limited, though the entire expenditure was to be met from the agencies' funds. Some agencies placed much emphasis on these programmes, even neglecting subsidiary occupations. Road construction and minor irrigation were the most common items in this programme. A complete picture of employment to agricultural labourers and marginal farmers is not available. However, as observed by the PEO the percentage of identified agricultural labourers provided with employment under this scheme ranged from 0.4 to 19.0, and for marginal farmers from 0.2 to 6.2.

Proportion of Beneficiaries of SCs and STs

Data on the number of Scheduled Castes (SCs) and Scheduled Tribes (STs) identified, enrolled as members and benefited by one scheme or the other are available for 150 SFDAs surveyed out of 168 existing in the country (NIRD, Hyderabad, Rural Development in India, p. 28). SCs and STs are about 23.7 per cent of the Indian population, but in the identified categories they are 16.6 per cent, in enrolment of membership 13.5 per cent, and in beneficiaries 18 per cent only. Thus they are not taken at least in existing proportion for various benefits by the other sections. The expenditure incurred on these two classes in 1979-80 was 13.3 per cent of the total for the agencies. Out of a total 7,198,721 beneficiaries, 7,071,883 (98.3%) were from agricultural pursuits such as improven agriculture, minor irrigation and animal husbandry. In village industries and other occupations (form the tertiary sector) there were only 11,160 (1.7%) beneficiaries. Thus the SFDAs were working for small and marginal farmers only, and not for landless agricultural labourers (among whom Untouchables are concentrated) and rural artisans. Rural works programmes were beneficial to landless labourers, but they were not undertaken except in a few instances.

Defects in the Working of SFDAs

Following were the prominent defects in ths working of the SFDAs:

1. Trying to cover under one scheme all weaker sections, including small farmers and marginal farmers, was not calculated to promote efficiency in implementation. Merging SFDAs and MFALs was again improper, because the issues relating to the different classes are hardly likely to be identical. The problems and needs of the different categories of the rural poor—such as small farmers, morginal farmers, agricultural labourers, Scheduled Castes, Scheduled Tribes, Notified Tribes, Denotified Tribes, non-farm workers and rural artisans—are different and require specific programmes to be chalked out for meeting them. Even among the Scheduled Castes and Scheduled Tribes, there are poorer and indigent sections, neglected and suppressed sections. Identical programmes for the upliftment of all the weaker sections will not yield results.

2. The members of better-off sections, such as landlords, managed to infiltrate the target groups of weaker sections to usurp the benefits bestowed by these agencies by producing false certificates issued by the colluding bureaucrats. Naturally, to accommodate them the genuine poor were elbowed out. The entire set-up is such that even among the poor, the relatively better placed were more readily covered and indigent sections tended to be ignored.

3. The landless labourers, who were amongst the poorest of the weaker sections and generally hailed from the Untouchable communities, actually received negligible or no benefits from the agency. The benefits of the agency were denied to these people by operating their schemes—such as rural works programmes, goat-and sheep-rearing, and poultry schemes—rarely or too late.

4. The commercial and co-operative banks did not exhibit any inclination or enthusiasm to finance the schemes of the weaker sections in general and that of Scheduled Castes and Scheduled Tribes in particular. The Reserve

Bank of India stipulates that at least 20 per cent of the total outstanding credit should be loaned to the weaker sections. There is also a scheme for outright grants for the benefit of these sections, which also has not been operative for the most part. The co-operative banks, which are dominated by the better-off classes, have played an even smaller role in helping the poor than the commercial banks. The assistance received by SFDAs from all fnancing agencies has been declining.

5. The contribution of the concerned government departments such as Revenue, Agriculture, Animal Husbandry, Co-operation, Fisheries, etc., towards the smooth operation of the agencies was insignificant.

6. Infrastructural facilities comprising marketing, storage, transport facilities, feed stocks, veterinary hospitals, banking, post office, etc., were woefully inadequate for subsidiary businesses like dairy, animal husbandry, poultry, etc., which adversely affected their progress.

7. The implementing officers of the agencies were generally drawn from the better-off classes who lacked knowledge of the intricacies of problems at grass-roots level and genuine sympathy for the lowly. Perhaps public-spirited officers belonging to weaker sections might have given a better performance.

8. Last but not least, representatives of Scheduled Castes and Scheduled Tribes were not taken on to the managing committees of the agencies. Members of Parliament and State Legislative Assemblies generally hailing from better-off sections dominated these committees and tried to manipulate the agencies to promote their vested interests.

Conclusions

As experienced by the agencies, the problems of weaker sections in rural areas are complicated and they need closer attention on a long-term basis than attempted by the agencies.

A thorough examination of eligibilities, needs constraints and assistance required is needed, if the rural poor are to be helped. Obviously this cannot be accomplished by a small team of three or four officers to cover about 50,000 people, and that too within five years. A systematic individual-centred and broad-based approach is essential.

The indicators used for measuring the performances of programmes have all been statistical indices like number of potential beneficiaries identified, number of these covered under some subsidy scheme, amount spent, equipment distributed etc. These are only indirect indicators and are not necessarily able to show the change in incomes and the quality of life of beneficiaries.

4

Dalit in the Modern World: Search for Identity

A constitution is never a culmination is ever a commencement in the long navigation a nation makes, from generation to generation, guided by the governing values of a given era. By this canon, our Constitution is a project for the dignity and development of a nation, a blueprint for raising the worth of the human person in the hallowed land of Bharat.[1] The higher motivation of our Constituent Assembly was highighted by Nehru when he said:

> "The first task of this Assembly is to free India through a new constitution, to feed the starving people, and to clothe the naked masses, and to give every Indian the fullest opportunity to develop himself according to his capacity."[2]

Our societal goal is an emphatic Destination Man. This massive development dynamics, in the context of a status bound, hierachical polity of 600 millions, compels "a fundamental change in the structure of Indian society" Social democracy is not midwifed through soft therapeutics, especially when the down-trodden numbers of scheduled tribes and scheduled castes involve a staggering 135 millions and the resistance to change takes refuge in 500 thousand villages, primitively oriented to anti-Harijan Reaction. To fight this hard core of rural India where untouchability rules untouched is a giant task and an urgent imperative. One evidence of why we should burn with social rage, we will mention. Imagine acharyas[3] preaching and practising touch-me-notism, and worse, wet scavanging and night-soil carrying by Bhangis,[4] especially their womenfolk, through stinking public streets as a ubiquitous urban spectacle, even over 25 years after the burial of untouchability by Article 17 of the Constitution and the banning of head-load carriage of human excreta by municipal laws and Central directives! It is an unspeakable survival of the Past that even today, in the Socialist Republic of India, the right to get scavanging done for villages and towns is regarded by an unconscionable Indian law a profitable right, inflicting a double exploitation on the humiliated Bhangis! The long limbs of the law hang limp and uncivilized where social will wilts. The politics of platitude and the law of the Constitution have yet to pierce the armour of primitivism in life.

A scientific approach to this colossal socio-legal problem must become a national plan in itself—defining the objectives, refining the strategies and orienting the cadres so that the castles of conservatism might be beseiged by the joint forces of law and politics. The objective is quite plan—the dismanling of the hierarchical social system and the spreading of distributive economic justice. The engineering process is equally clear—the use of legal fire power to remould the social and economic order and of the thrust of the political power to make such revolutionary legal mandate strong enough to break the walls of orthodoxy. The competence of the cadres is equally noteworthy. Lenin long ago said, "Cadres are everything". Gandhiji set the tone for the spirit we must summon in this campaign for uplift when he said:

> "I shall work for an India in which the poorest shall feel that it is their country in whose making they have an effective voice; an India in which there shall be no high

class or low class of people; an India in which all communities shall live in perfect harmony."[5]

Prime Minister Indira Gandhi underscored the new stragegy when she articulated the need for a planned attack on this grave human problem:

> "We have evolved the strategy of sub-plans and have systematically identified the areas of tribal concentration. Sometimes these strategies and plans become bottlenecks. We should see that whatever is decided is implemented straightway.[6]
>
> The most important element is the personnel. We should find out dedicated persons who have the competence and the correct attitude, the correct emotional involvement with this work . . . People should be urged to do something because it is in the national interest and it is something worth doing and it is a rewarding thing even for the individual.
>
> A simple situation requires a simple organisation so that the unsophisticated people with whom one has to deal can understand and not get confused by complicated procedures."

The political decision is that social justice to the backward classes is a time-bound 'must'; the legal projection of this political resolution is the erection of an infra-structure operating on legislative wheels for the betterment of the culturally, economically and socially weakest sections of the general community. The constitutional reflection of this time is found in Article 38 which directs the creation of a social order in which justice social, economic and political—shall inform all institutions of the national life. The cornerstone of the Dalit revolution is Article 46 which nobly enounces:

> "The State shall promote with special care the educational and economic interests of the weaker sections of the people.

and, in particular, of the Scheduled Castes and Scheduled Tribes, and shall protect them from social injustice and all forms of exploitation."[7]

Special care is called for, not routine attention. Both their education and economic interests, in their broadest connotation, must receive State protection and promotion. The weakest sections are the target group. They deserve the greatest assistance who need help most. Dalit justice is integral to social justice. Therefore, areas of chronic social injustice must be identified as the enemy and battle tactics must be adopted to fight down exploitation, neglect and suppression with the focus on equalisation and homogenisation. This philosophy and plan must find organisational statutory expression as the National Human Dignity and Development Authority with special responsibilities and comprehensive powers and annual accountability to Parliament. Even the Special Officer for Scheduled Castes and Scheduled Tribes appointed under Article 338 and the Commission appointed under Article 339 and Article 340 can be integrated with this high powered Authority which may also work in close liaison with the Planning Commission for formulation and implementation of the Sub-Plan for Scheduled Castes and Scheduled Tribes and Scheduled Areas. The ministries at the State and Central levels charged with the welfare of Scheduled Castes and Scheduled Tribes can be welded into this national machinery. Even special tribunals to enforce welfare and protective legislation may be organised by this super-body manned by appropriate personnel with deep commitment to the cause—the cause of social transformation.

It is fair to project the contemporary position as a starting point for further discussion. The 22nd Report of the Commissioner for Scheduled Castes and Scheduled Tribes begins beautifully with a general observation which aptly sums up the conscience of the Constitution, the efforts made to eradicate backwardness and a realistic appraisal of success and failures—rather, the balance-sheet of the socio-economic business of the nation in the area of uplift of the depressed classes:

"1.2 The makers of the Constitution were quite consccious about the prevailing miserable and appalling living conditions of a large section of our population, particularly the Scheduled Castes and Scheduled Tribes who have remained far behind and regregated from our national and social life and have continued to be socially suppressed and economically exploited for centuries due to various types of social disabilities created by socio-religious taboos like untouchability in the caste-ridden structure of the Hindu Society. This is apparent from the special provisions and safeguards provided in the Constitution for the development of the economically and socially weaker sections, particularly the Scheduled Castes and Scheduled Tribes—the weakest amongst them.[8]

"1.3 There is no doubt that during the past two and a half decades, efforts have been made for the social upliftment and educational and economic development of these communities. A number of useful schemes to achieve that end have also been introduced through various Five-Year Plans which have benefited these people to some extent. In the field of general development, however, the country has made tremendous progress in various spheres and in some of them we have achieved spectacular results of which one can feel proud of. No doubt due to all these efforts there has been general prosperity in the country but only a few have been benefited by it and no one should complain about the prosperity of such persons. These benefits have not percolated to the desired extent to the weaker sections. The question is whether we really planned things in such a manner as to enable the weaker sections to get their due share as envisaged in our Constitution, so that they also feel that they are equal partners in the prosperity of the Nation."[9]

The Commissioner quotes the Prime Minister to say:

"While I am fully conscious of the slowness of this work, I do not think we should belittle the progress which has been made in the last twenty years. There is, for example, remarkable achievement in the field of education. We have today a large number of doctors, engineers, administrators and professors coming from these groups. Within a few years some of them will be in the top rung of their professions. They have important positions in all the political parties, and I have no doubt that they will hold a much larger number of such positions as time goes on. In fact, I think that it is their active role in the legislatures and in the Government which has done so much to wipe out many of the old prejudices. The growth of industries and urban communities is also helping in this progress. Yet we realise only too poignantly that much more needs to be done."[10]

Self-criticism and recognition of shortcomings are essential if we are to avoid pitfalls and accelerate the pace. There is, to be candid, considerable work done but the undone—The Great Divide—is big too. The facts of contrast between the Raj[11] and the Republic are extraordinary. I shall quote an official statement in this behalf:

> "Untouchability has been abolished by law, and no discrimination is allowed on the ground of caste, creed or profession.
>
> Literacy has gone up significantly among the Scheduled Castes since Independence. It is now 14.71 per cent as against 1.9 per cent in 1931.
>
> From 1964 onwards in the IAS, and IPS, as also in Class I and Class II Central Services, to which recruitment is made on the basis of the IAS etc. Examinations, all the reserved vacancies are being filled up by candidates belonging to Scheduled Castes. The number of Scheduled Castes in IAS and IPS was 18 and 7 respectively as on 1.1.1954 which rose to 252 and 130 on 1.1.1974. Out of 717 cannidates, 22 Scheduled Caste candidates were selected for IAS and 72

Scheduled Caste candidates for IPS and other Central Services during 1975.

More than three lakhs of post-matric scholarships are awarded to Scheduled Caste students as against 114 scholarships given in 1944-45. The rates of these scholarships have also been enhanced.

Finance corporations for the economic development of Scheduled Castes have been set up in Andhra Pradesh, Assam, Kerala, Punjab, Uttar Pradesh and Haryana.

6,93,567 acres of land were allotted to 35,732 landless workers amongst the Scheduled Castes during 1970-71.*

In Fourth Plan Rs. 32.05 crores was spent on the housing scheme for the Scheduled Castes and 1,21,811, houses were constructed."[12]

Where have we failed and why? Remembering that there are over 135 million people in this humble category what has been achieved makes us blush. Untouchability abolition has been more in law than in life. Very few prosecutions, fewer successful convictions and fewest effective sentences, are the cynical tale of an important enactment which the beneficiaries do not know, the offenders openly violate and the law agencies regard as a nuisance. So it is that the Prime Minister exhorted:

"Fight against Untouchability must continue. . . . Untouchability was poison for the progress of the country and anybody believing in it must be condemned irrespective of his status in social or religious life."[13]

A revolutionary measure, in some respects, is the passage of the Civil Rights Protection Act, 1976[14]—a reincarnation with sharper legal claws, more realistic attack on the evil and some serious thought for community responsibility in ending the

*For the Eighth Plan perspective, see excerpt from the Plan Document at Appendix-I.

practice of untouchability. But revolutionary legislation can be dismal disaster unless militant legal literacy, aware enforcement cadres, supportive auxiliary forces of social reform, sensitized backing of public opinion and relentless punitive strategy, can be ensured. The new measure is, anyway, a landmark legislation where Parliament has dared to wound the vicious practitioners collectively and individually whether found guilty in private or public places, preaching or practising. Indeed, violations in private shrines and private lives are, by far, the largest and the law reaching out to catch them is commendably original. Many loopholes of the earlier law have been sealed, the sentencing has been made stern and probation leniency taken away. The new provision Sec. 10A empowers the State Government to impose collective fines on the inhabitants of an area vicariously involved in the offence of untouchability. More importantly and quite realistically, the Act goes at the public servants who wilfully neglect investigation into these anti-social crimes. The escalation of crime is often due to the gross inaction of law agencies. Another touch of realism is in the mild distrust of ordinary criminal courts with legalese and the 'sacred cows' of the forensic system. It is good that Special Courts can be set up for trial of these offences. Another wholesome innovation consists in making convictions for untouchability offences disqualificatory of membership of the legislatures. Yet another progressive provision is in See 15 (2) (i) which states:

> "The provision of adequate facilities, including legal aid to the persons subjected to any disability arising out of "untouchability" to enable them to avail themselves of such rights."

Legislations are not self-acting remedies for social sins. The victims intended to be benefited must be given legal literacy, afforded legal aid and provided facilities for setting the law in motion. Positive action in this behalf is a sine qua non for social success of ameliorative laws for the weaker sections. Indeed this great legislation is a pioneering effort in affirmative and effective State action in tracking down anti-social offenders and may well be a model for other statutory projects.

What more should be done to make this penal law more potent? A few unorthodox suggestions may be ventured for serious reflection. The Special Courts must be located in villages where Harijans mostly live. The distance between the crime and the court is often the distance between law and justice. Special Courts must be sitting solely for cases under this Act and the composition must be of two laymen of whom one must be a member of Scheduled Caste and the third a lawman. There must be mobile courts and activist judges; procedures must be simple and summary and the Evidence Act inapplicable. The law of evidence is so sophisticated that when artless people are parties or witnesses, its operation is often self-defeating. The commonsense of common men is good enough. Preponderance of probabilities, as against proof beyond reasonable doubt, must be enough. A single appeal to the High Court should be sufficient—not a tiring series of appeals and revisions and further appeals. The traditional, over-judicialised life style of our criminal system has claimed a dear price from the community in the sense of acquittals of the really guilty and delays productive of injustice. The failure of the Act in another area is in the welcome provisions of Sec. 7A.[15] It reads perfect:

> "7A. (1) Whoever compels any person on the ground of 'untouchability' to do any scavanging or sweeping or to remove any carcass or to do any other job of a similar nature, shall be deemed to have enforced a disability arising out of 'untouchability'.
>
> (2) Whoever is deemed under sub-section (1) to have enforced a disability arising out of 'untouchability' shall be punishable with imprisonment for a term which shall not be less than three months and not more than six months and also with fine which shall not be less than one hundred rupees and not more than five hundred rupees."

It may prove a damp squib in practice. To prove compulsion is difficult; to prove that it is on the ground of untouchability is more difficult; to leave the local bodies to hire Harijans for all these same mean jobs but to punish private people for the same acts looks strange. Is it for pleasure or under implicit compulsion of starvation that Bhangi women foul themselves in the mornings in municipalities by removing flowing night-soil from many houses? Can public bodies be models for criminals without societal demoralisation? The remedy is more radical. Is social conscience ready for it? And rehabilitation of displaced persons must be part of penal projects. Why have the draftsmen forgotten to define inclusively and comprehensively what is 'untouchability' instead of leaving it to be truncated or distorted by literal interpretations in courts? Wisdom comes, if it comes, from experience. To leave the cornerstone shaky is to build weak.

However, we must congratulate the Dalit parliamentarians and Parliament itself for this heroic measure—a homage to Baba Saheb Ambedkar! The title and many clauses suggested by Ambedkar himself once, are a great tribute to his memory twenty years after his death—We honour our great by posthumous fulfilment of their militant noble mission.

If total eradication of untouchability is the basic condition of social democracy, the economic imperative of democracy, so far as the Dalit proletariat is concerned, will not be a living reality unless a transformation in their economic way of life is achieved. It is a notorious fact that untouchability which is a social stigma, is closely associated with demeaning occupations traditionally allotted to the Dalit Proletariat. They are inter alia scavanging, sweeping, removing carcasses, flaying animals, removing umbilical cords and other similar degraded vocations. A bulk of this community constitutes India's landless labour, living under near-serf conditions. They are the bonded labour whom the 20-point programme[16] seeks to redeem. They are the landless drudges in the villages for whom land reform laws will be a blessing. In short, they are degraded both economically and socially. Therefore, the Sub-Plan which the Union

Government has evolved as a specialised strategy to salvage the Dalit Proletariat must zero in on projects peculiarly adapted to the uplift of these classes. The delivery system must not be lost in officialese or drowned in litigation or be allowed to be exploited by the upper layers of the Scheduled Caste groups but must reach the target groups intended to be served. This is so important that if there is one lesson from the failures of social legislation it is this that the third reading of a Bill or its final validation by the Supreme Court or the lovely drafting of an executive project pursuant to it is but the beginning and not the end of Operation Amelioration! A classic instance is our land reform measures; for, with no court or constitution coming in the way, land reforms tantalise and remain a far cry even today. And the harrowing tale of bonded labour defies the abolition legislation.

We have earlier mentioned about the cream of Scheduled Castes lapping up the cream of benefits. This is confirmed by the observations of the Assembly Committee (of West Bengal) on the Welfare of Scheduled Castes and Scheduled Tribes. A recent report says:

> "The assembly committee on the welfare of the Scheduled Castes and Tribes has observed that the benefits granted to them by the Central and State Govrenments have largely been usurped' by the vocal and economically more privileged sections.
>
> The Committee wants the newly-constituted West Bengal Scheduled Castes Development and Finance Corporation to pay greater attention to the 'silent majority of the people of these communities who have been forced to live in abysmal poverty'.[17]
>
> Once a group of beneficiaries is economically settled, it should be required to carry on with its own resources, the Corporation extending help to the next group of waiting people."[18]

These guidelines are contained in the committee's report tabled in the House today. The report also notes another disquieting feature—gradual displacement of the members of the Scheduled Castes from the traditional occupations under the impact of modern technological development.[19]

In the course of formulation of its policies, the Corporation should endeavour to remove the imbalance in the economy that has 'crippled a section of the Scheduled Castes on account of their displacement from traditional occupations, and to ensure technological advancement of these under-privileged people engaged in the production process.'

But the committee emphasised the Corporation, apart from granting loans to potential entrepreneurs, should also serve developmental and promotional purposes; its task should generally be to 'change the basis of privileges from concession to facilities and to remove the special barrier blocking the mobility of the weaker sections of the community into the mainstream of socio-economie life.'[20]

The Corporation should have a separate cell for collecting commercial intelligence in various fields of economic activity in the rural and urban areas and draw and elaborate extension service for the economically unorganised."[21]

Prosperity of ideas and penury in performance is Indian genius.

Bonded labour is quasi-slavery. Its stronghold is the agrarian mediaevalism of modern India. The manpower of this dismal system is the Dalit Proletariat. Landlessness of agricultural workers is the fertile condition for this flourishing custom. Caste-based chores and the social exclusion of the panchama[22] humanity from the mainstream of national life thrive on the land system, the brahmin[23] to the bhangi being assigned proper places in the vertical societal scheme. The temples the rituals, the myths, bigotries and obscurantist mannerisms which make up the mores of the bulk of the community are regulated in their graded importance and access by the land system from a distance. Feudal ways of life, which have bent into shape even village democracy survive on agrarian dharma. After all, caste continues to be politics in village India. The economy of rural agriculture remains grossly unproductive because the creative energies of the masses are frozen by the land pyramid. If you want to fly into the past and glory over the primitive greatness, keep this agrestic injustice intact; but if you do mean to modernise, democratise and constitutionalise the values of half a million villages do ignite the grass-roots revolution by blowing up the backwardness of the land law with the bomb of a new agrarian jurisprudence. Indian stagnation and Dalit servitude will keep company with us in this century unless we sentence to transportation for life this land-locked Reaction. If we are to legitimise our societal ethos by our constitutional creeds and write on it the values of social justice we must radicalise our land law, abolish landlordism, invest landless labour with land, make the tiller the owner and create a system of incentives and facilities to kindle self-respect and passion for production. The strategy of Indian transformation is the redemption of the village from the vampire of primitive land ownership. The strategy of distributive justice for Dalit proletarians must begin with humanising agrarian jurisprudence. This programme was part of our Freedom Struggle. This compulsion was strong enough to amend the Constitution one year after it was grandly inaugurated. And the Prime Minister's best point is the stress on land distribution. Yet the bourgeoisie are playing hide and seek with land reform, making laws in the books and defeating them, not in the courts now but in pragmatic politics and in the enforcement field. The Man with the Hoe—see him and listen to him:

> "Bowed by the weight of centuries he leans
> Upon his hoe and gazes on the ground,
> The emptiness of ages on his face,
> And on his back the burden of the world.

"Through this dread shape the suffering ages look
Time's tragedy is in that aching stoop.
Through this dread shape humanity betrayed,
Plundered, profaned and disinherited,
Cries protest to the powers that made the world
A protest that is also prophecy."[24]

If the Indian Constitution is the title-deed of peaceful socio-economic revolution and the Indian land reform laws are the guidebook for the process, the time is ripe for youth power in alliance with Dalit wrath to midwife the birth of the New Order of land justice and kulak obituary. This is the dialectics of the situation. My plea is that the land revolution through the law must be operated by organizing an army of Dalit youth—the proletariate of the proletariat. Legal constructs which will involve these new forces alone produce the true synthesis of economic justice. The days of double think, double talk and double do are numbered and the era of ambivalence is dying.

Why legal power to the tribals and the Panchamas? Because law not merely sets the norms; its engineering can be effective if it is vested in the hands of the consumers. In our social conditions laws will flop if administered by a class belonging to or corrupted by the proprietariat. The lands given to Adivasis[25] have been snatched away, the lands formally given to Harijans never got into their hands, the lands effectively given were wrested from them by litigation and many other ailments afflicted well-intentioned legislations because the enforcement cardres were unsympathetic and the structures and processes were complicated. Distribute all the lands and you dissolve feudalism—not till then.

We say so because it is elementary in the history of the world that the feudal property regime linked estates in land with status in society. This involved a power-combination of political and proprietary relations, 'a fusion of public and private law'. So it is that in all early systems, 'dominium' meant both ownership and lordship—even spiritual supremancy and military rank. This design to link 'land law' with political, military and religious power and even family headship is at the root of para-feudal jurisprudence. So, cut the root and the trunk will wither, not till then.

Mere distribution is not distributive justice. The sinews of Development must be there. Give them—the 135 million people—education, credit, fertilisers, cooperatives, market facilities, occupational training. And then Dalit power will make its best contribution to national reconstruction. We have to get out of the rut and be ideologically conditioned for the change.

In the Operation Civil Revolution, the legal process, geared to people's justice, has a constructive role to play. It is well known that welfare legislation has no wings and effective publicity is needed to create literacy in such law in the largest group before they can claim to be consumers of social justice through social legislation. Mere creation of consciousness is not enough. The Dalits have to be helped by legal-aiders with free facilities for asking, getting and keeping their rights from courts and administrative agencies. To secure rights to the weak with special care is to provide, all along the 'route, every needed assistance and further to ensure that the benefits obtained are held secure because otherwise, they will be cheated of their rights by social swindlers waiting round the corner by means of inducement, threat and the like. The social responsibility of the State, through the legal aid agencies, is to enforce effective performance of the legislative programmes, even by reform of the law if, in its working, defects are found. The metabolism of democratic legality is complete only when the legislative nutrients are fully absorbed by the weaker limbs of the body politic. The vistarama of 'juridicare' is thus a democratic imperative of a progressive rule of law.

In these sectors much remains to be done. Our land reforms laws are inadequate, ill conceived and not even straight-forward in some cases. To illustrate is to injure and I pause. Our

Harijan welfare programmes have a socialist finish on paper but performance auditors have a nasty report to make. May we expect a dramatic seriousness and a new drive with verve in organising this beneficient mission? Law and politics must combine for success.

Confusion in court decisions caused by absence of social thrust in the judicial bosom; mixing up backward classes with Scheduled Castes and Tribes resulting in the less backward lapping up the free milk from the administrative table; vocal domination by forward classes in legislative houses drowning the less strident voices of the Harijans; the staffing of Harijan projects by non-and-anti-Harijan cadres; the politicizing party-wise, of Harijan organizations creating disruption, corruption and bogus leadership; the temptation to help oneself at the expense of the silent innocents and to swindle government money earmarked for Harijan housing, Harijan scholarships, tribal welfare and the like and the absence of adequate or quick-acting or efficacious special punitive remedies or free legal services programmes, have made the valiant saga of administrative jack-up and legislative life-up of the Dalit proletariat a historic failure. The slogan of land for the landless, considering how great a blessing for Harijans and how strategic a blow on feudal headquarters it could have been, has had cynical impact except in official hand-outs, political speeches and some annual reports. The many Commissions, the Central and State heads of Harijan welfare departments, why, most Harijan Ministers, have, over the decades, confessed, in private, how the untouchables remain untouched by welfare measures and how, to the depressed classes, the three great instrumentalities of State still remain 'untouchable' and 'unapproachable'. Welfare programmes have reached a point of no return so that the sooner we change the human engineers who work the Harijan projects and involve Dalit humanity in the legislative and administrative processes, the better. Harijan welfare should not be harijanised in administrative priorities.

There is a new stir during the last few years. Those who know the Constitution and the provisions relating to

Emergency Powers will know that it is folly to lug in better enforcement of measures as part of the gains of Emergency. The truth is that a new seriousness has dawned on the political leadership; consequently, a new speed and sincerity have invigorated the administrative echelons and a new confidence among the scheduled castes and scheduled tribes is creeping in. A new sociological awareness has affected the noetic altitude of the judiciary. But the political resistance, especially to land distribution, abolition of bonded labour and rural indebtedness, mounted covertly by small and not-so-small Party bosses and ubiquitous kulaks makes pessimism current coin. Not statistics, but veracity, not new projects, but new will—these are the considerata. For, when the big tomes of our history are written with sociological acumen and independent candour, the huge officialese on Dalit betterment may shrink into a few pages, with sardonic footnotes suggestive of hypocriticalhomage to the Father of the Nation. Even our fashionable researchers, except for micro-studies, have forgotten Dalit brothers. Et tu brute!

Therefore, what? The awakening has come. There is a new administrative wave, legislative awakening and juridicare sensibility—all to the activist credit of the Prime Minister Indira Gandhi, whose 7-point action plan for national cohesion may bode a new deal. Equally importantly, a welcome militancy amongst the panchamas, warning that they be not taken for granted is showing up, lying low during the Emergency but sure to blow as a storm if the old tape-recorded tunes do not give place to massive, orchestrated marching songs of the brave Dalit youth. 'Scheduled' Power is emerging—ala Dalit Panthers[26] —to wipe out the indelible stains and incurable wounds of our mediaeval mores! The days of morganatic alliance with Harijans are gone and a new homogenisation is on the way.

This hope of Indian history needs a closer study. The ends must animate the means, in any social manoeuvre. What are the objectives? Homogenise socially, not perpetuate compartmentalization. Equalise, not profess equality, when inequality is writ large on social reality. Accelerate socialism in land, desegregate residence and economic equity through distributive justice and promote the living doctrine of each according to his needs and ability to work. We then honour Gandhi, Nehru and Ambedkar.

Speaking in socio-spiritual terms, the Hindu ego, encrusted in chatur varna,[27] must go, and the sheen of Sarvam-brahma mayam[28] must light up life in the raw. Thereby we pay tribute to human unity, to reformers and rishis, contemporary and of yore. These broad generalisations will cut no ice unless a more deliberate policy takes hold of the situation, more probity and imperativeness possess execution of policies and periodic performance audits, followed by self-criticism, are built into the system. The hortative era has vanished.

A national newspaper summarised the present situation with fair insight. To quote:

> "The problems of the tribal face—the expropriation of their lands, the conditions of virtual serfdom under which so many of them labour, their indebtedness to usurers—are deeply rooted in their past. Trying to resolve them is not simply a matter of efficient and compassionate administration. It entails nothing less than tackling head-on the vested interests that thrive on the present set-up. But while a strong positive and sympathetic administration which throws its full weight behind the tribals in their struggle against their over-lords is not a sufficient condition on ameliorative change it is nevertheless a necessary one. Where an official responsible for administering a tribal area has been indifferent to the inhabitants' problems, or, even worse, has made it plain by his behaviour and attitude that he identifies with those he should be fighting against, the result has been the perpetuation of the status quo. Because, unfortunately, this has tended to be the general experience so far, the Union Home Minister has found it necessary to exhort tribal development project administrators to look upon their work not as a duty but as a mission. But

exhorting them isn't enough. The government itself is at least partly responsible for the undesirable attitudes . . . ."[29]

The signs of the change are seen on the skies. New economic and social know-how is being put to use with a drive not discerned in the past.

What, more concretely, are they? Here I am interested in highlighting the functional—not the formal—role of the legal process in bringing about social justice. The work, wealth and happiness of the entire people being the goal of the developmental struggle, we cannot afford, in the very interests of the health of the nation, a large laggard group or a three-legged race. Let me confine myself to the legal architecture and the social justice sculpture. There are very original economic betterment schemes, the target group being the Scheduled Castes and the Scheduled Tribes. I do not purpose to dilate on them here. But the legislative and legal initiatives which bear upon these classes must claim my attention. The most significant legislation has been the Untouchability (Offences) Act, 1955.

We have need for socio-legal research, forward-looking and fact-finding. Based on fresh juristic thinking inspired by political and economic programmes, legal models and legislative constructs have to be fashioned. They must be intelligently designed for effective operation, with built-in audit mechanism, self-correcting and control systems and properly oriented manpower. Social engineering is not the haphazard handiwork of politicians but painstakingly expert action of specialists with vision.

Courts must rise to the occasion. Affirmative legal action to enforce State obligations, as American Courts have sometimes done for the coloureds, is a good example. New canons of interpretation to fulfil the social mission of crusade legislation must be creatively innovated. A new awareness in enforcement must be manifest—a helpful attitude, not a pedantic neutrality. The court must become the centre of home, even when Government and its minions mismanage or fail. The dynamic rule of law is the last refuge of the weak in a real democracy. Therefore, members of the Scheduled Castes and Scheduled Tribes must be given easy access to courts of justice and administrative agencies. Apart, free legal services in multiform ways, new types of proceedings, representative suits and prosecutions, test actions by legal aid agencies, new torts creating liability in the changed socio-legal situation, quick-acting legal methodology and other substantive and processual changes must be creatively brought about. People's law must become the potent delivery system of People's Justice.

The political warfare also has to be waged with fresh, flexible and unorthodoxly aggressive methods, decisions and strategies. If homogenisation is the aim you may achieve it by many and varied tactics, attuned to the given circumstances. Making Harijan priests and trustees of temples by force of law, decastifying those vacations traditionally the miserable monopoly of the panchama proletariat by bringing other castes into them, promoting trans-Harijan marriages by legally sanctioned inducements, enforcing mixed residence in hostels and housing colonies on a massive scale and banning caste-based residential exclusivism in villages and towns, giving leadership to Dalit members in clubs, societies and other organs by official blandishments and legal sanctions are some of the many methods worth trying. A casteless comes into being, not by constitutional piety nor by political manifestoes but by socially designed strategies sincerely executed. While we do not have segregated schools as is done in other countries, we have two patterns of public schools, one for elite and aspirants for elitism and the other for the common brood—and worse, some for Harijans. Apartheidisation has subtle incarnations

The vast private sector remains to be invaded and occupied for and by Harijans by cautiously shaped policies legally implemented. It is within the powers of Parliament to enforce Harijan intake in private employment, subject to efficiency and other sensitive considerations.

The considerable general development plans of the country have been neglecting the Scheduled Castes and Scheduled Tribes, by and large. True welfare and development projects geared to Harijan welfare, are part of the national plans and increasing sums being spent during the several plan periods. But what about the general development programmes—industrial, agricultural and other? Rural electrification programmes often bypass Scheduled Castes cheries. Drinking water supply provided for village often forgets Scheduled Caste ghettoes. Housing programmes are for the common lower middle class and higher categories. When it comes to Harijans, the concept of housing suddenly shrinks into single-room hovels at petty cost although propaganda paints a rosy picture of these bhangi bungalows. They are beneath our construction engineering skills. Even minor irrigation projects, small scale industries, cooperative cultivation training, institutes of technology and other humble economic schemes run past, without remembering. Even cutcha[32] village roads are too proud to touch Harijan dwellings! Why, the raucus yer very critical population control programmes do not turn their benignant and persuasive sound and fury on the darknest and the weakest! We may multiply the catalogue of neglect but the focus is on redesigning programmes for national reconstruction so as to secure participation of the Dalit sector. Equal partnership springs from equal participation in community development.

We have dwelt on the basics, leaving specifics in law, economics and politics to be filled in by specialists. My thesis is that the socio-economic emanicipation of India truly comes through a joint enterpise of law and politics endeavouring to equalise, homogenise integrate the Dalit proletariat, animated by the social mission of our Constitution and processed by the dynamics of orderly transformation.

22 per cent of Indian humanity, 135 million citizens of our country, are a great asset if we exploit their talent potential and a distressing drag if allowed to suffer stagnation. Nothing short of a cultural revolution can achieve the absorption by

stages of these derelict chunks of our countrymen the genial current of whose soul has remained frozen over the centuries. The challenge is not whether we accepted the democratic responsibility for raising this down-trodden minority but whether our choices are the humane ways to channel change to bring them into the mainstream or the myopic alternatives of evasion, hoodwinking and half-hearted healing, only to be expropriated by the Dalit proletariat when history is ripe for forced change. For their strength is in numbers and their chronic subjection is the trigger for explosion, now that 'organise or perish' has a validity for them. The politico-legal blue-print for a just society by forging a union of the weak with the rest for a can answer our history's criminal charge on the guilty generations. Let us cultivate these values and attitudes in action.

We have made some effort to articulate the policy objectives—not micro, but macro-considerations—and to define the broad parametric implications of these objectives on a Human Plan, motivated by social justice and operated by legal techniques and technologies. The constitutional perspectives have been settled but our laggard law and will-less politics have to move in that direction geared to decisive victory before 2000 A.D. The 20th Century has made India free; the 21st Century must make Indians free.

We are conscious of the stamp of hurry in this presentation. We are acutely aware of the shortcomings of my approach and coverage. For instance, considerable emphasis is necessary on a massive educational campaign among the Dalit proletariat. Education can be a revolutionary force and when huge numbers of backward people are involved only a tearing and raging campaign with social motivation and mass mobilisation can succeed. Our student power must be harnessed to this task and a new level of equalisation in educational status must be established before long. The multiform socio-legal methodology in this programme depends on the specific conditions of each state.

Another confusing feature about my thesis is the lugging together of Harijans and Girijans. While both share chronic backwardness at the social level, their problems are different and the degree of their disabilities also varies. Naturally, the solutions must be discriminately different to hit the target groups sharply.

The psychological and sociological thrust of my thesis is a passionate plea for a rediscovery of India and its disabled humanity. The inhuman Yesterday and the less-than-human Today must be supplanted by a human Tomorrow. Parliamentary methods may go some way but not all the way. Extra-Parliamentary militancy, displayed through mass organisations and contained within civil limits, must back up parliamentary pressure. The focus—at once fierce and constructive—must be on the deliverance of the Dalit proletariat from their down-trodden state. Our system will be doomed to an adaptatioual breakdown if we do not adopt activist socio-legal and politico-legal Darwinism. If we use law for social change, the transformation will be peaceful. It has been rightly said: The function of law is to conserve the past, to assimilate the present and to anticipate the future. Law not only embodies past history but is impregnated with the seeds of future history. We need a New Testament whereby the system which thrives on slave and serf and the toiling Labour but keeps power with the slave-owner, squire and capitalist, is replaced by a set of rules governing social relations where the classes-masses dichotomy will gradually vanish and equal justice under the law will prevail. In short, our economic and legal system shall be becoming of a socialist republic.

We conclude on the critical theme that the imperative of democracy, the social conscience of the Constitution and the soul of national solidarity coverage on the necessitous note of a socially sensitized rule of law strengthened by a socially honest political will. In India, the word revolution has lost its revolution and we can only hope that history will avenge itself upon us bloodlessly if we do not adapt ourselves, through socio-legal Darwinism, to new mutations of life's values where the Dalit brother is at least a first cousin. Dalit Power is a fact; Dalit Panther is a portent; Dalit Deliverance a certainty. It is a matter of human rights, of human order, of human spirit, of human truth. It is a choice between the trauma of future shock and the truth of Human Tomorrow. Before that TRUTH that all humans are divinely one and born equal and have title to dignity and development of personality. We offer these fading flowers of thought and word, remembering those great ones gone by, who have fought for Truth and Justice and, on this occasion, offering anjali[31] particularly to Baba Saheb Ambedkar.

NOTES AND REFERENCES

(Kindly note that the lectures referred to here under are the Baba Saheb Ambedkar Memorial Lectures.)

1. Bharat: See foot not No. 11 of Lecture 1.
2. From the concluding speech of Jawaharlal Nehru in Constituent Assembly on 25th November, 1949.
3. Acharyas: Refers to the 'teachers' of yester years. One who imparts knowledge to the people.
4. Bhangi: See foot note no. 11 of Lecture 2.
5. From the speech of Mahatma Gandhi given as a reply to Rabindra Nath Tagore. Published in Youngh India of 13th October, 1921.
6. From the speech of Mrs. Gandhi at Madras on May 22, 1976 (unpublished).
7. Article 46. Constitution of India.
8. Dalit: See foot note no. 1 of Lecture 1.
9. 22nd report of the Commissioner for Scheduled Castes and Scheduled Tribes, Government of India, Section 1, 2 and 1, 3,
10. *Ibid.*
11. Raj: See foot note no. 62 of Lecture 1.
12. 22nd report of the Commissioner for Scheduled Castes and Scheduled Tribes, Government of India.
13. *Ibid.*

14. Civil Rights Protection Act, 1976—Sec. 15A (2) (i).
15. Civil Rights Protection Act, 1976—Sec. 7A (1) and (2),
16. 20 Point Programme: See foot note no. 29 of Lecture 2.
17. Fourth Report: Presented to the Assembly on 29th November, 1976, pp. 2-5.
18. *Ibid.*
19. *Ibid.*
20. *Ibid.*
21. *Ibid.*
22. Panchama: See foot note no. 29 of Lecture 1.
23. Brahmin: See foot note no. 18 of Lecture 1.
24. Nehru, J.—An Autobiography. The Bodley Head, London, 1936, p. 349.
25. Adivasis: See foot note no. 8 of Lecture 1.
26. Dalit Panthers: See foot note No. 13 of Lecture 1.
27. Chatur Varna: Literally means four colours. Here refers to the Indian Social hierarchy of four varnas—Brahmins, Kshatriyas, Vaisyas and Sudras.
28. Sarvam Brahma Mayam: Brahman is not Brahma, the creator—one of the Trinity—but is the Absolute, the Supreme, the Imperishable Primordial Being of which the phenomenal Universe is a projection. Hence Brahman is the only all-pervasive substance in all creation.
29. The Times of India: editorial, 22nd November, 1976.
30. Cutcha Road. . .Cutcha Literally means raw. Here it refers to the fair weather roads, not suitable for transportation, particularly during Monsoon.
31. Anjali: Literally means offering, refers to offerings given by hand.

5

Constitution and Politics of Reservations

The Constitution (85th Amendment) Bill to include the Tamil Nadu Reservation Act in the Ninth Schedule of the Constitution was passed by both Houses of Parliament in August, 1994. The Tamil Nadu Act ensures the continuation of 69 per cent reservation in educational institutions and jobs in the state, a matter that is sub-judice.

The Tamil Nadu quota system violates the existing Supreme Court ruling that the total reservations should not exceed 50 per cent. The Supreme Court expected the states to limit the reservations for all categories to a maximum of 50 per cent as laid down by a nine-judge Constitution Bench in the Mandal judgement on November 16, 1992. The apex court also ruled that 'creamy layer' should be kept out and that quotas should only apply to recruitment and not to promotions. The decisions of the Union Government to give assent to the Tamil Nadu Reservation Act and subsequently to move a Constitutional Amendment to take it out of the jurisdiction of courts seems to have opened a pandora's box, with one state government after another rushing through similar legislation.

Madhya Pradesh has raised the quota for other backward classes (OBCs) by 18 per cent, thus stretching the overall quota limit to 63 per cent. Andhra Pradesh also included 14 groups including Muslims and the Kapu community in the list of OBCs. But the high court admitted two writ petitions and put the government order on hold.

Bihar Chief Minister Laloo Prasad Yadav has vowed to raise the ceiling of reservation to 80 per cent through an ordinance as against the existing 50 per cent. Uttar Pradesh has already made 27 per cent reservation for backward classes in addition to the 23 per cent earlier available to scheduled castes and scheduled tribes. The reservation of 27 per cent for OBCs sparked protests in the 8 hill districts which have only a 2 per cent OBC population.

The Karnataka government raised the quantum of reservation from 68 per cent to 73 per cent in April this year. The state assembly on September 20 passed a bill seeking to provide 73 per cent reservation in employment and education and in a resolution called upon the centre to include it in the Ninth Schedule.

Union Welfare Minister Sitaram Kesri has already signalled to the States wanting to increase the quota percentage that the Centre will not obstruct them.

At present, the reservation quota exceeds 50 per cent in Tamil Nadu, Karnataka, Aurnachal Pradesh, Meghalaya, Negaland, Madhya Pradesh and Gujarat. The quota touches 50 per cent in Bihar, Manipur, Punjab, Sikkim, Uttar Pradesh, Kerala, Orissa and Rajasthan.

Significance of Court Ruling

Within three weeks of Parliament amending the Constitution to place Tamil Nadu's Act for 69 per cent reservation in the Ninth Schedule, the Supreme Court has once again reiterated that the quota cannot exceed the ceiling of 50 per cent.

On September 9, 1994, the apex court directed Karnataka not to exceed the limit and also confirmed the stay of its 1986 notification which provided for 68 per cent reservation for the Scheduled Castes. Scheduled Tribes and Backward Classes.

The ruling comes at the time when several states, with an eye on the approaching elections, are making moves towards hiking quotas in contravention of the Supreme Court ruling.

The ruling has given rise to the apprehension that the apex court could even now strike down as unconstitutional the Tamil Nadu Act providing for 69 per cent reservation, which has been challenged before it. Normally, it is rare for Acts which are placed in the Ninth Schedule to be struck down but such an eventuality is not altogether ruled out; the Supreme Court can do it in case it feels that the basic structure of the Constitution is in any way altered.

The moot question now is whether the basic structure has indeed been altered in the light of the Supreme Court noting that the dictum of reasonable restriction on the fundamental right to equality ceased to operate if the quota exceeds 50 per cent.

While the laws in the Ninth Schedule cannot generally be challenged in courts, the Supreme Court has ruled in the past that the governmemt cannot use this Schedule as a protective dumping ground for laws that may violate the "basic structure" of the Constitution. And this basic structure is enshrined, among others, in Articles 15 and 16 which protect a citizen from discrimination on grounds of caste and religion. These provisions, nonetheless, allow reservation for backward castes as an exception, to promote social justice. And it is on this that the Supreme Court has relied in fixing the 50 per cent limit.

Exceeding this is an obvious violation of the "basic structure" because the exception now becomes the rule. And the Supreme Court is unlikely to rule that the new quota is entitled to Ninth Schedule protection, according to some jurists. But if the reservation hikes are struck down, the politicians can always pass the blame on to the Centre and Supreme Court. If the hikes are not struck down, they have everything to gain politically.

85th Amendment Bill

The Constitution (85th) Amendment Bill to save from judicial scrutiny the Tamil Nadu law on 69 per cent reservation, which is under challenge before the Supreme Court, was passed by Parliament at remarkable speed.

The Tamil Nadu Government, desperate as it was to circumvent the Supreme Court's directive requiring it to adhere to 50 per cent quota limit in admissions to professional colleges, hit upon the rather dubious strategy of statutorily mandating, with retrospective effect, the 69 per cent quota scheme and then getting the law included in the Ninth Schedule of the Constitution under Article 31-B, a provision that affords protection against judicial scrutiny to certain types of enactments.

How exactly the apex court will view what prima facie amounts to defying its specific injunction against crossing the 50 per cent bar remains to be seen, although it chose to take a soft line in its interfere order by deciding not to interface with the admissions to professional colleges made this year on the basis of 69 per cent reservation and granting relief to the limited extent of accommodating the 62 'merit' students who had been denied seats as a consequence. A less objectionable option for the Government would have been to stick to the 50 per cent limit and create additional seats to provide for the prospective beneficiaries of the 'other' 19 per cent.

In any event, the mere fact of inclusion of a law in the Ninth Schedule will not totally preclude judicial scrutiny, as the nature and scope of Article 31-B are subject to varying constructions. For instance, it is a moot point whether the 'protection' available under the Article is restricted to certain specific areas or is open to any and every law that may be passed by legislation and without any time bar. Above all, there is the larger and more vital question whether the Tamil Nadu Act does not seek to alter the "basic structure" of the Constitution to the extent that it provides for quotas at a level that far exceeds 50 per cent, the point beyond which, as noted by the Supreme Court, the dictum of reasonable restriction on the fundamental right to equality ceased to operate.

It is true that the apex court did say in its Mandal case judgement that "some relaxation on this strict rule (of 50% ceiling) may become imperative" in certain "extraordinary situations inherent in the great diversity of this country and the people." But it seems very unlikely that the court had States like Karnataka and Tamil Nadu in mind when it spoke of the "extraordinary situations." Surely, these issues will be agitated before the Supreme Court and, as such, the last word is yet to be said on the much abused quota system.

The Central government's decision to place the Tamil Nadu Reservation Act under the Ninth Schedule of the Constitution threatens to reopen once again the reservation controversy, reviving memories of those dark days when the Mandal report had split society and youths immolated themselves in a protest which nad no precedent in North India.

The Centre's move is bound to upset the consensus the Supreme Court had evolved over the reservation issue. The apex court, in its famous judgement upholding the implementation of the Mandal report, had laid down the following principles:

1. Reservation for socially and educationally backward classes other than Scheduled Castes and Scheduled Tribes is constitutionally valid.
2. Reservation should not cross the maximum limit of 50 per cent, except in those areas where a extraordinary situation prevails.

3. The creamy layer among the other Backward Classes (OBCs) should be excluded from the reservation pool.
4. It implicitly recognised the principle of dereservation of those castes that cross the threshold of backwardness.

In the absence of a cogent central policy on reservation, it was generally assumed that the Supreme Court judgement on the Mandal report would henceforth form the basis of any affirmative action that a government may decide to undertake. This view was buttressed not only by the government's udequivocal acceptance of the Supreme Court verdict but also because several intellectuals hailed the Justices for striking a fine balance between merit and social justice.

Sociologist Yogendra Singh explains, "The Supreme Court reiterated the constitutional position that while there is a case for reservation for the OBCs, this policy should not and cannot neglect merit." The Supreme Court thus laid down that reservation should not exceed 50 per cent, quoting Dr. B.R. Ambedkar who had wanted the government to reserve only a minority of seats and posts.

This created a piquant situation for those states that had reservations beyond 50 per cent. A Consumer Action Group petitioned the Supreme Court pointing out that the Tamil Nadu government was violating the 50 per cent ceiling. The Jayalalitha government in return gave a written commitment to scale down reservation to the statutory limit.

Such a step was obviously fraught with serious political consequences, and the Chief Minister got the Assembly to pass unanimously the Tamil Nadu Reservation Bill protecting 69 per cent reservations. The Bill became law when the President's assent was obtained following a meeting between Chief Minister Ms. Jayalalitha and Prime Minister P.V. Narasimha Rao.

Janata Dal ideologue Surendra Mohan says "The Centre's decision to place the Tamil Nadu Reservation Act under the Ninth Schedule is extremely short-sighted. Not only will the other southern states, which have reservation above 50 per cent, follow suit, but even states like Uttar Pradesh and Bihar are likely to raise reservations above the 50 per cent limit.

The Supreme Court has already admitted a writ petition challenging the Moily government's decision to increase reservations to a whopping 80 per cent in Karnataka (it is now down to 73% again). Bihar Chief Minister Laloo Prasad Yadav, too, has announced his government's intention to raise reservation to 80 per cent.

These developments have predictably split the votaries of reservation into opposing camps. The political class finds nothing wrong in having reservation in excess of the Supreme Court limit. Says Mr Surendra Mohan, "Why did the Supreme Court fix the limit at 50 per cent? It should have realised that reservation much above 50 per cent was already in existence in some states when the Mandal case came up."

Opposing them are those intellectuals who had unabashedly supported reservation for the OBCs, even daring to go against the popular anti-Mandal sentiments of those days. They feel the Tamil Nadu Act and the Karnataka experiment threatens to put the philosophy of reservation on its head. For instance, Mr. D.L. Sheth, a member of the National Commission on Backward Classes, said "This will render the whole policy absurd."

The moot question is: What does the reservation policy aim at? Reservation is essentially a socially affirmative action armed at removing backwardness arising from historical disabilities and injustices which certain sociol groups suffer from. These disabilities create backwardness which, unlike those resulting from development processes, are structural in nature. These groups, when freed from historically debilitating conditions, are then expected to compete with others on equal terms.

Rajya Sabha Approval

In a rare display of unity, the Rajya Sabha on August 24, 1994 approved without debate the Constitution (Eighty-Fifth Amendment) Bill for inclusion of the Tamil Nadu Reservation Act in the Ninth Schedule under Article 31-B of the Constitution.

Mr. Chimanbhai Mehta (Ind.), the lone dissenting voice, made a futile attempt to oppose the Bill and stood isolated on the subject alongwith Mr. Sharad Pradhan (Shiv Sena) when Rajya Sabha K.R. Narayanan ordered a division.

The division on the clause-by-clause consideration of the Bill, showed 148 members in favour and two members against it. All the end of the exercise, the Chairman declared the Bill, amid much thumping of desks from all sides, as adopted.

The 90-minute exercise was not without its share of drama with the members of the ruling party and the Opposition lapsing into a prolonged wrangle over Mr. Kesri's desire to make a formal statement on the rationale and philosophy behind the Constitution Bill.

Several Opposition members took exception to the statement from the Welfare Minister on the plea that since the Business Advisory Committee (BAC) of the Upper House had decided to adopt the Bill without any discussion, Mr. Kesri should not be allowed to make a formal speech and if he was given an opportunity to explain the Government view-point on the subject, the Opposition could not be deprived of a similar privilege.

As a result of the row over the ticklish issue. Deputy Chairperson Najma Heptullah adjourned the House for 15 minutes and invited the floor leaders into her chambers to sort out the problem. The issue was resolved with the floor leaders agreeing that the Minister only make a statement on the statement of objects and reason's for the Constitution Bill and drop his proposed speech.

A visibly disappointed Mr. Kesri had to content himself with this. The Welfare Minister traced the history of policy of reservations in Tamil Nadu and how it had to be increased to 69 per cent consistent with the needs of the majority of the people.

Mr. Kesri gave the sequence of events beginning with the Supreme Court observations in the Mandal case in November 1992; the direction of Madras High Court to the Tamil Nadu Government to stick to the 50 per cent celling prescribed by the Supreme Court from the academic session 1993-94; enactment of the Tamil Nadu Reservation Act by the State Government for continuation of the 69 per cent reservation and the subsequent Presidential assent to the Bill.

The Minister quoted from the July 22, 1994, representation of the Tamil Nadu Government asking the Centre to give constitutional protection of the Tamil Nadu Reservation Act so that it was put beyond the jurisdiction of the courts.

As per the letter quoted by the Minister, "now it has been decided to address the Government of India for including the Act in the Ninth Schedule to the Constitution, so that the law cannot be challenged as violative of any of the fundamental rights contained in Part III of the Constitution including Article 15 and 16, and gets protection under Article 31-B of the Constitution."

Mr. Kesri informed the House that since the Union Government has already supported the Tamil Nadu Reservation Act, as a corollary to the decision it was now necessary to bring the Act within the purview of the Ninth Schedule.

Earlier, when the Deputy Chairperson called on Mr. Kesri to introduce the Bill, Mr. Chimanbhai Mehta rose to raise objections to its introduction under Rule 57 on the ground that Parliament was not competent to enact legislation which violated the very spirit of the Constitution.

Lok Sabha Assent

With the Lok Sabha approving the Constitution (85th Amendment) Bill on August 25, 1994 Parliament extended legal immunity to the Tamil Nadu Reservation Act.

However several Opposition members were not sure whether the measure was "100 per cent" foolproof, as CPI leader Indrajit Gupta put it. His apprehension was that the Supreme Court could "intervene", if it felt "affronted" by Parliament's attempt to circumvent its ruling that reservations should not exceed 50 per cent. Wondering if the move was "really watertight", he urged the Government to tell the House what "exactly are we legislating."

His fears were shared by Mr. Buta Singh (Congress I) and the Janata Dal (G) leaders Chandrajit Yadav and Syed Shahabuddin, who argued that the Supreme Court's ruling emanted from the case involving larger issues, some of which were still pending before it. The legal dimensions of the legislation needed to be considered, lest it later be struck down by the court, they pointed out.

After a nearly two-hour discussion, during which the Opposition demanded a comprehensive constitutional amendment on reservations for all states, the House approved the Bill without a single dissenting voice. The impressive voting figure—all the 348 members present at the time of the division voting for the Bill—did not reflect the misgivings expressed by almost all Opposition members about the Government's "intentions" to give social justice to the weaker sections.

The Welfare Minister, responding to the points raised during the discussion, hinted that if under similar conditions other states came forward with legislation on the lines of the Tamil Nadu Act,—envisaging more than 50 per cent reservations—the Centre would seriously consider them. Indirectly, he let it be known that other states could successfully emulate the

Tamil Nadu "model". He told the more vocal supporters of "social justice" that instead of concentrating all their fire on the floor of the House, they should raise their voice outside to mobilise opinion in support of measures intended to help the weaker sections.

Earlier, the Opposition, while supporting the Bill, used the occasion to accuse the Government of not being serious about raising the status of the disadvantaged sections. The political will needed to give them a share in power was lacking, the Government should formulate a more coherent policy for the uplift of the backward classes, and "piecemeal" measures such as a Constitution Amendment Bill would not do in the long run.

Janata Dal leader Ram Vilas Paswan told Mr. Kesri to "stop dangling lollipops" and come forward with a comprehensive bill. He suggested amendment to Article 15(4) and 16(4) of the Constitution, thus allowing each State to fix its own reservation quota depending on its perceived need. Such an amendment would settle all the problems relating to reservations, he said, echoing the known position of the various Janata Dal factions.

Mr. Nitish Kumar (JD-G) said the amendment was only a "limited measure" restricted to one State and did not address the needs of other states. It was simply an attempt to "defuse" tension in Tamil Nadu and indicated that the Centre did not have a clear-cut policy. The Left parties sharply differed on the question of amending Articles 15(4) and 16(4)

Mr. Indrajit Gupta, while extending "whole hearted" support to the Tamil Nadu Act, opposed the proposal to allow every State to fix its own quota. If such a principle was accepted there would no longer be "one India", he said. His CPI(M) colleague Saifuddin Chaudhury too qualified his party's support to the Tamil Nadu Act, His party was supporting it because the level of reservations in Tamil Nadu exceeded 50 per cent before the Supreme Court imposed the ceiling. His party did not want to give the impression that it favoured taking away the rights which people already enjoyed.

Return of the Quota Raj

Parliament's seal of approval on Tamil Nadu's bid for constitutional safeguards to its Act on reservation has once again pushed the issue to quotas to the top of the country's political agenda.

With assembly elections in 10 states round the corner, several other states are queuing up to step on the plank of social justice by hiking quotas for backward classes.

Andhra Pradesh, which goes to the polls in December, 1994, along with Karnataka, is the latest to announce inclusion of more communities in the BCs list. Karnataka has already enhanced reservation to 80 per cent with a Bill to give effect to its resolve, just as Tamil Nadu did.

In the North too, chief ministers are going all out to woo the OBCs. In Bihar, Mr. Yadav, who is expected to face a tough fight in the elections due next year, has spoken of 80 per cent quotas. Uttar Pradesh is on the boil with the forward castes taking to the streets against the state government's decision to provide 27 per cent reservation in the eight hill districts.

In such a scenario, the passage of the Constitution (85th Amendment) Bill is considered significant as it has thrown up several legal and political questions.

For instance, what happens to the Tamil Nadu Act if it struck down by the Supreme Court? And will the Centre oblige other states if they come up with similar legislation? Or will the Centre be forced to bring amendments to Articles 15(4) and 16(4) of the Constitution to allow the states to vary quotas ignoring the apex court's ceiling of 50 per cent?

Constitutional experts are of the opinion that normally courts do not strike down those Acts which have been included in the Ninth Schedule, but they refuse to rule out such a possibility. They cite the Keshavanand Bharti case to buttress their point.

Says Mr. Shanti Bhushan, "If the Supreme Court feels that the Tamil Nadu Act is in some way altering the basic structure of the Constitution, it could choose to strike it down. But if it does not, it will be very difficult for the court to strike it down, especially in view of the universal consensus behind the Bill."

It is not as if the legal questions did not bother the Centre, but political compulsions proved too strong.

While the crisis over the so-called reservation tangle may have blown over, the inclusion of the Tamil Nadu Reservation Act in the Ninth Schedule has serious implications at both the political and Constitutional levels.

The move, which is intended to provide the Reservation Act with immunity from judicial review under Article 31(b) of the Constitution, raises two fundamental sets of questions.

Among the first of political questions is whether this will lead other states, which want to enhance reservations over the maximum 50 per cent, to enact similar legislation. What will be the political fallout of such demands? And how will the Centre react to them?

The constitutional question is what impact the Tamil Nadu Reservation Act will have on the distributive legislative system. The Act is a unique piece of legislation in as much as it is based on the premise that a State Government may, under Article 31(c), enact legislation aimed at implementing the Constitution's Directive Principles.

So could it set a precedent by leading other state governments to make laws under Article 31(c) on issues other than reservation and justify them on the ground that they are directed at securing any of the Directive Principles?

The possibility of other State governments enacting a similar quota bill is real. Karnataka Chief Minister Veerappa Moily's recent attempt at increasing the reservation level to 80 per cent was stymied by the Supreme Court. The State assembly on September 20 passed a bill providing for 73 per cent reservation. The bill had originally sought 80 per cent reservation. Mr. Laloo Prasad Yadav too has proclaimed his intention to raise the reservation limit.

The implications of the Tamil Nadu Act for the distributive legislative system, are very important. Those who had doubts about the legal validity of the legislation argued that the scope of Article 31(c), under which the Act was passed, was limited to securing or implementing Articles 39(b) and (c) of the Directive Principles, which deal with the distribution of property and wealth. Also, more generally, that a State Government was not empowered to legislate on reservation.

Legal proponents of the legislation maintained that it could be used to secure any or all of the articles in the Constitution's Part IV (Directive Principles of State Policy).

The States

Election year compulsions have finally caught up with the ruling Congress Party in Andhra Pradesh. The state joined Tamil Nadu and Karnataka in hiking the reservations by including Muslims, Kapus and 12 other castes and communities in the list of Backward Classes on August 25, 1994.

Since the government made it clear that these newly included communities would not cut into the existing quantum of reservations, the total reservations after this announcement may exceed 70 per cent, bringing the state at par with Tamil Nadu.

Speaking to newsmen after the meeting of the State Cabinet, which ratified the hike, Chief Minister Vijaya BhaskaraReddy said the State Government had considered legal and all other aspects before taking the decision and added that, if necessary, the existing law would be amended to uphold the Government decision.

The communities included in the backward castes list by the latest government order are Muslims, Kapus, Balijas, Telegas, Ontari, Ayyakaras, Kasi, Kapidi, Patra, Ajulabalijas, Nagaralu, Pondara, Kurakalas, Quresh and Palaekari.

According to official estimates, Muslims comprise 12 per cent and Kapus account for 17 per cent of the state's population, whereas the remaining 12 cases account for 8 per cent of the State's populace. So today's order brings an additional 37 per cent of the State's population under the reservation category.

The decision would have wider political ramifications. It is noteworthy to mention that the Kapus are the most vocal group in coastal Andhra Pradesh and play a decisive role in as many as 60 Assembly constituencies in the state. They have been demanding, for quite some time their inclusion in the BC list.

The Government had asked the State BC Commission headed by Mr. Justice Puttuswamy to give its interim report early so as to facilitate a decision in the matter. As the commission expressed its inability to submit its interim report in such a short time, the Government decided not to wait but include them in the BC lists.

The Government order stated that the commission would decide about the percentage of reservations and economic criteria subsequently.

It further stated that the order would have no bearing in respect of admissions in education institutions for the academic year 1994-95 or selections to services of which the process had already been started. As regards the demand of other communities and castes for inclusion in the BC list, the statement said that the Commission would examine them separately.

The decision regarding inclusion of Muslims has come as total surprise for the community leaders. Though there had been demands from time to time there was no immediate provocation as in the case of Kapus. They felt that the decision was clearly aimed at winning over the Muslims, who had deserted the Congress after the Ayodhya episode. Andhra Pradesh, incidentally, became the third state in the country after Utter Pradesh and Karnataka in extending BS status to Muslims.

The Andhra Pradesh High Court granted an interim suspension of the government order including Kapus, Muslims and 12 other communities in the backward classes list. The court granted the interim suspension while admitting two writ petitions on August 29 filed by the Andhra Pradesh Backward Classes Association and an advocate.

The Madhya Pradesh Government's decision to reserve an additional 14 per cent of vacancies for the other backward classes (OBCs) in Government service has taken the total percentage of reservation in nine tribal districts of the State of 64.

Asked if the State Government directive raising the total percentage of reservation to as high as 64 would not violate the Supreme Court ruling restrictiug it to 50 per cent, an official spokesman said he could not say whether it was violative of the apex court's ruling. "If anyone went to the court, the latter could decided upon it. The grounds for reservation have been already been listed in the notification," he added.

The 69 per cent reservation applies to all educational institutions in Tamil Nadu, but it is the medical and engineering seats which have been the subject of controversy. The reason is that arts colleges are aplenty, with the availability of seats more or less equal to the demand.

A statement filed by the Advocate-General in the Supreme Court shows that of the 300 students admitted against the open competition quota (OC) of 31 per cent this year, the candidates belonging to backward classes, most backward classes and scheduled castes are 213,29 and 2 respectively. The number of students not belonging to any of the reserved categories admitted against the OC quota is 56, that is, less than 6 per cent of the 970 seats available.

The Supreme Court judges said, "This shows and affirms the trend disclosed last year—a trend both heartening the highly significant. The candidates belonging to Backward Classes are getting 80 per cent of the seats in merit quota on the basis of their merit alone. In addition, they are getting 50 per cent of the total seats (excluding All India Merit Quota) under the rule of reservation."

The Supreme Court has also directed the Tamil Nadu government to release 52 extra seats under the merit quota. The reason is that had the government scaled down reservation to the 50 per cent limit, these students would have been on the merit list.

Even those in the Backward list have to get 90 per cent or more to be in the reckoning for professional courses. There is much talk in academic circles that parents manipulate marks to ensure admission for their wards to engineering or medical colleges. The manipulation is done at the university level, with the amount to be paid linked to the increase in percentage.

This year admissions to engineering and medical colleges were held up until the President gave his assent to the Tamil Nadu Reservation Act. Subsequently, the list of selected candidates was announced under the 69 per cent quota.

UP Chief Minister Mulayam Singh Yadav has announced a 27 per cent reservation in jobs and in educational institutions for the OBCs in the State. Initially, the UP government had said that even if the reserved seats meant for the backward classes were not utilised by them these would remain vacant. However, under mounting public pressure the State government has had to amend this. Mr. Yadav has also announced a two per cent reservation in State government services for the people of the hill districts. But these steps have failed to pacify the agitating people in the hilly region of Uttarakhand. In fact, the agitation is spreading both in intensity and the area affected.

The grievance is not against the reservation policy as such as against the implications of what will happen when the quotas are enforced in the hill areas. It is believed that in this region the OBCs constitute not more than two per cent of the total population. And that 27 per cent reservation for such a tiny population would be unfair for the other sections who have remained backward in terms of other considerations. If the composition of the backward classes in the region is really so, the grievance of the agitating people has substance. People in different parts of the country have varying characteristics. Casteism of the plains may not be a sure winner of votes in Kumaon or Garhwal. The OBC politics of the plains of Bihar and UP cannot be replicated in all parts of the country. Regional differences should have been taken into account. But, unfortunately, instead of admitting this, the UP Chief Minister has taken a tough stand. He is reported to have threatened that the agitation in the Hills might produce another agitation in the plains.

Legal Issues and Debate

The Tamil Nadu Backward Classes, Scheduled Castes and Scheduled Tribes (Reservation of Seats in Educational Institutions and of Appointments or Posts in the Services) Act 1993 (Tamil Nadu Act 45 of 94) providing for 69 per cent reservation in educational institutions and appointments in the services raises certain important legal issues.

The Supreme Court in its judgement in the Mandal case, delivered in November 1992, inter alia laid down that the reservations should not exceed 50 per cent.

At the same time the Court observed that "while 50 per cent shall be the rule, it is necessary not to put out of consideration certain extraordinary situations inherent in the great diversity of the country and the people. It might happen that in the far-flung and remote areas the population inhabiting those areas might, on account of their being out of the mainstream of national life and in view of conditions peculiar to and characteristical to them, need to be treated in a different way, some relaxation in this strict rule may become imperative. In doing so extreme caution is to be exercised and a special case made out."

A legal question that arises is whether the Tamil Nadu Act is in accordance with the apex court's ruling in the Mandal case (on the limit of reservation). In this connection reference might be made to Articles 142 and 144 of the Constitution. Article 142 deals with enforcement of decrees and orders of the Supreme Court throughout India, while Article 144 says that all civil and judicial authorities in the country shall act in aid of the Supreme Court.

Another issue is whether the 'relaxation' in the matter of reservation (of 69 %) is in conformity with the observations of the apex court in the Mandal case.

A question is whether the Tamil Nadu Act is in conformity with the "equality clauses" in the Constitution namely, Article 14 (equality before law), 15 (prohibition of discrimination on grounds of religion, race, caste, sex or place of birth) and 16 (equality of opportunity in matters of public employment).

The total percentage of the population of SCs, STs and BCs in Tamil Nadu is reported to be around 88. The question is whether the reservation of 69 per cent in Tamil Nadu, having regard to the socio-economic conditions of the SCs, STs and

BCs in the State, can be described as being on the 'high side.' Should the percentage of reservation in favour of specified classes of citizens bear reasonable proportion to the total population of the classes of citizens concerned in the context of the public interest and public purpose underlying public services and higher education?

The apex court, in its interim orders made on August 18, 1994, in the Tamil Nadu reservation case, inter alia noted that the candidates belonging to BCs had got 30 per cent of the seats in the medical colleges in the "merit quota" during 1993-94 and 1994-95. In addition, they were getting 50 per cent of the total seats (excluding all India quota) under the rule of reservation. The percentage of candidates "not belonging to any social reservation categories" who got admission in the "merit quota" this year was not even six per cent of the total seats. Should not policy planners and state authorities examine this aspect and do justice to those not belonging to any of the social reservation categories?

The Tamil Nadu Act contains a 'declaration' that it is giving effect to the policy of the State for securing the principles laid down in Part IV of the Constitution, namely, "Directive Principles of State Policy" and in particular, Article 38, clauses (b) and (c) of Article 39 and Article 46 of the Constitution.

Article 46 deals with the promotion of educational and economic interests of SCs, STs and other weaker sections by the State.

Article 38 deals with obligation of the State "to secure a social order for the promotion and welfare of the people," clause (b) of Article 39 says that the State shall, in particular, direct its policy towards securing "that the ownership and control of the material resources of the community are so distributed as best to subsecure the common good." According to clause (c) of Article 39, "the operation of economic system does not result in the concentration of wealth and means of production to the common detriment."

Under Article 31 C, no law giving effect to the policy of the State towards securing any of the principles in the "Directive Principles of State Policy" shall be deemed to be void on the ground that it is inconsistent with any of the rights conferred by Article 14 (equality before law) or Article 19 (personal freedoms).

A important question that arises is whether the subject matter of the Tamil Nadu Act bears reasonable and rational "nexus" with the specified Directive Principles of State Policy.

According to noted constitution expert Nani A Palkhivala, an appropriate petition should be filed in the Supreme Court to declare the latest constitutional amendment void. It is well settled that an amendment of the Constitution which purports to affect its basic structure is void; and the insertion of the Tamil Nadu Act in the ninth schedule does impinge upon the basic structure of the Constitution. Reservations of the type sought to be made in Tamil Nadu can be allowed to prevail only by scrapping what Chief Justice Mahajan called "our sublime Constitution" and promulgating a backward Constitution for a backward nation.

Mr Palkhivala said there are five important reasons in support of the view that the insertion the Tamil Nadu Act in the Ninth Schedule violates the basic structure of fundamental law. First, the basic structure of the Constitution envisages a cohesive, unified casteless society—in which casteism, petrified and ossified for centuries, should become merely the dust on the shelf of Indian history. The right to equality before the law and to the rule of meritocracy was allowed by the majority judgment to be encroached upon only to the extent of maximum reservations of 50 per cent in other words, even according to the majority view which stretched the law to bursting point, it is not parmissible to cross the limit of 50 per cent when caste is given precedence over merit and calibre, is common knowledge that already reservations in different states have resulted in the substandard replacing the standard and the reins of power passing from meritocracy to mediocrity.

"Do we intend to re-enact the pre-independence tragedy with the roles reversed—the erstwhile under-privileged now becoming the privileged? (The desperate tale of the forward caste woman in Kerala who, merely with a view to gaining admission for her son in a medical college, deposed before a magistrate in the presence of her husband that the son was her illegitimate off-spring by a harijan, does not seem to have attracted the attention of our lethargic and indifferent citizenry)." Mr. Palkhiwala said.

Secondly, the Supreme Court is the final arbiter of constitutional issues and every executive and legislative authority has to respect the Supreme Court's verdict, it is absurd beyond words to suggest that a state legislature can sit in judgement over the Supreme Court. If the Supreme Court lays down that 50 per cent reservations on the ground of caste represent the ultimate constitutional limit of reservations, which State government can claim the right to revise that limit? In the words of studied moderation, the Tamil Nadu Act represents the ultimate in contempt for the Supreme Court. There is already a scramble among state politicians to vie with one another in prescribing larger reservations. Karnataka and Arunachal Pradesh are talking of 80 per cent reservations for the backward classes. The backlash in the U.P. hills and the move in Karnataka to gave OBC status to two advanced castes, are "grim portents of the chaos to which casteism has already reduced this benighted country." Mr. Palkhiwala said.

Thirdly, flexibility is available to the States to decide what percentage should be reserved on the basis of caste, but only subject to the overall ceiling of 50 per cent which is not to be exceeded in any case. If the latest amendment to the Constitution is valid, every state would be entitled to ignore the overall ceiling and have its law specified in the Ninth Schedule prescribing any percentage of reservations for its backward castes. India has already becomes the laughing stock of the civilised world as the only country which has reservations for the majority of its citizens, while in the rest of the world reservations are known only for minorities.

Fourthly, the unity and integrity of India is one of the prime objectives of the Constitution, as expressly set out in the Preamble. This basic objective would be set at nought by laws like the Tamil Nadu Act.

Fifthly, the preservation of the sovereignty and security of India is again one of the paramount aims of the Constitution. If the State can ignore with impunity the express ruling of the Supreme Court that reservations should not exceed 50 per cent in the aggregate, with far greater impunity would it feel emboldened to ignore the mere "advice" of the Supreme Court that the armed forces and same higher civilian posts should be outside the purview of caste reservations.

The Mandal report envisages not only reservations in civil service on the ground of caste but also reservations in the armed forces on the same ground. Further, not only appointments but even promotions are to be reserved for the privileged (euphemistically called "backward" class). Mr. Palkhiwala said the country's armed forces are the pride of the nation—the only institution which has not been devalued and degraded. "What kind of an army, navy and air force shall we have when field marshals and generals, and admirals and air marshals, have secured admissions and promotions on caste considerations? This raises the most momentous of all issues—the security of the state if the bitterest enemy of India were to be in charge of amendments of our Constitution, he could do no more disastrous job than to put laws like the Tamil Nadu Act in the ninth schedule and ensure the trumbling of the fundamental law of India."

Wiser Framers

The framers of the Constitution were infinitely wiser than our so-called leaders of today. The forbade reservations based exclusively on caste—as if a poor Brahmin or a rich Dalit is a contradiction in terms. They harkened to the reality that there are no backward castes but only backward individuals. The only known solvent of casteism is a change in the national consciousness: harmony among, and social intermingling of, the anachronistic castes." Mr. Palkhiwala said.

During the 207 years of its existence, the U.S. Constitution has been amended only 27 times; while the Indian Constitution has been amended 76 times in 44 years. "Let us ask ourselves in despair the question—Do we deserve our noble Constitution."

Reservation Policy—An Alternative

The issue of reservation needs to be oriented in a scientific and rational manner. Due to prejudices or biased discussion either in favour or against reservation, it is very difficult to judge what is wright or wrong, just or unjust? The basic context of reservation has been sidelined. The historical necessity of reservation to give Bhagedari (share) in Satta (power) and the current stress on social justice through reservation has been undermined in the wake of highly surcharged atmosphere during the anti-mandal stir and self-immolation bids by some youngsters. Most of the intellectuals and mediapersons were also emotional.

Inherent Lacunae

The present reservation policy has certain inherent lacunae. The most important among them is the lack of any restriction on those who have received benefit from it. Whether they are in scheduled castes and tribes or backward classes, most of them have bothered the least for their disadvantaged brethren. It has led to severe criticism of the basic foundations of reservation. Even politicians admit it. But they are under pressure because of fear of vociferous opposition from the beneficiaries and its impact on their uncertain vote bank.

Simultaneously, reservation policy has failed to pave way for large scale social changes and even bridging the increasing gap between the deprived and the beneficiaries. The importance of a job in economic terms has deliberately undermined and attention from it continues to be diverted by the beneficiaries. It is a matter of serious concern.

Socio-Economic Justice

Any reservation policy should be oriented to social and economic justice. The former Prime Minister Mr. Vishwanath Pratap Singh after implementing Mandal report suddenly raised, the issue of social justice ignoring the process of social change and economic justice. It is relevant today because the situation of pre-independence India has almost changed. During the last four decades the social and economic scenario of Dalits and backwards has also undergone tremendous changes. They have also emerged higher in the field of education. Despite severe paradoxes of development, it has benefitted all.

If caste system is an evil, it needs to be abolished. In that case the present caste based reservation policy has to be modified with a more just, scientific and far-reaching policy. The question is how can it be achieved? What should be the alternative in a casteless society? How for reservation can be oriented towards economic justice?

Powerful Options

There are powerful options to move in this direction. Firstly, use of all the caste identification marks and surnames—*i.e.*, Mishra, Singh, Yadav, Reddy, Ansari, Khan, Majumdar, Naiyer, Subrahmaniam, etc.—should be banned. It will be just a beginning to dismantle the inhuman caste system. Since caste feeling is deep-rooted and has developed over thousands of years as an institution of the society, it will take a few generations to wither away. Secondly, all the caste based groups, societies, organisations, name plates, etc. should be prescribed. Thirdly, effective law should be made to discourage the caste rituals and practices. Fourthly, the conduct of marriage should be regulated through scientific data, information and match-making technics. Job seekers should be given incentives to adopt data-bank facilities for better choice. The marriage should no longer remain the matter of chance, it be made a matter of choice. They need to be given priority In getting job, promotion, loan and house accommodation. It should be made legally binding on everyone.

First Generation

Reservation on the basis of caste should be altered on the following pattern:

(a) The first generation of a family should get 50 to 70 per cent exclusive reservation;

(b) Women should get 40 to 50 per cent share in all category of jobs—reserved over unreserved;

(c) First generation of women should also get 50 per cent reservation;

(d) If any first generation candidate comes in the general merit list, he or she should be counted in that category;

(e) If seats remain unfilled it should be given to the respective category candidates;

(f) This should be made legally binding on the private sector also;

(g) All the national languages should be given equal opportunity as medium of examinations in jobs or job-oriented vocational-cum-technical education including private sector. It is essential to attract the best talents from different corners of the country. It will ensure due representation to all linguistic and ethnic groups;

(h) The backward section mostly from rural background of schooling and landless section should be given additional weightage *i.e.*, 3 to 5 per cent grace and deprivation marks/points—in vocational education and employment. So that they can complete in the run of unequals till the conditions of inequality in opportunity persists;

(i) Job-oriented education system should be developed at the matric or higher secondary level and incentives in terms of financial, technical support, managerial skill developments, scholarships, post-training facilities to establish profession, etc. should be provided to the candidates. The crave for history, philosophy, politics type unproductive education should be discouraged. More and more traditional schools and colleges should be converted into employment-oriented productive education and skill development centres. More stress should be given to promote work-culture. Indeed, we do not need millions of unskilled graduates every year.

Check on Corruption

Even after that what is the guarantee of getting justice in a bureaucratic set up which is afflicted with corruption, nepotism and red-tapism? It is quite obvious. Therefore, strict rules and clear-cut guidelines will be necessary. It is therefore essential to make tough anti-corruption laws where meaning or relative and subjective merit also needs to be clearly defined. No scope should be left for nepotism and corruption.

Unless all these conditions are met a healthy, unified and development-oriented society cannot be built-up and promises of share in power, socio-economic changes and Justice through reservation will remain mere slogans.

6

Bonded Labour in India

After the introduction of the concept of ownership, exploitation of man by man started. The property relationship was such that one who owned it dominated one who did not, and in the process the latter was made a slave by the first. The present bonded labour system is the same slave system which existed for centuries together in India. It is not only the culmination of the debtor-creditor relation into a slave and master relation, it is also an outcome of the unequal social-economic system prevailing in India. The system provided a built-in mechanism for continuation of exploitation of the under-privileged sections by the privileged sections of the society. The caste system functioned as a transmission belt to pass on such slavery from one generation to another.

The system was glorified by giving it the religious colours of Karma theory and Varnashrama Dharma. The seat of power and the legal system also perpetuated the evil of this system. Consequently, it continued without interruption, in one form or the other. For the first time in India, the British restricted the slave system by passing the Bengal Regulations Act in 1806, but allowed forced labour by Act VI of 1825. Unfortunately, Section 6 of the Madras Compulsory Labour Act 1858 even legalized forced labour. However, the Indian

Penal Code 1862 banned the bonded labour system and made it a punishable offence. Many State governments passed laws banning the bonded labour system like Kamia Agreement Act, 1920, of Bihar; Money Lender Act, 1938, of Bihar; Debt Bondage Abolition Regulation Act, 1940, of Orissa and Madras; Bombay Money Lenders Act, 1946; Article 23 of the Constitution of India made bonded labour a punishable offence. Rajasthan Agricultural Relief Act, 1954, and Sargari Abolition Act, 1961; Lecadives, Minicoy and Amindivi Islands Revenue and Tenancy Regulation Act, 1965; Bonded Labour Abolition Act of Kerala, 1972; Scheduled Castes/Tribes and Denotified Tribes Debt Relief Ordinance of Uttar Pradesh, 1974, were some of the important acts passed in response to the constitutional provisions against bonded labour. Yet this evil practice continued. Hence, the President of India promulgated the Bonded Labour System (Abolition) Oridance, 1975, in order to wipe out the evil of the bonded labour system.

In response to this ordinance, bonded labourers were released for a shortwhile, but due to lack of alternative sources of living many of them again became bonded labour. Nearly 3 per cent of the households, mostly from landless households and from lower castes, were bonded labourers. By and large, bonded labourers stay in the farms or in the places desired by their masters. They are confined to one place; consequently they are cut off from the changing outside world. Many of them did know about the ban on the bonded labour system and yet could not take advantage of it due to fear of their master and lack of alternative sources of living.

Bonded labourers are paid nominal wages. Moreover their family members cannot take remunerative jobs eleswhere without prior permission of their masters, who normally would not grant permission as they get free work even from them. Thus their poverty aggravates and forces them to borrow from their masters at exorbitant rates of interest. Normally all contracts between master and bonded labour are oral, and even in written agreements most of the masters take undue advantage of the illiteracy of the bonded labourers and enter excess amounts in the agreements. Consequently, a bonded labourer cannot clear off his debt during his lifetime and he is forced to renew his bondage throughout his lifetime. After his death the bondage is passed on to his children. This is why even children below ten years of age are working as bonded labourers. Children are made to believe that accepting liability of bondage of their father is a sacred duty. Thus the bondage is passed on generation to generation. Bonded labourers can be mortgaged, purchased or exchanged by their masters.

The remedy lies in providing minimum productive assets to the bonded labourer before he is released. To stop ugly practices like this all productive assets should be owned and operated by the society and not by an individual or a group of individuals.

Servey Methods

I know the household and economic conditions of the bonded labourers and the mechanism of the operations of the system, as currently practised, a survey was conducted.

Selection of the Survey Villages. Tunkur district in Karnataka state was selected for the present study. According to the Census of India, there are 2,725 villages spread over 10 talukas of Tunkur district. Out of 2,725 villages, 2,454 villages are inhabited. Out of these inhabited villages, 20 villages. constituting 0.75 per cent of the total villages, were surveyed, as listed in Table 6.1. These village were randomly selected from all talukas in proportion to their number in each taluka. After selecting at random these 20 villages, each village was visited to identify the number of bonded labour households in them.

Selection of Households. After visiting the selected 20 villages it was found that . . . 10 villages reported having 36 bonded labour households. All these bonded labour households are taken for the present study.

TABLE 6.1

Selected Villages

Taluka	*Sl. No.*	*Villages*	*Village Code No.*	*No. of Households* *No. of Bonded Labourers*	*No. of Masters*
Tumkur	1	Doddagolla Halli	04	1	1
	2	Kuruvelu	07	4	3
	3	Doddanaravangala*	031	—	—
Tiptur*	4	Nonavinakere*	118	—	—
	5	Kadushettyhalli*	120	—	—
Kunigal	6	Vanigerakaval*	219	—	—
	7	Hulivana	225	7	1
Pavagada	8	Devalakere	301	5	5
Chickanaya-kanahalli	9	Navile*	403	—	—
	10	Tarabenahalli*	409	—	—
Turuvakere	11	Kallanagattihalli*	502	—	—
	12	Kodihalli*	514	—	—
Gubbi	13	Herur	623	2	2
	14	Kunaghatta	629	7	5
Sira	15	Devarahalli*	702	—	—
	16	Ranganahalli	709	2	2
Madhugiri	17	Thondoti	801	1	1
	18	Dodderi	824	17	16
Korategere*	19	Bhaktarahalli*	911	—	—
	20	Kambadahalli	909	—	—
Total	20			46	36

*No bonded labour households.

Methodology. Besides personal interviews with each bonded labourer, a structural questionnaire was also introduced to elicit information from the bonded labour households. However, more emphasis was laid on the personal interviews than the structural questionnaire because of the delicate nature of the problems and the involvement of the bonded labourer in supplying information which might be disliked by his master and therefore might put him in a serious situation. Since the study was sensitive to the socio-economic structure of villages, sufficient care was taken to see that the bonded labourers were not harassed on account of their giving information. As far as possible the interviews were taken when their masters or the family members of the masters were away.

> The survey found forty bonded labourers from thirty-six households belonging to the Scheduled Castes (Untouchables); Artisan, Lingayat and Vokkaliga castes; and the Muslim community. Of the bonded labour households, 50 per cent were Untouchable families, although Untouchables are only 13 per cent of the population in the state in which the study was conducted.

Master-Slave Relationship

Master's Occupation. It will be interesting to know something about the occupation of the masters of the bonded labourers. It was generally expected that the money-lenders-cum-landlords who could not cultivate their lands themselves would trap poor landless agricultural labourers or marginal farmers and make them bonded labourers, for working on their agricultural lands. However, it is not only the landlords, but even businessmen and men in services who keep bonded labourers. According to Table 6.2, 14 per cent of the bonded labourers' masters were businessmen and the remaining 86 per cent were landlords. Businessmen while they are in business cannot cultivative their lands so they prefer banded labourers to free agricultural labourers.

TABLE 6.2

Particulars of Masters

Bonded Labour's Status	*Master's Caste*				*Master's Occupation*			*Master's Official Panchayat* Position*		
	Lingayata	*Vokkaliga*	*Muslims*	*Total*	*Agriculture*	*Business*	*Total*	*Chairman*	*Member*	*Total*
Former	—	10	—	10	9	1	10	3	2	5
Current	6	22	2	30	26	4	30	2	5	7
Total	6	32	2	40	35	5	40	5	7	12

*The Panchayat at is now the officially recognized unit of local government.

The impact of tenancy reforms was marginal, as most of landlords distributed their lands among their family members, relatives and even to fake members, so as to escape from land reforms. There were some cases in Bihar where lands were recorded even under the names of animals; such dodging of the government was possible because of their collusion with government officials.

We also found such fake transfers in the sample villages. However, we found that on records for official purposes the lands were distributed among the members of the landlords' family and their relations, though all the documents as well as lands were retained by the landlords. Thus in reality the lands are owned by the landlords themselves. Such landlords got hold of the cheapest labour, like bonded labour, and cultivated their lands.

Social and economic status has a very high correlation with political position in rural as well as urban areas. For example Table 6.2 shows that out of the total number of matters, five masters (constituting 1 2%) were chairmen of the village Panchayats, and seven masters (constituting 18%) were members of the village Panchayats. Thus political power and economic power are going hand in hand. In such a situation how can a bonded labourer go against the master or think of coming out of the clutches of bondage? Politicians are boasting that they have released bonded labourers and some of them say that the landlords are not responding to them. In reality, in such siuations both landlords and politicians are one and the same. How is it possible to introduce change against the landlords who are also politicians? The tragedy of execution of such reformative laws lies in the dual personality of the law-makers. When executors of the laws are also victims of the laws, then it is not surprising if they do not execute such laws. Thus the makers of laws, executors of laws, and the persons against whom laws are made, by and large are the same people. Hence, such laws normally become only decorative pieces of the legislatures.

Caste of Bonded Labourer and His Master. The caste factor in India plays an important role in determining intercaste relations, so also in determining the relationship between the bonded labourer and his master. If a bonded labourer belongs to his master's caste, he is likely io get relatively less harsh treatment than a bonded labourer belonging to a caste lower than that of his master. It is normally found that a bonded labourer belongs to a caste lower than that of his master, and at times to the same caste as the master. But there was not even a single incidence where a bonded labourer belonged to a higher caste than his master.

Payments to Bonded Labour. The bonded labour system, as known today, has been aggravated by poverty and inequality. Most of the poor and underprivileged people are made bonded labourers or one type of the other, in one place or the other. For many centuries such evil practices in India were systematized and legalized for the benefit of a few privileged and rich people. Since political and economic powers were concentrated in a few hands of socially privileged sections they managed to create, pass and execute certain laws protecting their own interests but detrimental to the interests of the under-privileged masses. Even religion came to their rescue in providing myths for strengthening the system. Even non-payments of wages or remuneration were supported by the socio-religious laws rather than condemned by them: for example, nothing belonged to the Sudras (labouring castes), and if anything was possessed by them it could be calmly taken away by the privileged higher castes without any fear (Manu Smriti, Chapter VIII Verse 417). Such laws were continued in different forms with modifications according to the necessity of changing circumstances.

In the present study nearly one-fourth of the bonded labourers are paid once a month, but not in cash. Some of them are paid in grain or clothes, but charged according to the will of the master. Many times, in the agreement, the bonded labourer is given for every year, one pair of clothes, sometimes a pair of shoes and food grains to sustain him, but these were

TABLE 6.3

Payment of Wages to the Bonded Labourer

Bonded Labour's Status	*Payment time*			*Monthly Wages (Rs.)*						*Goods*		
	Monthly	*Yearly*	*Total*	*50-100*	*100-200*	*200-300*	*300-500*	*500& abave*	*Total*	*Grain*	*Cloth*	*Total*
Former	7	1	8*	—	3	—	4	1	8	—	6	6
Current	21	9	30	5	10	8	7	—	30	1	20	21
Total	28	10	38	5	13	8	11	1	38	1	26	27

*Two persons worked for food only.

always inadequate to support his family. Nearly 97 per cent of the bonded labourers were paid below Rs. 500 per annum while one-seventh of them were paid only Rs. 50 to Rs. 100 per annum, which comes to only 28 paise per day, which is not sufficient even to have a cup of tea in a hotel. Such a nominal wage is nothing but total exploitation of the bonded labourers. Some were not paid at all. Is it possible to remain at least alive at such a low wage level? In such conditions how can a weak bonded labourer revolt against such a tyrannical system? For raising one's voice against any tyranny, minimum strength is required; that too is absent. If this is so, how can a bonded labourer dream of freedom ? Only out and out help from outside, for his complete liberation, will help, father than passing half-hearted laws and making legal provisions practically beyond their reach. Moreover, the judicial system is costly, and it can be misused by money and other powers. The poor bonded labourer cannot afford to hire a pleader to defend himself. It is unlikely that even the guilty will be punished with the help of a good pleader, but of course such so-called good pleaders charge exhorbitant fees. Only the rich can afford to pay it. Hence the poor have to submit meekly like animals to the tortures of the exploitative socio-economic system.

Table 6.3 further shows that most of the bonded labourers who are still working get coarse clothes from their masters which do not last even for a few months; as a consequence they have to forego even clothes for the rest of the year. Since food grains are not given to all of them they have to buy food grains from outside or force their family members to work elsewhere for food grains. As a result most of them work only for food grains or only for food. Such acute poverty leading to exploitation and oppression is a blot on a democratic society. It needs to be wiped out early, not by hypocritical slogans of 'Garibi Hatao' (remove poverty), but by taking positive steps.

It is in the interest of the country to relieve them of bondage and poverty. They are underfed; hence, their working capacities are low, they are exposed to diseases, and their life is short. Their poverty prohibits them from taking treatment, and contagious diseases spread in society. Landlords/masters of bonded labourers about extracting work around the clock from bonded labourers bother, and not about their living conditions. It is striking to note that two bonded labourers were working only for food and nothing else. It is like feeding a bullock for extracting work. In such a situation what can a bonded labourer give to his family? It is no wonder if his family is also exploited and oppressed by the cruel elements in society. This type of exploitation of human labour is not different from slavery. The bonded labourers are treated like cattle; hence, this system should be condemned by all means.

Out of forty bonded labourers from thirty-six households, thirty bonded labourers are still working; ten were released in response to the President's Ordinance, but because of the absence of alternative occupations, they again preferred to be bonded labourers. Neither the bonded labourers themselves nor their masters reveal the fact of their being bonded, because neither did the bonded labourers want to face the risk of unemployment and starvation nor did the masters want to lose their bonded cheap labourers. Thus the system of bonded labour, in spite of its legal abolition, is continuing. In the absence of subsistence, bonded labourers cannot but remain bonded labourers. There is no point in releasing bonded labourers and throwing them on the roads without subsistence or an alternative source of living. Many of them did not like being bonded labourers, but cannot help being so because of the lack of an alternative source of livelihood. Many of them prefer to be half fed and over-exploited rather than be free without any source of living.

Years of Bonded Labour. All the bonded labourers under study were under bondage for more than two years. In fact, one Scheduled Caste and one Vokkaliga bonded labourer were bonded for more than ten years, which reflects their exploitation for a long period by the landlords. Out of forty bonded labourers, sixteen were bonded for two to four years, eleven were bonded for four to six years, seven were bonded for six to eight years, four were bonded for eight to ten years and two were bonded for more than ten years. The contract of a bonded labourer can be broken by repayment of the entire debt by the bonded labourer after borrowing from another landlord. This means while getting rid of one landlord, the bonded labourer becomes bonded to another landlord. Thus the bondage continues in the same manner except with a change of master. The borrowed money could hardly be repaid, resulting in their perpetual bondage.

Place of Residence. Since the master of the bonded labourer wants to extract work round the clock, he keeps him in a place from which his services would be easily extracted. For this reason practically all bonded labourers were residing either in their master's houses or on their farms. Generally, the bonded labourers are required to reside on their master's farms by constructing, themselves thatched huts. A large number of the bonded labourers, particularly those belonging to Scheduled Castes, were residing on the landlords' farms. Such physical location of huts of the bonded labourers on the landlords' premises enables the landlords to command services from bonded labourers and their family members at any time, mostly without payment. Thus the exploitation of bonded labour is not confined to the labourer himself, but it also covers both old and young, men and women members of his family. Often, family members of the bonded labourer feel obliged to work for the landlord even without his command. Their residence on the farm helps to protect the farm produce from being stolen or grazed by cattle or destroyed by mischievous social elements. The benefits derived by the landlords from the bonded labourer and his family members are many. Bonded labourers are not only labourers on the farm of the landlords, but they also work in the houses of the landlord and elsewhere at the command of landlords.

On the basis of observations made earlier, it may be stated that the bonded labour system very definitely exists, in spite of passing laws against it, because of collusion between the masters of bonded labourers and executive machinery which seems to be sympathetic towards the masters. The social system is such that the masters are also socially privileged high-caste men who have economic power and access to political power. Loopholes in the law help the masters rather than the serfs. The bonded labourers are so weak that they cannot take advantage of legal provisions. Moreover, they do not have alternative sources of living even if they are released from bondage, so they are compelled to continue as bonded labourers.

The hammering of bondage since childhood on the bonded labourer kills his imagination and aspiration for freedom. Even if he is released from bondage he may not appreciate the value of freedom; on the contrary, he may prefer bondage to a free climate because of his acclimatization. Surprisingly, bondage is sometimes treated as an ornament by some of them. Some of them take pride in the richness and power of their masters. While talking, many of them refer to their landlords as 'My master' and 'My owner' and 'My sir', etc. Even their children and wives use similar honorific words for their landlords. Thus even while talking in normal conversation, they consciously or unconsciously accept slavery and help to strengthen the system instead of challenging it. Even if someone talks about freedom from bondage, bonded labourers themselves do not appreciate it and some of them feel it an insult to their masters and treachery on their part. One who tries to convince them to get rid of the bondage is disliked by some bonded labourers. Nevertheless, some of them feel like getting rid of the bonded labour system, but they have to accept it because of their helplessness. Day-to-day living in a village becomes practically impossible for them if they leave their masters, because the masters are economically powerful and socially belong to higher castes, so they can declare a total boycott of bonded labour families. In some villages, bonded labourers sided with their masters to please them, even against their bonded labour fellows who were released.

This was precisely because they have to remain in the villages. Otherwise their fate would be like those released bonded labourers who were compelled to leave their native places and go elsewhere for work. One family which left the village and went to Hospet City for work in an iron ore company feels happier in spite of its being uprooted from the village. It is because the family members get better treatment and much higher wages than they were getting in their native village. However, the family being away from relations at times feels sorry because of absent kith and kin. Particularly females and old people feel very badly about leaving the places of their ancestors where kith and kin resided for generations, while youths feel happy after leaving the bondage and village. From this point of view, the younger generation seems to be more awakened than the older one.

> Flight to the cities has indeed become a common alternative to social and economic oppression in the small world of India's villages. Untouchables are not alone in this voluntary 'diaspora', but a recent survey of 'jhuggi jhompri' (shanty) dwellers in the capital city of Delhi showed 65 per cent were Untouchables (Majumdar, 1983). The following commentary and exhortation appeared as an editorial in Dalit Voice (1-15 April, 1983), a fortnightly newspaper that is published in Bangalore, a city in south-central India. Articles and letters to the editor come from Untouchables and other minorities who write from points as distant as Calcutta; Birmingham, England: and Three Rivers, Texas.

BOMBAY: WHOSE GRANDFATHER'S PROPERTY?

J.R.D. Tata's speech in reply to a special reception accorded by the Mayor of Bombay has received very wide publicity for two reasons. He once represented India's richest business house, now occupying the number 2 position after the Birlas overtook the Tatas. Secondly, he gave expression to something that is very much worrying India's entire ruling class: that the bigger Indian cities are exploding with over-population because of the exodus of the poor and destitute from the countryside, and life in the metropolis is becoming unbearable to the rich and leisured class. Hence the flow into Bombay, Calcutta, Delhi, Madras and Bangalore must be stopped. If possible the urban slum and pavement dwellers, beggars, etc., must be forcibly evicted and bundled out mercilessly.

JRD might not have spoken these very words but he meant exactly this when he said 'the Government's failure to tackle the problems of Bombay was not due to inefficiency or ignorance but a misconceived populist posture and partly no doubt to safeguard votes from the masses'. Bombay, which he described as his much-loved home, had become a victim of unending influx from the rural areas. 'As the millions who poured into Bombay in the last 30 years came in a legitimate search of employment and a better life for themselves and their families than rural India could give them, our politicians claimed that no democratic Government could prevent them from coming into the (Times of India, 12 March). He said the influx perhaps could have been reduced if from the beginning the people had discovered that they would not be allowed to occupy and build hutments on any open ground with impunity. The bulk of the Bombay slum dwellers had well paid jobs. He felt sorry that in the distorted interpretation of social justice, they were allowed to enjoy all these benefits virtually free. It is deplorable to find that this misconceived idea now finds sympathy even among our judges.' Tata demanded a control on the population of Bombay or else it 'will become the greatest collection of slums by the turn of the century'. Tata only asked the government to pack up the poor, but Antulay, then Chief Minister of Maharashtra, actually hounded them out and was stopped only by a sane judge of the Bombay High Court in a rare gesture towards the poor. This is what Tata meant when he criticized 'the distorted interpretation of social justice finding sympathy even among judges'. When the courts side with the poor, the ruling class never likes it.

Since Tata has raised a very important issue of checking the city population which affects Dalits. OBCs [low-ranked bu non-Untouchable castes] and minorities, we want to deal with it here. Tata is echoing what India's ruling class sincerely feels. We respect Tata and acknowledge his contribution to India. But this is a disastrous policy for Dalits. The government may any time re-enact Antulay. Already under different names such as city beautification, slum clearance, urban development, etc. the different governments are virtually driving the poor beyond the city limits. The urban rich often complain that the poor are creating all sorts of problems by occupying gardens, play-grounds, any open space, and dirtying the area. This is true. All of Calcutta is fast turning into one vast slum. Bombay is following. If Calcutta is already a dead city, Bombay is dying.

Why this exodus from the villages? In Trombay (suburb of Bombay), we visited a vast slum (Cheetah Camp) exclusively of Tamil Dalits and Muslims from Tamil Nadu's southern-most district. In Dharavi, considered Asia's largest slum, it is again the Dalits and Muslims who live cheek to jowl. Why are these two large persecuted minorities of India becoming urban slum-dwellers? As more and more people of India are slipping below the poverty line, these two communities, the poorest of the destitute, will naturally be the first to be affected when pauperization grows. Muslims have already become an urban community. But does Tata know why Dalits are making a beeline for the cities? Being mostly landless agricultural labourers, they find it impossible to live in villages. Not only are more and more Dalits losing their lands and becoming farm workers, the rapid rural decay is making it difficult for them even to get jobs as landless labourers. That means stravation. In many villages, aggressive landlords are boycotting local farm hands and bringing labour from outside as a punishment. On one side starvation, but more than that their very life, their little property and the honour of their women are in danger. It is no longer possible for the poverty-stricken, unarmed Untouchables to live in villages. Hundreds of Dalits who fled to Bombay during the 'Marathwada Caste War' [a series of anti-Untouchable riots in 1977] have not yet returned even after so many years. There are one hundred and one reasons why the Dalits prefer the city.

It may be an animal existence, miserable in the congested, dirty slums, but in the villages even the very existence of the Dalits is threatened. Dalits and Muslims have realized this and hence for the past three decades they have migrated to the cities. As insecurity and pauperization increase in the countryside, this trickle will turn into a flood. And it is a healthy sign. No power on earth can stop this natural process. Not even one hundred Tatas. We have long been advocating the shifting of Dalit population to bigger cities. We call upon Dalit organizations and leaders to take up this work seriously and make it an organized mass migration, come what may. Every Dalit employed in cities must try to shift his entire family if not the entire Dalit population of his village to the city. Always prefer bigger cities, not small ones. Since Dalits are in a minority in every village, with minor exceptions, their very existence is threatened. How can they think of organizing themselves under such circumstances? Therefore if the widely-scattered Dalits are brought together in cities, it becomes easier to educate, agitate and organize. Number is strength. Dr. Ambedkar [an Untouchable leader] had spoken about India's stinking 'village republics'—the cesspool of caste politics. Where [high-caste] Hindus are in brute majority, Dalits have no salvation. Therefore he demanded the organized shifting of Dalits to bigger cities. Transfer of Dalit population from the jaws of Hindu hounds should be undertaken in a very big way. The ruling class will put forward one hundred and one obstacles. We must fight it out. Who is Tata to say that the poor should be thrown out of Bombay? Why is he silent about the villages turning into war camps, the landed gentry becoming warlords? It is to escape from them that Phoolan Devi, a Dalit girl, rightly turned into a dacoil [robber]. We want more such Phoolan Devis.

The bluff of land reform and distribution of surplus lands to the landless has been called. Nobody talks about it today. Not even the Marxist governments of Bengal and Tipura. When there is no attraction for the Dalits to stay on in villages, what right has Tata to say the poor have no right to enter Bombay? Does he mean to say that the cities must be reserved as the pleasure house of the parasites? He must know that the urban boom is the result of rural decay for which the ruling class is directly responsible. In the name of slum clearance, city beautification, urban ecology, etc., the ruling class is only trying to throw out the poor to make way for the rich. We know this. The ruling class has no plan to cure the disease, the poverty of India. On the other hand, it is foolish enough to mistake the symptom for the disease (or it is just to fool us? and spend all its time and energy curing the symptom of this creeping paralysis. The urban slums are boils on the body of the dying, decaying society of India. But the ruling class wants to cure the boil, its symptom, not the disease. We shall not allow this non-sense. We are as much part of this country as any of the elite. It is we who shall decide, not Tata. We shall resist this non-sense with all our might. We have any number of tree-lovers, animal-lovers, cow-lovers, nature-lovers. But alas, no human-lovers in India. Whose grandfather's property is Bombay, to say that the poor should be thrown out?

> Where mobility has come for Untouchables, it is largely through special access programmes to scholarships, scarce seats in higher education, and employment in public sector industry and civil service. (No significant anti-discrimination policies apply in the private sector.) These programmes have been some antidote to the pervasive effects of limited family backgrounds and to prejudice that blocks Untouchables who do have skills to compete as equals. An antidote —but a limited one. The number of jobs in the organized sector is limited, and Untouchable access is still greatest at the level of menial and semi-skilled jobs. In 1980, official figures showed Scheduled Caste representation in Central Government public industries as follows: Class A jobs, 2.9 per cent, Class B, 5.1 per cent; Class C, 18.0 per cent: Class D (exclusive of sweepers), 22.4 per cent. Representation in Central Government ministries/departments at corresponding job levels was 4.9 per cent, 8.5 per cent, 13.4 per cent and 19.4 per cent. (Indians officially classified as Scheduled Castes are 15 per cent of the population.)

In spite of continuing limitations in the search for more-than-menial jobs, the appearance of a few Untouchables so outrageously out of place as to compete for skilled jobs or higher education has triggered increasingly violent resistance, including months of riots in several states in 1985. The pattern was set during three months of riots in Gujarat in 1981, which began with hostility to Untouchable medical students and then engulfed private sector factory workers (not covered by the special reservation policies) and Untouchable villagers. Subsequent studies showed that Scheduled Caste and Tribe students together held only 507 (11 %) of a total of 4,500 medical school seats at the time of the riots, though they constitute 21 per cent of the state's population (Desai, 1981). Throughout the state, there was a close correlation between the incidence of violent attacks and Untouchable mobility through any channel, including rural co-operatives or small businesses (Bose, 1981).

Some observers have pointed out that one significant development the riots was Dalit mobilization of effective resistance in some urban areas. However, a representative of the People's Union for Civil Liberties has reported that as of late 1983 no legal action had been taken against those accused of the murder of Untouchables during the riots (Yagnik and Bhatt, 1984).

The following description of the riots and Untouchable losses was made available to the editor a few months after the riots by an Untouchable elected official, and was used by Dr. Laxmi Berwa, an Untouchable human rights activist, in testimony to the United Nations in 1982 on behalf of a coalition of Untouchable organizations from India and Western countries. The data have been cross checked with reports of both the People's Union for Civil Liberties, a national association with a predominantly higher status Indian membership, and the Bharatiya Depressed Classes League, a national Untouchable organization. The human details of the attacks form a protest poetry of their own.

CASTE WAR IN GUJARAT

The caste war in Gujarat started as a result of agitation by medical students of B.J. Medical College (Ahmedabad) for removal of 'carry forward system' of unfilled seats reserved for Scheduled Castes and Scheduled Tribes students. Later on they extended their demand to total abolition of reservation system from education and services too. In 1978 the government had implemented a 'roster system' in postgraduate courses which includes carry forward and inter-changeability of SC [Scheduled Caste, *i.e.* Untouchable] and ST [Scheduled Tribe] seats.

The agitation started from B.J. Medical College on 4 January 1981. On 5 January 1981 the agitating students resorted to stoning, damaged college furniture and raised slogans to abolish the reservation system for SC and ST. On 12 January, these students hijacked four Ahmedabad Municipal Transport Service buses and also resorted to stoning the students of Dental College, who were not in support of their agitation. On 22 January 1981, three government vehicles, including two jeeps of the Public Health Department, were set on fire by the agitating students in B. J. Medical College campus. On 22 January 1981, the agitating caste Hindu students tried to prevent the non-clinical students from entering the college. On 24 January 1981, the SC and ST students were beaten by the agitating students while they were going to attend a conference at B. J. Medical College. On 26 January 1981, the caste Hindu agitating students addressed a caste Hindu meeting in 'Asarwa Chakla' and thereafter attacked the Harijan [Untouchable] Chawl [tenement building], Aryoday Mill Chawl, with burning missiles and lethal weapons.

On 28 January 1981 the government of Gujarat closed State Medical Colleges. Agitating students went to the High Court of Gujarat but their petition was rejected. The Division Bench of the High Court, comprised Judges Justice M.P. Thakkar and Justice R.C. Anand, held a bench on holiday and appealed to agitators as follows: 'We appeal to the medicos to withdraw their agitation against reservation which could result in disintegration of the country. Doctors have to heal the wounds of the society and not to cause them.'

On 5 February 1981, the agitating caste Hindu miscreants attempted to topple the statue of Dr. B.R. Ambedkar [the late Untouchable leader] at Sarangpur Darwaja (near Ahmedabad Railway Station) and the statue's spectacles were knocked down. Thereafter riots followed on a large scale.

Many riot-hurt areas, listed below, have a high density of 'Dalits' (SCs): Rajpur, Gomtipur, Omnagar, Chamanpura, Meghaninagar, Girdhar Nagar, Pritampura, Baliya, Limbi, Asarwa-Hasipura, Nirmalpura Chawl, Fulchand Chawl in Saraspur, Naroda and Behrampura, Majoor Gaon, Gitamandir Road, Ramapir Tekra, Vaday, Ranip, Rupa Pari of Dariyapur and Patni Sheri.

Attacks on Dalits were from five Ps: Pocket, Public (mostly the Patel community, a high caste), Press, Police and Politicians. All these Ps were in the hands of the Patel community, who are the landlords in all areas of Gujarat state.

The press, instead of giving the correct situation, twisted the matter in police reports and published the news 'Harijan mobs attack on caste Hindus'; 'Police were forced to open fire and burst tear gas shells to disperse attacking mob of Harijans', etc.

Incited by this 'news', caste Hindus attacked and murdered Harijans, and threw stones on Harijans. Police too rushed to Harijan streets and chawls and severely beat the Harijans.

In Girdharnagar-Pritampura, police opened fire. In Girdharnagar-Parsini Chawl, police rushed into the chawl, dragged the Harijans and beat them severely with lathis. In Meghani Nagar, the Harijans were beaten by caste Hindus. In Bhimraonagar, the police opened fire—one dead. In Ganpatnagar, police beat innocent Harijans. The Tirupati Society of

Harijans in Ranip was attacked by caste Hindu Patels and burnt. In Rajpur-Gomtipur, police fired and created a scene of terror to crush Harijans. One young boy (SC) died. From Shivanand Nagar, Harijans fled their houses and their furniture was burnt by caste Hindus. Baherampura, Majjorgaon, police beat up Harijans of the chawls and resorted to firing—death of two Harijans. Police and caste Hindus entered Saraspur-Nirmalpura and beat Harijans. Five persons were stabbed to death on the road by caste Hindus in the presence of police. Saraspur-Fulchand chawl, Harijans fled the locality. One Harijan social worker was murdered with a knife by caste Hindus. Saraspur-Vankarvas—New Cloth Market was attacked by caste Hindus and Harijans were severely beaten. In Bharadia police beat up Harijans. Women and children were not spared.

7

Educational Development Among Scheduled Castes

In this paper on educational development among scheduled castes the extent and level of literacy, inter-district variation in literacy, inter-caste variation in literacy and variation in literacy between males and females have been analysed and compared with the general population on the basis of quantitative information from the Census and other sources. The problems of stagnation and wastage have been discussed, and enrolment trends at different stages of education of the scheduled castes have been indicated. The programmes in the plans for the educational development of scheduled castes at pre-matric and post-matric stages have been described and certain suggestions made so as to accelerate the pace of their educational development.

Education is one of the most significant instruments for the equalization of opportunities for development and for the removal of the social and economic disabilities of the scheduled castes. Although the general level of literacy in the country continues to be low, educational backwardness of the scheduled castes is more pronounced than that of the general population as will be evident from the data in Table 7.1 giving the extent of literacy in different states. The data show fairly large inter-state variation in literacy in the general population (standard deviation 8.4) as well as in the scheduled caste population (standard deviation 6.5).

TABLE 7.1

Extent of Literacy in Scheduled Castes Population and the General Population

State	*Percentage of literates in total population*	*Percentage of literates in scheduled caste population*
1. Andhra Pradesh	21.2	8.5
2. Assam	27.4	24.4
3. Bihar	18.4	5.9
4. Gujarat	30.5	22.5
5. Jammu and Kashmir	11.0	4.7
6. Kerala	46.8	24.4
7. Madhya Pradesh	17.1	7.9
8. Madras	31.4	14.7
9. Maharashtra	29.8	15.8
10. Mysore	25.4	9.1
11. Orissa	21.7	11.6
12. Punjab	24.2	9.6
13. Rajasthan	15.2	6.4
14. Uttar Pradesh	17.6	7.1
15. West Bengal	29.3	13.6
India	24.0	10.3

Source: Census of India, 1961. Nagaland has not been included because the population of scheduled castes in the State is not significant.

The gap between extent of literacy in general population and scheduled caste population varies from state to state. In some of the states, such as, Assam and Jammu and Kashmir, the difference between the percentage of literates in the scheduled caste population and general population is not very significant, but in others such as Kerala, Madras, Mysore and West Bengal, it is more than 15 per cent. The coefficient of correlation between percentage of literacy in general population in a state and the percentage of literacy in scheduled caste population is +0.796 which indicates that states in which the extent of literacy in general population is high tend to have a high literacy in the scheduled caste population also. However, the co-efficient of correlation between extent of literacy of general population and the gap in literacy between general population and scheduled caste population is +0.648 indicating that states with higher literacy tend to have a larger gap.

Level of Literacy

There is variation not only in the extent of literacy in different states but also in the level of literacy in the scheduled caste population as compared to the general population. This is evident from the data in Table 7.2 which gives the number of scheduled caste persons per 1,000 of the general population in each educational category. In all the states, then umber of scheduled caste literates (without educational level) per 1,000 literates or scheduled caste persons with primary or junior basic level of education per 1,000 with this educational level is lower than the proportion of scheduled caste population in the state. The data further show that the proportion of scheduled caste persons in each educational category falls with a rise in the educational level and the decline is particularly sharp in the category, matric and above. There is also considerable inter-state variation in the level of literacy; in states with low literacy, the number of scheduled caste persons, matric and above, per 1,000 with this educational level is the lowest compared to the number of scheduled caste persons per 1,000 of the total population in the state. For instance, in Bihar, Madhya Pradesh, Orissa and Rajasthan the number of

TABLE 7.2

Number of Scheduled Caste Persons Per 1,000 Persons in each Educational Level

State	*Number of scheduled caste persons per 1,000 persons*	*Illiterate*	*Number of scheduled caste persons per 1,000 persons in each educational level*		
			Literate (without educational level)	*Primary or Junior basic*	*Matric and above*
1	*2*	*3*	*4*	*5*	*6*
1. Andhra Pradesh	138	161	61	51	23
2. Assam	62	64	59	51	17
3. Bihar	141	162	50	38	13
4. Gujarat	66	74	63	44	14
5. Jammu and Kashmir	80	85	44	22	9
6. Kerala	85	121	49	37	17
7. Madhya Pradesh	131	295	68	50	8
8. Madras	180	224	95	72	24

9. Maharashtra	56	67	36	26	9
10. Mysore	135	141	32	41	24
11. Orissa	157	178	90	61	16
12. Punjab	204	142	100	76	32
13. Rajasthan	167	184	75	66	15
14. Uttar Pradesh	209	235	94	77	37
15. West Bengal	107	241	114	73	23

scheduled caste persons per 1,000 in the category matric and above is less than one-ninth of the number of scheduled caste persons per 1,000 persons in the state.

Inter-District Variation

There is also variation in extent of literacy in different districts within a state. This will be evident from Table 7.3. The data

TABLE 7.3

Variation in Extent of Literacy in Different Districts within a State

State	*Lowest percentage of literacy in scheduled caste popuIotion in a district*	*Highest percentage of literacy in scheduled caste population in a district*	*Range*	*Standard deviation*
1. Andhra Pradesh	2.90	17.18	14.28	3.23
2. Assam	11.07	32.32	21.25	5.47
3. Bihar	3.60	16.00	12.40	2.88
4. Gujarat	9.14	40.44	31.30	9.70
5. Jammu and Kashmir	2.49	5.64	3.15	1.30
6. Kerala	13.81	41.68	27.87	9.15
7. Madhya Pradesh	1.44	23.00	39.25	8.88
8. Madras	8.34	39.68	30.31	9.12
9. Maharashtra	4.32	35.09	80.77	6.51
10. Mysore	3.85	15.46	11.61	3.32
11. Orissa	6.55	15.49	8.94	2.73
12. Punjab	5.47	20.47	13.00	4.88
13. Rajasthan	2.09	13.87	11.58	2.21
14. Uttar Pradesh	2.82	19.02	16.20	3.61
15. West Bengal	7.05	22.23	15.18	5.58

show that in some of the states like Gujarat, Kerala, Madras and Maharashtra, the range (the difference between highest percentage of literacy in a district in scheduled caste population and the lowest percentage of literacy in a district in scheduled caste population) is more than 25 per cent. The standard deviation of percentags literacy in scheduled caste population in different districts is also fairly high in these states which, incidentally, rank among the first five in regard to the spread of literacy in the scheduled caste population.

To ascertain the degree of association between extent of literacy in the general population and extent of literacy in the scheduled caste population in different districts correlation co-efficients were calculated for all the states. The data given in Table 7.4 show that in almost all the states the correlation is high, suggesting that districts with a higher level of literacy in general population also have higher level of literacy in scheduled caste population. However, the coefficient of correlation between extent of literacy in a district in general population and the gap in literacy between a district in general population and scheduled caste population is high in most states suggesting that districts with higher literacy tend to have a larger gap.

A study of problems of extension of primary education in rural areas by the Programme Evaluation Organisation (Planning Commission) too found considerable inter-district variation in enrolment of Harijan children. For instance, the percentage Harijan children on roll to total in the sample schools varied of from 8.7 per cent in Burdwan district to 29.4 per cent in Amravati district.[1] A study on post-matric education among the scheduled castes by the Cultural Research Institute, Government of West Bengal, also showed that out of the 16 districts in the state, about 57 per cent of the post-matric scholarship awards in 1966-67 were availed of by scheduled caste students of two districts although only 24 per cent of the scheduled caste population in the state lived in these two districts.[2]

TABLE 7.4

Association between Literacy in General Population in a District and Literacy in Scheduled Castes Population

State	*Correlation between percentage of literacy in general population in a district and percentage of literacy in scheduled caste population*	*Correlation between percentage of literacy in general population in a district and gap between percentage of literacy in general population and in scheduled caste populat ion*
1. Andhra Pradesh	+0.942	+0.854
2. Assam	+0.922	+0.297
3. Bihar	+0.489	+0.734
4. Gujarat	+0.629	+0.294
5. Jammu and Kashmir	+0.549	+0.947
6. Kerala	+0.783	—0.031
7. Madhya Pradesh	+0.545	+0.588
8. Madras	+0.936	+0.399
9. Maharashtra	+0.617	+0.555
10. Mysore	+0.659	+0.948
11. Orissa	+0.668	+0.922
12. Punjab	+0.559	+0.764
13. Rajasthan	+0.727	+0.875
14. Uttar Pradesh	+0.868	+0.803
15. West Bengal	+0.655	+0.868

Inter-Caste Variation

Another important feature of the educational development of scheduled castes is the difference in extent of literacy between castes. This will be evident from the data in Table 7.5 compiled for numerically large castes, *i.e.*, those with a population of more than 25,000. The data show that in five states, *viz.*, Andhra Pradesh, Gujarat, Kerala, Madras and Maharashtra the inter-caste variation in extent of literacy is high. Incidentally, these states rank high in regard to spread of literacy among scheduled castes.

TABLE 7.5

Variation in Extent of Literacy Among Different Scheduled Castes in a State

State	*Lowest percentage of literacy in scheduled caste*	*Highest percentage of literacy in a scheduled caste*	*Range*	*Standard deviation*
1. Andhra Pradesh	2.97	25.98	23.01	7.42
2. Assam	18.37	36.89	18.52	5.49
3. Bihar	1.32	12.47	11.15	3.49
4. Gujarat	9.11	43.00	33.89	10.66
5. Jammu and Kashmir	3.35	5.51	2.16	0.94
6. Kerala	11.07	49.64	38.57	12.60
7. Madhya Pradesh	2.24	22.64	20.40	5.57
8. Madras	3.50	34.20	30.70	7.55
9. Maharashtra	9.87	27.14	17.27	6.93
10. Mysore	3.20	19.17	15.97	4.97
11. Orissa	6.37	19.31	12.94	2.83
12. Punjab	3.00	16.01	13.01	4.75
13. Rajasthan	3.24	11.58	8.34	2.47
14. Uttar Pradesh	2.23	11.57	9.34	2.28
15. West Bengal	5.33	21.68	16.35	4.98

Source: Census data. Only castes with a population above 25,000 were taken into consideration.

For three states, *viz.*, Bihar, Madras and Gujarat, the level of education among scheduled castes with a population of over 50,000 was calculated. The extent of literacy among the scheduled castes in these three states is 5.9 per cent, 14.7 per cent and 22.5 per cent respectively and may, therefore, be considered as representing different levels of spread of literacy among the scheduled castes. The data in Table 7.6 show that in Bihar, among all the scheduled castes, the percentage with matric or higher education is less than 0.5 per cent and in only six of the 13 castes more than 1 per cent have education up to primary or junior basic levels. In Madras and Gujarat, too, in only one caste the percentage with an educational level of matric and above is more than 0.5 per cent. However, in the educational level, primary or junior basic, the situation in Gujarat for most of the scheduled castes is much better than in Madras and Bihar. Eor instance, of the 13 numerically large scheduled castes in Bihar, in seven castes the percentage of population with primary or junior basic level of education is less than 1 per cent while in the remaining six it is more than 1 per cent but less than 2 per cent. In Madras, of the 10 numerically large scheduled castes, in only one caste is the percentage of population with primary or junior basic level of education less than 1 per cent; in three castes it is between 1 and 2 per cent; in 5 castes it is between 2 and 5 per cent and in one caste it is more than 5 per cent. In Gujarat, in four of the six numerically large scheduled castes, the percentage of population with primary or junior basic level of education is more than 9. Thus, while there is inter-caste variation in the level of literacy in states with low as well as higher levels of literacy, the range of variation at the level of primary junior basic and above appears to be greater in the case of states with higher literacy.

The Cultural Research Institute of the Tribal Welfare Department, Government of West Bengal, which made a study of the progress of secondary education among scheduled castes in West Bengal,[3] too, found considerable variation in the extent to which different scheduled castes have availed themselves of educational facilities. Data for 1950-61 showed that

TABLE 7.6

Percentage Distribution of Level of Education Among Scheduled Castes in Bihar, Madras and Gujarat

Caste	Total	Illiterate	Literate without education level	Primary or Junior basic	Matric and above
1	2	3	4	5	6
Bihar					
1. Bauri	100.00	94.21	5.08	0.64	0.07
2. Bhogta	100.00	95.89	3.56	0.53	0.02
3. Bhuiya	100.00	98.68	4.17	0.14	0.01
4. Chamar	100.00	93.68	5.15	1.06	0.11
5. Dhobi	100.00	89.97	7.76	1.92	0.35
6. Dom	100.00	95.19	4.15	0.59	0.07
7. Dusadh	100.00	92.94	5.72	1.23	0.13

(*Contd.*)

1	2	3	4	5	6
8. Ghasi	100.00	90.89	7.19	1.68	0.24
9. Hari	100.00	89.48	9.11	1.28	0.13
10. Musahar	100.00	97.88	1.94	0.17	0.01
11. Pasi	100.00	89.97	7.76	1.46	0.38
12. Rajwar	100.00	95.11	4.16	0.67	0.06
13. Turi	100.00	95.33	4.01	0.63	0.03
Madras					
1. Adi-Dravida	100.00	83.32	12.10	4.20	0.38
2. Arunthathiyar	100.00	86.88	9.40	3.34	0.36
3. Chakkiliyan	100.00	96.50	2.42	1.02	0.03
4. Kudumban	100.00	85.48	12.38	1.91	0.28
5. Kuravan, Sidhanar	100.00	86.81	9.97	2.96	0.26
6. Madari	100.00	93.10	5.95	0.91	0.04
7. Pallan	100.00	83.87	12.90	2.86	0.37
8. Paraiyan, Parayan	100.00	84.97	12.03	2.75	0.25

9. Samban	100.00	88.11	10.13	1.68	0.08
10. Valluvan	100.00	65.00	25.99	7.42	0.79
Gujarat					
1. Bhambi	100.00	75.19	11.19	13.30	0.32
2. Bhangi	100.00	80.93	7.82	11.11	0.14
3. Chamar, Nalia or Rohit	100.00	89.75	4.24	5.94	0.07
4. Mahyavanshi	100.00	67.43	12.68	19.26	0.63
5. Meghwal	100.00	90.89	4.98	4.10	0.03
6. Voukar, Dhedh or Antyaj	100.00	85.89	4.89	9.14	0.13

Source: Census data. Only castes with a population of more than 50,000 were taken into consideration.

the percentage of the students in school-going age in secondary stage who are actually attending schools is 16.48 per cent among the scheduled castes and 45.45 per cent among other communities excluding scheduled tribes. Among the Namasudra, Pan and Poliya castes more than 50 per cent of the number of students of school-going age in secondary stage are actually attending school; in more than 32 castes, however, the percentage is less than 17. The study further reports that the number of students from different castes attending school is increasing, but the progress is not uniform among all.

Another study on post-matric education among the scheduled castes of West Bengal by this Institute[4] showed that out of 63 scheduled castes in the state, students from 50 scheduled castes received post-matric scholarships. Four scheduled castes (Namasudra, Poundra, Sunri and Rajbansi) got 84 per cent of the total awards, although they comprise only 42 per cent of the total scheduled caste population in the state. Comparison of the situation showed that more than 84 per cent of the total post-matric awards went to the same four castes (Namasudra, Poundra, Sunri and Rajbansi). However, while in 1959-60, 21 scheduled caste communities did not get any post-matric awards, in 1966-67 the number came down to 13.

The Maharashtra State Government which undertook a study of the scheduled castes who were getting post-matric scholarships reported somewhat similar findings. The progress of post-matric education was very low among some scheduled castes even though they were numerically fairly large. The Mahars, for instance, were getting 85.8 per cent of the scholarships awarded to scheduled caste students although they comprise 35.1 per cent of the total scheduled caste population in the state, while the Mang were getting only 2.2 per cent of the scholarships although they comprise 32.6 per cent of the total scheduled caste population.[5]

Literacy Among Females

The extent of literacy among scheduled caste women is only

3.29 per cent as compared to 16.96 per cent among scheduled caste men. Thus the gap at the all-India level is 13.67 per cent, but the position varies significantly from state to state. The data in Table 7.7 which gives the percentage literacy among scheduled caste males and females and the gap between the two in each state show that in two states less than 1 per cent of the females are literate and in ten states less than 5 per cent

TABLE 7.7

Extent of Literacy in Scheduled Caste Male and Female Population

State	*Percentage of Literacy in Scheduled Caste Males*	*Percentage of Literacy in Scheduled Caste Females*	*Gap in Literacy*
1. Andhra Pradesh	13.43	3.10	10.03
2. Assam	31.74	16.08	15.66
3. Bihar	11.13	0.92	10.21
4. Gujarat	33.87	10.72	23.15
5. Jammu & Kashmir	7.95	1.09	6.86
6. Kerala	31.61	17.38	14.23
7. Madhya Pradesh	14.26	1.33	12.93
8. Madras	23.56	5.69	17.87
9. Maharashtra	25.46	5.71	19.75
10. Mysore	14.87	3.04	11.83
11. Orissa	19.82	3.43	16.39
12. Punjab	16.18	2.16	14.02
13. Rajasthan	11.63	0. 7	10.84
14. Uttar Pradesh	12.79	1.14	11.65
15. West Bengal	21.80	4.61	17.19

Source: Census data.

of the scheduled caste females are literate. In educationally backward states like Jammu & Kashmir, Bihar, Madhya Pradesh, Rajasthan and Uttar Pradesh, the picture is particularly depressing. The co-efficient of correlation between extent of literacy in a state among scheduled caste males and scheduled caste females is +0.893 indicating that states with higher literacy among males tend to have higher literacy among females as well. The co-efficient of correlation between extent of literacy among scheduled caste males and gap in literacy between scheduled caste males and females is fairly high (+0.788) indicating that states with higher literacy among males tend to have a larger gap.

The difference in level of literacy between scheduled caste males and scheduled caste females is also fairly pronounced as will be evident from Table 7.8 giving the number of scheduled caste females per 1,000 scheduled caste males in each educational category. The data show that the gap increases considerably in the category of matriculation and above. There is, however, considerable inter-state variation; in states with low literacy, the number of scheduled caste females per 1,000 scheduled caste males, matric and above, is much lower compared to the sex ratio in the scheduled caste population in the state.

The co-efficient of correlation between extent of literacy among females in general population in a state and extent of literacy among scheduled caste females is +0.822, showing that states with higher literacy among females in general population tend to have higher literacy among scheduled caste females. However, the co-efficient of correlation between extent of literacy among females in general population and gap in literacy between general population females and scheduled caste females is +0.601 suggesting that in states with higher literacy among females the gap tends to be larger.

Table 7.9 gives the number of scheduled caste females for every thousand females of the general population in each educational category in different states. The data show that the comparative position is extremely unsatisfactory, particularly at the higher levels. Thereis, however, a large variation in this regard between states.

Stagnation and Wastage

The problem of stagnation and wastage in education is acute in India, more so in the case of the scheduled castes. The Education Commission has made pointed reference to this aspect of Indian education.[6] It stated that stagnation is highest in class I; it is reduced considerably in class II and then remains fairly constant in classes III and IV. At the higher primary stage stagnation decreases still further; stagnation is greater among girls, and there are considerable variations form area to area. In the case of wastage, it reported that 'wastage is very large at the lower primary stage—about 56 per cent for boys and 62 per cent for girls. About two-thirds of the wastages occurs in class I. Moreover, it has remained fairly constant in the case of boys while there has been a slight improvement in the case of girls. At the higher primary stage, wastage is much less—about 24 per cent for boys and 34 per cent for girls; and what is more important, it is decreasing consistently, although at a slow rate. The study on wastage and stagnation in primary and middle schools of India by the National Council of Educational Research and Training also showed that the total rate of wastage and stagnation is 65.30 per cent by the time children reach grade V and 78.35 per cent by the time they reach grade VIII. Of 100 pupils enrolled in grade I, about 39 drop out or stagnate in grade I, 11 in grade II, 8 each in grades III and IV, 7 in grade V, 3 in grade VI and 2 each in grades VII and VIII. As is evident from these figures, about 50 per cent of the total wastage and stagnation at the elementary stage is in grade I itself and the incidence decreases as the pupils move from lower to higher grades.[7] Separate data for scheduled castes are not available in this Report but the data on the difference between drop-outs and stay-ins in relation to caste structure of families showed that children

TABLE 7.8

Number of Scheduled Caste Females per Thousand Scheduled Caste Males in Each Educational Level

State	*No. of Scheduled Caste Females per 1,000 Scheduled Caste Males*	*Number of Scheduled Caste Females per 1,000 Scheduled Caste Male in Each Educational level*			
		Illiterate	*Literate without Educational Level*	*Primary or Junior basic*	*Matric and above*
1. Andhra Pradesh	980	1,093	247	267	121
2. Assam	882	1,085	460	428	135
3. Bihar	1,031	1,149	92	53	68
4. Gujarat	972	1,314	313	312	57
5. Jammu and Kashmir	889	956	131	91	63
6. Kerala	1,014	1,225	573	533	331
7. Madhya Pradesh	973	1,119	95	74	81
8. Madras	993	1,225	236	269	127

9. Maharashtra	962	1,216	253	168	97
10. Mysore	965	1,098	196	237	88
11. Orissa	1,015	1,223	182	125	36
12. Punjab	874	1,021	147	89	25
13. Rajasthan	923	1,036	63	88	54
14. Uttar Pradesh	941	1,066	92	62	52
15. West Bengal	916	1,117	21	169	62

Source: Census data.

TABLE 7.9

Number of Scheduled Caste Females per 1,000 Females in Each Educational Category

State	*Number of Scheduled Caste Females per 1,000 Females in the Population*	*Number of Scheduled Caste Females per 1,000 Females in Each Educational Level*			
		Illiterate	*Literate without Educational Level*	*Primary or Junior basic*	*Matric and above*
1. Andhra Pradesh	138	152	40	38	22
2. Assam	62	62	64	59	15
3. Bihar	143	152	20	15	13
4. Gujarat	67	74	49	33	5
5. Jammu and Kashmir	81	83	27	10	4
6. Kerala	85	114	42	30	14
7. Madhya Pradesh	133	140	29	21	2
8. Madras	180	207	63	46	15
9. Maharashtra	57	65	24	15	4

10. Mysore	133	150	30	26	12
11. Orissa	150	167	66	43	8
12. Puniab	205	234	42	23	5
13. Rajasthan	168	177	24	20	7
14. Uttar Pradesh	213	227	82	29	10
15. West Bcngal	202	232	66	39	16

Source: Census data.

from Brahmin, Kshatriya and Vaishya families do not drop out in the same proportion as those from the 'backward classes' and scheduled caste or scheduled tribes.

A study on wastage and stagnation in Satara district by the Gokhale Institute of Politics and Economics[8] reported that among higher castes like Brahmins, Jains, etc. 'the absolute minima in education of their children are kept considerably higher than the primary third standard, so that even in the face of rather disappointing progress, the children are not usually withdrawn from school'. In the case of lower castes, the Report states that 'education of children is difficult to obtain and almost impossible when the children, for one reason or the other, fail to keep the normal progress.'

The Cultural Research Institute of the Tribal Welfare Department, Government of West Bengal, too, made a study of the extent of wastage and stagnation among the scheduled caste and scheduled tribe students at high school stage.[9] The extent of stagnation found by it is glven below:

Percentage of stagnation for 1962

	Class				
	V	*VI*	*VII*	*VIII*	*IX*
Scheduled tribes	27.9	31.2	34.7	38.5	50.1
Scheduled castes	28.2	30.0	30.7	34.8	45.4
Other communities	19.9	22.4	27.2	29.8	35.9

It is apparent that the extent of wastage increases in the higher classes and is the highest for scheduled tribes followed by scheduled castes and the rest of the population. Among both scheduled castes and scheduled tribes the extent of wastage shows a significant rise from class VIII to class IX.

The information collected by the Directorate General of Employment and Training, Government of India, from returns submitted by 38 University Employment Information and

Guidance Bureaus (UEIGB) about students getting post-matric scholarships also show that wastage and stagnation is very high. Each UEIGB was asked to collect from a representative college in its jurisdiction data relating to the number of scheduled caste students enrolled and passed during the years 1960 to 1966. The number of colleges covered was 54. The findings show that one-half to two-thirds of scheduled caste candidates enrolled in most of the post-matric courses failed to complete them successfully. In the general education courses, the average rate of wastage was more than 40 per cent for all courses and was even as high as 80 per cent for some courses. In professional courses like medicine and engineering, the wastage was 62 per cent and 45 per cent respectively.[10] Despite the limited base from which the above data have been collected, it could, nevertheless, be inferred that the rate of drop-outs and failures in post-matric scholarships is very high. The result of a study made in Madhya Pradesh by the Office of the Commissioner for Scheduled Castes and Scheduled Tribes also points in the same direction. Out of 314 students of B.A. Part I who were awarded fresh scholarships only 94 (30%) were awarded renewals in B.A. Part II. In the case of B.Sc. Part II, the percentage renewals was only 24.3 and in the case of B. Com. Part II it was 35.3 per cent.[11]

Thus all these studies report the high incidence of wastage and stagnation at all levels. The Education Commission attributed this to a number of economic, educational and social causes. The NCERT, in its study on wastage and stagnation in primary and middle schools in India, classified the causes of wastage in relation to school variables, pupil variables and family variables and also took into account the causes given by drop-outs, theirparents and their teachers. It reported that 'in primary education, the first six variables in order of importance which maximally discriminate drop-outs from staying are: attendance in school, parents' view of the child's educational performance, motivation for learning from home, pupil's academic performance, caste and age at the time of admission to school. At the middle stage, the corresponding order of first six variablesis: attendance in school, pupil's academic performance, interestin education, motivation for learning from home, age at the time of admission to school and parents' view of child's educational performance. Thus, it is evident that among the first six variables, five are common to both the primary as well as middle stages of education, although the ranks of some of these variables are not exactly the same'.[12]

Separate studies on the causes of stagnation and wastage in education among scheduled castes are not available, but it may be assumed that most of the causes pointed out by the Education Commission and the NCERT study apply with greater intensity in the case of scheduled castes. Most of the students from these communities are first-generation school-goers and so parental help, support and encouragement are generally lacking. Other important reasons are the poverty of parents and the difficulties they face in sparing their children to attend school since their services are required either for some assistance in the family enterprise or for looking after the younger children when the parents are out for working. Malnutrition, ill health and an unattractive school environment and school curriculum lead to the waning of interest of the child in school. There are also deficiencies in admission policies in lower primary level, in school equipment and in teaching methods. Overcrowding, non-availability of the right type of teachers motivated to teach students from these communities, and weaknesses in suprevision of the school system in backward areas are other reasons. Hardly any attempt has been made to motivate the parents to send children to school or to try and remove the handicaps of the child who is lagging in studies, irregular, in attendance or not interested in studies.

Enrolment Trends

An encouraging feature in the education of scheduled castes is the significant progress in recent years in enrolment of children from these groups in educational institutions.[13] Data collected by the Education Ministry on enrolment of scheduled caste students at different levels is available. This gives a comparative picture of the percentage enrolment of scheduled caste children at each level compared to the proportion of the population of these castes in the total population. The data in Table 7.10 show that whereas in 1960-61 in only three states, namely, Assam, Kerala and Maharashtra, the percentage enrolment of scheduled caste children at primary stage was higher than the proportion of scheduled castes in the total population, in 1964-65 in six states, the percentage

TABLE 7.10

Percentage Enrolment of Scheduled Caste Children to Total Enrolment at Primary/Junior Basic Level

State	*Percentage of scheduled caste population*	*Percentage enrolment of scheduled caste children*	
		1960-61	*1964-65*
1. Andhra Pradesh	13.8	12.3	14.0
2. Assam	6.2	7.7	7.1
3. Bihar	14.1	9.8	10.4
4. Gujarat	6.6	6.1	7.6
5. Kerala	8.4	10.9	10.6
6. Madhya Pradesh	13.1	9.3	9.9
7. Madras	18.0	17.0	18.1
8. Maharashtra	5.6	10.0	10.3
9. Mysore	13.2	10.5	12.6
10. Punjab	20.4	12.3	13.5
11. Rajasthan	16.7	4.4	12.4
12. Uttar Pradesh	20.9	14.3	13.3
13. West Bengal	19.9	17.5	16.4

Source : Education Ministry, Government of India; information is available for only 13 states.

enrolment of scheduled caste children was higher than the proportion of scheduled castes in the total population. In the other states the gap between the percentage enrolment of scheduled caste children and the percentage of scheduled caste population in the state is becoming reduced.

A study by the P.E.O.[13] on the problems of extension of primary education in rural areas was also reported an increase in the enrolment of scheduled caste children. It found that the proportion of schools having Harijan children on roll registered an increase from 60.3 per cent to 69.2 per cent and 74.2 per cent. The enrolment of Harijan children also increased more than two and a half times. The proportion of Harijan children on roll to the total children on roll showed an increase from 13.6 per cent to 16.1 per cent. A significant finding reported by this study is that the growth in enrolment of Harijan children was higher in each of the two plan periods than that of the non-Harijan children, as will be evident from the following figures giving the percentage incrase in enrolment of Harijan and non-Harijan children in sample schools:

Harijan children	*Other children*
80.0	50.3
48.5	34.3
167.2	101.10

Data on enrolment at middle/senior basic high/higher secondary and higher levels is given in Table 7.11. At the middle/senior basic stage, in four states the percentage enrolment of scheduled caste students to total enrolment in 1964-65 is higher than the percentage of scheduled caste population in the state. In most states, the percentage enrolment of scheduled castes tends to increase but in a few there is a marginal fall. At the higher secondary level, in most of the states there is a marginal increase in percentage enrolment of scheduled castes. In three states, however, which are educationally backward, namely, Bihar, U.P. and Punjab, there is a fall in the percentage of scheduled caste enrolment. In the case of enrolment at higher levels, while in eight states there is a marginal increase, in five states there is marginal fall.

Table 7.12 gives the gap at different levels of education between percentage enrolment of scheduled caste children to total enrolment and the percentage of scheduled caste population in the state.

The data show that the gap increases at the higher levels except in Maharashtra where at all levels the percentage enrolment of scheduled caste students is higher than the percentage of scheduled caste population in the state. In seven out of thirteen states for which data are available, the gap at primary/junior basic stage is either less than 1 per cant or the percentage enrolment of scheduled caste students is higher. In the other states the gap varies from 3.2 to 7.6 per cent. These are, incidentally, the states which the educationally backward. In Assam, Gujarat and Kerala at the primary/junior basic and middle/senior basic level, the pereentage enrolment of scheduled caste children is higher than the percentage of their population in the state, but at the higher levels it is less. In six states, namely, Bihar, Madhya Pradesh, Rajasthan, Uttar Pradesh, Punjab and West Bengal, the gap between percentage enrolment of scheduled caste children and the percentage of scheduled caste population is high at all levels of education.

The extent of enrolment of scheduled caste students in professional, vocational and technical courses is rather low. The Maharashtra Gorernment, in its study of scheduled caste and scheduled tribe students getting post-matric scholarships, found that nearly 87 per cent of the seheduled caste scholarship holders took art, science and commerce courses while the percentage taking up professional and technical courses is comparatively low.[14] The study on post-matric education among scheduled castes ia West Beagal, too, showed that 70 per cent of the post-matric scholarships were awarded for courses in arts and commerce, about 20 per cent for science subjects and about 10 per cent for other technical subjects.[15]

TABLE 7.11

Percentage Enrolment of Scheduled Castes to Total Enrolment at Middle/Senior Basic, High/Higher Secondary and Higher Education Levels

State	*Percentage of Scheduled caste Population*	*Percentage Enrolment of Scheduled Castes*					
		Middle/Senior Basic		*High/Higher Secondary*		*Higher Educational Level*	
		1960-61	*1964-65*	*1960-61*	*1964-65*	*1960-61*	*1964-65*
1. Andra Pradesh	13.8	9.2	9.6	8.2	8.2	5.1	5.4
2. Assam	6.2	6.2	6.4	6.6	6.1	4.8	4.4
3. Bihar	14.1	7.6	7.9	6.0	5.9	3.4	3.8
4. Gujarat	6.6	6.8	7.9	3.8	5.0	2.3	2.2
5. Kerala	8.4	8.5	9.2	7.6	8.0	3.5	3.7
6. Madhya Pradesh	13.1	8.1	8.4	4.2	5.3	2.6	3.7
7. Madras	18.0	11.6	14.9	8.1	12.8	5.1	5.0
8. Maharashtra	5.6	10.2	8.3	7.3	7.9	6.9	7.5
9. Mysore	13.2	6.3	8.9	5.3	5.7	3.1	2.8

10. Punjab	20.4	9.2	8.9	8.5	8.4	5.8	4.6
11. Rajasthan	16.7	3.6	8.7	3.2	8.1	1.5	1.9
12. Uttar Pradesh	20.9	12.2	10.8	9.6	8.8	4.3	4.6
13. West Bengal	19.9	12.2	11.4	6.2	6.2	4.4	5.6

Source: Education Ministry

The same trend is evident from data on post-matric scholarships awarded to scheduled caste students in 1966-67 in Gujara and Orissa.

TABLE 7.12

Difference Between Percentage Enrolment of Scheduled Caste Children to Total Enrolment in 1964-65 at Different Educational Levels and Percentage Population of Scheduled Castes

State	*Primary/ Junior Basic*	*Middle/ Senior Basic*	*High/ Higher Secondary*	*Higher Education*
1. Andhra Pradesh	+0.2	—4.2	—5.6	—8.4
2. Assam	+0-9	+0.2	—0.1	—1.8
3. Bihar	—3.7	—6.2	—8.2	—10.3
4. Gujarat	+1.0	+1.3	—1.6	—4.4
5. Kerala	+2.2	+0.8	—0.4	—4.7
6. Madhya Pradesh	+3.2	—4.7	—7.8	—9.4
7. Madras	+0.1	—3.1	—5.2	—13.0
8. Maharashtra	+4.7	+2.7	+2.3	+1.9
9. Mysore	+0.6	—4.3	—7.5	—10.4
10. Punjab	—6.9	—11.5	—12.0	—15.8
11. Rajasthan	—4.3	—8.0	—10.6	—14.8
12. Uttar Pradesh	—7.6	—10.1	—12.1	—16.3
13. West Bengal	—3.5	—8.5	—13.7	—14.3

Source: Based on Education Ministry data.

Although reservation of seats in indnstrial training insritutes set up in different parts of the country has been made for scheduled castes proportionate to their population in the respective states, and each scheduled caste candidate is given

TABLE 7.13

Course-wise Award of Post-matric Scholarships to Scheduled Caste Students

Course	Gujarat		Orissa	
	Number	*Percentage*	*Number*	*Percentage*
1	*2*	*3*	*4*	*5*
1, Inter Science/B, Sc/M. Sc.	704	18.56	162	25.47
2. Inter Arts/B.A./M.A.	1,877	49.49	303	47.64
3. Inter Com./B. Com./M. Com.	414	10.92	4	0.63
4. LL.B./Honours/Other Oriental Languages/Fine Arts/ Correspondence	110	2.90	6	0.94
5. D. Sc./D. Litt./Ph. D.	—	—	—	—
6. Diploma Certificate Course in Agriculture/Veterinary Science	7	0.18	—	—
7. Teachers, Training and Physical Education	54	1.43	1	0.16
8. B.Sc. Agriculture/B. V. Sc. diploma in Rural Science/Civil and Rural Engineering	7	0.18	13	2.04

(*Contd.*)

1	2	3	4	5
9. Post-graduate courses in Agriculture	—	—	—	—
10. Bachclor of Nursing and Pharmacy	3	0.08	—	—
11. Diploma Certificate Course in Engineering/Architecture etc.	60	1.58	84	13.21
12. Degree course in Engineering	123	3.24	63	9.91
13. Other Courses	434	11.44	—	—
Total:	3,793	100.00	636	100.00

a stipend of Rs. 45 per month, these are not filled as will be evident from the data in Table 7.14 giving the state-wise distribution of candidates undergoing training in I.T.I.'s in 1966.[16] The chief seasons for this non-utilization are restricted mobility undergoing a fresh period of training after schooling. Many scheduled caste students are also not fully aware of the potentialities of placement after training at these Institutes, and the pay scales available. Those who do continue education,

TABLE 7.14

Percentage Distribution of Scheduled Caste Candidates Undergoing Training in Industrial Training Institutes

State	*Percentage of Scheduled Caste Trainees to Total Trainees*	*Percentage of Scheduled Caste Population in the State*
1. Andhra Pradesh	10.0	13.8
2. Assam	3.9	6.2
3. Bihar	4.5	14.1
4. Gujarat	3.7	6.6
5. Jammu & Kashmir	6.5	7.5
6. Kerala	8.8	8.4
7. Madhya Pradesh	6.7	13.1
8. Madras	12.4	18.0
9. Maharashtra	8.5	5.6
10. Mysore	12.5	13.2
11. Orissa	6.8	15.7
12. Punjab	12.1	20.4
13. Rajasthan	10.0	16.7
14. Uttar Pradesh	11.1	20.9
15. West Bengal	7.7	19.9

therefore, tend to move towards general courses in the hope that by obtaining another degree they will be able to get a suitable job and acquire a higher status in their community.

Concessions in Admission

The Government of India, State governments, Union Territory Administrations and the Universities throughout the country, are expected to give the following concessions to scheduled caste candidates in the matter of admission to technical and other educational institutions under their respective control in compliance with the requests made in this regard by the Ministry of Education:

(i) Twenty per cent of seats in all technical institutions should be reserved for the scheduled castes and the scheduled tribes, with a distinct reservation of 15 per cent for scheduled castes and 5 per cent for scheduled tribes. This reservation can be interchanged;

(ii) Where admissions are restricted to candidates obtaining a certain minimum percentage of marks and not merely to his passing of a certain examination, there may be a 5 per cent reduction for scheduled castes, provided that the lower percentage prescribed does not fall below the qualifying examination;

(iii) If there is a maximum age limit, it may be raised by 8 years in the case of such candidates; and

(iv) A minimum qualifying standard should be prescribed for admission to any technical institution. Students belonging to scheduled castes should be eligible for admission to the reserved seats if they attain this minimum standard without any reference to the gap between their marks and the marks of the last person admitted in the open seats.

A number of ministries and institutions are giving these concessions in compliance with the request of the Ministry of Education.

Programmes for Educational Development at Pre-matric Stage

To provide educational facilities to the scheduled castes, a number of schemes have been undertaken in the backward classes sector of the Plan for pre-matric education. These are in addition to the exemption given to scheduled caste students in the payment of fees. They include grant of stipends/scholarships, midday meals, uniforms, exemption from payment of examinination fees, books grants and hostel facilities. In the Third Plan about Rs. 17 crores and during 1966-69 about Rs. 9.3 crores were spent in the state sector for the education of scheduled castes.[17] Seventeen lakh stipends/scholarships.were given to scheduled caste students in the Third Plan, midday meals were given to 71.862 scheduled caste students and book and equipment grants to 3.49 lakh scheduled caste students. Most of the states have been allocating about two-thirds of the outlay in the welfare of backward classes sector to education. Emphasis is being given in current education-programmes to the expansion of hostel facilities for both boys and girls in order to provide a better environment for studies. Boarding grants are also being given to enable students living in scattered areas to avail of facilities for middle and higher education. These hostels are run both by government and voluntary organizations and admit students from all communities. Chauhan[18] reported difficulties faced by scheduled caste students in adjustment with others in general educational institutions and hostels on account of indifference or resistance from the latter. He, however, suggested that 'corrective action would demand the creation of conditions under which the students from the general population accepted the students of lower castes willingly, and that they take an initiative in that direction rather than provide a negative or indifference response'. A study by the Office of the Commissioner for Scheduled Castes and Scheduled Tribes on the practice of untouchability in nine mixed hostels in Andhra Pradesh showed, however, that no form of untouchability was observed in both subsidized and government hostels, the students took their meals together and everybydy had free access to drinking water pots kept in the hostels.[19] The present policy is against the setting up of institutions exclusively for scheduled castes even if initial difficulties are faced by the students as this would not promote integration through group-living.

Programmes for Educational Development at Post-matric Stage

In the field of higher education, the scheme of post-matric scholarships is being implemented since 1944-45. In the Third Plan, about 3.19 lakh scholarships were awarded to scheduled caste students. The number of scholarships awarded has shown a phenomenal increase. In 1951-52, only 1,604 scheduled caste students got post-matric scholarships, but by 1965-66 the number rose to 78,548. In 1966-67, the number of scholarships awarded increased still further to 90,481, in 1967-68 to 1,06,869, and in 1988-89 to 1,49,313. These scholarships cover maintenance allowance, compulsory non-refundable fees, study-tour charges in professional courses and thesis-typing charges. The maintenance charges in the scholarships vary from Rs. 40 per month for hostellers and Rs. 27 for day scholars for under-graduate and graduate courses to Rs. 75 for hostellers and Rs. 60 for day scholars in professional degree courses in engineering, medicine, etc. Students whose parents'/guardians' income from all sources does not exceed Rs. 500 per month are awarded post-matric scholarships on a graded means test. Employed scheduled caste students are also given scholarships subject to the graded means test.

Table 7.15 gives the state-wise distribution of post-matric scholarships. The data show that in the educationally backward states of Andhra Pradesh, Bihar, Madhya Pradesh and Orissa the percentage of scholarships awarded is less than the percentage of scheduled caste population in these states.

The working of the scheme of post-matric scholarships has shown that a larger share of the scholarships goes to castes which are educationally more advanced than others. The extent of stagnation and wastage among students is high since most of the students come from poor families, their health and diet are often unsatisfactory, they are not able to devote full attention to their studies and have to join the family labour force or take up employment early in life. Hostel facilities generally lag behind. The rate of scholarship has remained static for more than a decade and does not take into account the difference in cost of living in different states in towns and cities. This has often meant that the scheduled caste students from poor families have to discontinue their studies or take up some part-time job for support. It has not been possible to provide for follow-up action in regard to future placement of students or give vocational guidance. Also, since students get scholarships from the state to which they belong rather than the state where they study, inconvenience has sometimes to be faced by them. Delay in the award of scholarships is one of the major difficulties experienced by students. The scholarships are sometimes given in a lump, which leads to the money being spent for meeting other expenses. The Commissioner for Scheduled Castes and Scheduled Tribes in his refort for 1966-67 stated that hardly 24 per cent of scholarships could be disbursed within a month from the receipt of application forms in the Directorate.[20]

Conclusion

It is necessary to consider measures to accelerate the pace of educational development among the scheduled castes, taking into account the differential needs of castes and the level of their educational development. The Education Commission (1964-66) which considered the problems of educational development of both scheduled castes and scheduled tribes felt that in so far as the scheduled castes are concerned, the existing programmes should be continued and expanded. It emphasized the importance of universal provision, universal enrolment and universal retention. It pointed out that while school facitities at primary stage exist, at the higher primary stage there is some inadequacy. It further emphasized that 'the most important programme to be implemented at the primary stage during the next ten years is to improve the quality of education and to reduce stagnation and wastage to the minimum. In

TABLE 7.15

State-wise Distribution of Post-matric Scholarships Awarded to Scheduled Caste Students

State	*Percentage of scheduled caste population*	*1st decade*		*3rd decade*		*6th decade*	
		No.	*%*	*No.*	*%*	*No.*	*%*
1	*2*	*3*	*4*	*5*	*6*	*7*	*8*
1. Andhra Pradesh	7.85	18,126	5.75	5,312	5.96	5,667	5.53
2. Assam	1.16	8,025	2.55	2,027	2.27	2,355	2.30
3. Bihar	10.32	16,771	5.32	4,595	5.16	6,052	5.91
4. Gujarat	2.16	9,555	3.03	3,793	4.26	3,759	3.67
5. Haryana	—	—	—	258	0.29	1,672	1.63
6. Kerala	2.25	5,819	1.85	2,442	2.74	2,442	2.39
7. Madhya Pradesh	6.72	8,971	2.85	4,018	4.51	3,780	3.69
8. Madras	9.59	15,42[illegible]	4.89	5,465	6.13	7,575	7.39
9. Maharashtra	3.52	50,501	16.03	13,264	14.89	15,277	14.91
10. Mysore	4.92	15,086	4.79	4,016	4.51	4,808	4.69

11. Orissa	4.36	2,183	0.69	636	0.71	781	0.76
12. Punjab*	6.54*	20,935*	6.65*	5,202	5.95	5,176	5.05
13. Rajasthan	5.30	3,859	1.22	1,310	1.47	1,767	1.72
14. Uttar Pradesh	24.34	98,263	31.18	24,813	27.85	29,021	28.32
15. West Bengal	10.97	41,607	13.20	11,855	13.30	12,351	12.25
Total	100.00	3,15,141	100.00	89,106	100.00	1,02,583	100.00

*Includes Haryana and Chandigarh.

fact, the task of universal education begins when children are enrolled in class I. It is completed only when they are successfully retained till they complete class VII. In this overall programme, the reduction of wastage and stagnation in class I is obviously the most important element'.[21]

At the pre-matric stage, it would be desirable to have a larger coverage of students for pre-matric scholarships/stipends, book grants, school uniforms and midday meals. At the middle and higher secondary stages the rate of expansion of hostel facilities would have to be accelerated. Special attention will be necessary to increase the enrolment and retention of girls at school. In order to reduce the incidence of drop-outs and wastage, apart from educating the community and motivating parents through increased parent-teacher contacts, it would be necessary to exercise greater care at those stages where the rate of drop-out is the maximum. Improvement of teacher-student ratio, greater regularity in the holding of classes and more individual attention to the needs of students would be essential. At the middle and higher secondary stages, coaching facilities for weaker students would be desirable while the brighter students should be chosen and special assistance given to enable them to realize their full potentialities for development. It would also be useful to extend facilities for career guidance. Greater care will have to be exericsed in the selection of teachers working in villages with a large scheduled caste population and measures devised for stimulating their interest. It would also be necessary to improve school equipment, introduce greater facilities for science education, encourage students from these commnnities to opt for science subjects and improve the machinery of supervision of school education of backward students. In view of the general constraint of resources, it is worth considering which of the different schemes for educational development should be given priority to obtain maximum returns.

For increasing the effectiveness of measures of promoting higher education, pre-matric education needs to be strengthened so that a strong foundation is laid, hostel facilities increased, new courses included for award of post-matric scholarships, book grants given and administrative and other delays minimized. It is also worth examining at what stage some form of graded merit test is applied so that the brighter students are given greater assistance in their academic pursuits.

REFERENCES

1. P.E.O., Problems of Extension of Primary Education in Rural Areas, Planning Commission, New Delhi.
2. A.K. Das and R.N. Saha, Post-matric Education among the Scheduled Tribes of West Bengal, Bulletion of Cultural Research Institute, 7(1 and 2).
3. Bidyut K. Roy Chowdhury, Comparative Study of the Progress of Secondary Education among the Scheduled Castes and Scheduled Tribes of West Bengal, Bulletin of the Cultural Research Institute, 2(1).
4. A.K. Das and R.N. Saha, Post-matric Education among the Scheduled Castes and Scheduled Tribes of West Bengal, Bulletin of the Cultural Research Institute, 7 (1 and 2).
5. Report of the Seminar on Employment of Scheduled Castes and Scheduled Tribes, Planning Commission, New Delhi.
6. Report of the Education Commission Ministry of Education, Government of India.
7. Wastage and Stagnation in Primary and Middle Schools in India, NCERT, New Delhi.
8. D.R. Gadgil and V.M. Dandekar, Primary Education in Satara District, Gokhale Institute of Politics and Economics, poona.
9. Bidyut K. Roy Chowdhury, Factors Retarding Tribal Education in West Bengal, Bulletin of the Cultural Research Institute, 3(2).
10. Report of the Working Group to Study the Progress of Measures for Land Allotment to Scheduled Castes and their Representation in Services, Ministry of Home Affairs, Government of India.
11. Report of the Commissioner for Scheduled Castes and Scheduled Tribes Manager of Publications, Delhi.
12. Wastage and Stagnation in Primary and Middle Schools in India. NCERT, New Delhi.

13. Problems of Extension of Primary Education in Rural Areas, P.E.O. Planning Commission, New Delhi.
14. Report of the Seminar on Employment of Scheduled Castes and Scheduled Tribes, Planning Commission, New Delhi.
15. A.K. Das and R.N. Saha, Post-Matric Education among the Scheduled Castes and Scheduled Tribes of West Bengal, Bulletin of Cultural Institute, 7(1 and 2).
16. Report of the Working Group to Study the Progress of Measures for Land Allotment to Scheduled Castes and Their Representation in Services, Ministry of Home Affairs, Government of India.
17. This is only the Plan expenditure. In addition, states spend sizable amounts as non-plan expenditure.
18. B.R. Chauhan, Special Problems of the Education of the Scheduled Castes, in The Sociology of Education in India, M.S. Gore, I.P. Desai and Suma Chitnis (ed.), NCERT.
19. Report of the Commissioner for Scheduled Castes and Scheduled Tribes Manager of Publications, Delhi.
20. Report of the Commissioner for Scheduled Castes and Scheduled Tribes, Manager of Publications, Delhi.
21. Report of the Education Commission, Ministry of Education, Government of India.

8

Scheduled Tribes: Educational Perspective

In this paper[1] on the educational development of Scheduled Tribes the extent and level of literacy, inter-district variation in literacy, inter-tribe variation in literacy and variation in literacy between males and females have been analysed and compared with the general population on the basis of quantitative information from the Census and other sources. The problems of stagnation and wastage have been discussed, and enrolment trends at different stages of education of the Scheduled Tribes have been indicated. The programmes in the plans for the educational development of Scheduled Tribes at pre-matric and post-matric stages have been described and certain suggestions made to accelerate the pace of their educational development.

The progress of Scheduled Tribes in India is closely linked up with their equcational advancement, more so in today's changing world in which education plays an increasing role, in everyday life apart from equipping a person with the necessary skills for more effective participation in different spheres of economic activity. The extent of educational development in the Scheduled Tribe population is, however, extremely low. According to the Census, only 8.5 per cent of the tribal population in India is lirerate compared to 10.3 per cent of the Scheduled Caste population and 24.0 per cent general literacy. In all the States except Bihar, the extent of literacy is lower in the tribal population than in the Scheduled Caste population. In some States like Gujarat, Kerala, Madras and Maharashtra, which rank high in regard to extent of literacy in the general population and Scheduled Caste population, the gap in extent of literacy in Scheduled Caste population and Scheduled Tribe population is the highest, namely, more than 7 per cent.

Table 8.1, which gives the extent of literacy in each State in the general population and the tribal population, shows that in seven States the gap in literacy is more than 15 per cent and in three States, namely, Kerala, Madras and Maharashtra, which are educationally more advanced, the gap is more than 22 per cent. With the exception of Assam, in all other States the gap is more than 9 per cent. The coefficient of correlation between extent of literacy in general population and extent of literacy in tribal population is +0.529 indicating that States with higher literacy in general population tend to have a higher literacy in tribal population. However, States with higher literacy in general population tend to have a larger gap with extent of literacy in tribal population, the coefficient of correlation between extent of literacy in general population and gap in literacy in general population and Scheduled Tribe population being +0.630.

There is also variation in the level of literacy in tribal population in different States as will be evident from the data in Table 8.2 giving the number of Scheduled Tribe persons per 1,000 in each educational category. In all States except Assam, even in the category 'literate without educational level', the number of Scheduled Tribe persons per 1,000 in this educational category is substantially lower than the number of Scheduled Tribe persons per 1,000 persons in the State. In all the States there is a sharp fall in the category matric-and-above, but there is no definite pattern which emerges in regard to the number of Scheduled Tribe persons matric-and-above per 1,000 in this educational category in relation to the educational development in the State. For instance, Gujarat which ranks third in regard to literacy in tribal population has a very small number of tribal persons per 1,000 matric-and-above compared to the proportion of tribal population in the State while in Bihar which ranks fifth, the representation of tribal people in this educational category is much more favourable.

TABLE 8.1

Extent of Literacy in Scheduled Tribe Population and the General Population

State	*Percentage of literates in the total population*	*Percentage of literates in the Scheduled Tribe population*
1. Andhra Pradesh	21.19	4.41
2. Assam	27.36	23.55
3. Bihar	18.40	9.18
4. Gujarat	30.45	11.69
5. Kerala	46.85	17.26
6. Madhya Pradesh	17.12	5.09
7. Madras	31.41	5.91
8. Maharashtra	29.81	7.22
9. Mysore	25.40	8.15
10. Orissa	21.66	7.36
11. Rajasthan	15.21	3.97
12. West Bengal	29.27	6.55

Source: Census of India, Uttar Pradesh, Jammu & Kashmir and Punjab have not been included here because in the Census, U.P. and Jammu & Kasemir had no tribal population while in Punjab the tribal population was very small.

TABLE 8.2

Number of Scheduled Tribe Persons per 1,000 Persons in Each Educational Category

State	*Number of Scheduled Tribe person per 1,000 persons*	*Number of Scheduled Tribe persons per 1,000 persons in each educational category*			
		Illiterate	*Literate without educational lavel*	*Primary or Junior Basic*	*Matrio and abovc*
1. Andhra Pradesh	37	45	10	6	1
2. Assam	174	183	172	106	46
3. Bihar	91	101	45	56	17
4. Gujarat	184	169	55	53	4
5. Kerala	13	20	5	4	1
6. Madhya Pradesh	206	236	68	56	Neg.
7. Madras	7	10	2	1	4
8. Maharashtra	61	80	22	9	1
9. Mysore	8	10	3	1	1
10. Orissa	241	285	83	89	16
11. Rajasthan	115	130	33	27	5
12. West Bengal	59	78	17	10	2

Source: Census data.

Inter-district Variation

There is not only variation between States in extent and level of literacy in tribal pepulation but also between different districts within a State as will be evident from Table 8.3 The data show that in three States the lowest percentage of literacy in tribal population in a district is less than 1 per cent. The range, *i.e.*, the difference between highest percentage of literacy in a

TABLE 8.3

Variation in Extent of Literacy in Scheduled Tribe Population in Different districts in a State

State	*Lowest percentage of literacy in Scheduled Tribe population in a district*	*Highest percentage of literacy in Scheduled Tribe population in a district*	*Range*	*Standard deviation*
1. Andhra Pradesh	1.37	13.54	21.17	2.91
2. Assam	10.88	43.34	32.46	8.08
3. Bihar	4.09	32.43	28.34	6.99
4. Gujarat	2.56	20.92	18.36	5.71
5. Kerala	4.46	38.57	34.11	9.90
6. Madhya Pradesh	0.72	12.72	12.00	2.61
7. Madras	3.90	40.97	37.07	11.34
8. Maharashtra	1.29	17.00	15.71	3.04
9. Mysore	0.30	15.56	15.26	4.75
10. Orissa	3.17	12.59	9.42	2.68
11. Rajasthan	0.92	13.34	12.42	3.07
12. West Bengal	2.51	33.61	31.10	7.26

Source: Census data; districts with less than 1,000 tribal population have not been taken into consideration.

district and lowest percentage of literacy in a district in a State, is more than 28 per cent in the States of Assam, Bihar, Kerala, Madras and West Bengal. The standard deviation of percentage literacy in tribal population in different districts in a State is also high in these States which, with the exception of Madras and West Bengal, rank high in regard to the spread of literacy in tribal population.

A study by the Cultural Research Institute of the Government of West Bengal on Scheduled Tribe[2] students getting post-matric scholarships also showed inter-district variation in regard to the extent to which tribal students from different districts availed of the scholarships. It was found that about 50 per cent of Scheduled Tribe students in the post-matric stage were from Darjeeling and Hooghly districts though only 11 per cent of the tribal population in the State lived in these two districts.

The degree of association between literacy in general population in a district and literacy in tribal population was computed from Census data. Table 8.4 which gives the coefficients of correlation, shows that in all the States it is positive and significant, indicating that districts with higher literacy in general population tend to have higher literacy in tribal population. The coefficient of correlation between literacy in general population in a district and gap between literacy in general population and in tribal population is also positive in all the States except Kerala.

Inter-tribe Variation

There is also variation in extent of literacy in different tribes. Table 8.5 indicates the position among the numerically large tribes in a State, *i.e.*, those with a population of more than 5,000. The data show that in three States, Andhra Pradesh, Madhya Pradesh and Orissa, the minimum percentage of literacy in a tribe is less than one per cent while in fiveStates, Andhra Pradesh, Madhya Pradesh, Mysore, Orissa and

Rajasthan, the minimum percentage of literacy in a tribe is less than 2 per cent. The highest percentages of literacy in a tribe are in Kerala and Assam which, incidentally, occupy the first two ranks in regard to the spread of literacy in the tribal population. The range is also the maximum in those two States. The standard deviation of percentage literacy in a State is the highest in those States which rank higher in regard to the spread of literacy in tribal population, namely, Assam and Kerala.

TABLE 8.4

Association Between Literacy in General Population in a District and Literacy in Scheduled Tribe Population

State	*Correlation between percentage of literacy in general Population in a district and percentage of literacy in Scheduled Tribe population*	*Correlation between percentage of literacy in general population in a district and gap between percentage of literacy in general population and Scheduled Tribe Population*
1. Andhra Pradesh	+0.794	+0.930
2. Assam	+0.794	+0.138
3. Bihar	+0.591	+0.113
4. Gujarat	+0.715	+0.776
5. Kerala	+0.889	—0.447
6. Madhya Pradesh	+0.323	+0.821
7. Madras	+0.792	+0.316
8. Maharashtra	+0.411	+0.918
9. Mysore	+0.526	+0.748
10. Orissa	+0.432	+0.918
11. Rajasthan	+0.623	+0.705
12. West Bengal	+0.771	+0.736

TABLE 8.5

Variation in Extent of Literacy in Different Scheduled Tribes in State

State	*Maximum Percentage of literacy in a Scheduled Tribe*	*Minimum Percentage of literacy in a Scheduled Tribe*	*Range*	*Standard Deviation*
1. Andhra Pradesh	10.71	0.94	9.97	3.37
2. Assam	49.02	8.89	40.13	11.68
3. Bihar	13.81	2.24	11.57	3.38
4. Gujarat	23.94	1.88	22.06	5.48
5. Kerala	53.17	2.17	51.00	14.80
6. Madhya Pradesh	14.25	0.34	13.91	3.26
7. Madras	9.63	3.29	6.34	2.40
8. Maharashtra	20.65	2.03	18.62	4.31
9. Mysore	10.16	1.89	8.27	3.12
10. Orissa	10.77	0.82	9.95	2.67
11. Rajasthan	5.16	1.30	3.86	1.59
12. West Bengal	25.06	3.57	21.49	7.30

Source: Census data. Only Scheduled Tribes with population 5,000 and above were taken into consideration.

A study by the Cultural Research Institute, Government of West Bengal, regarding the extent of utilization of post-matric scholarships by tribes too found variation in this regard between tribes. For instance, Lepchas and Bhutias who constitute about 2 per cent of the Scheduled Tribe population were awarded 27.40 per cent of the post-matric scholarship.[3] Ninetyeight per cent of the students getting post-matric schlorships came from eight Scheduled Tribes who constitute 91 per cent of the tribal population in the State. Twenty-six Scheduled Tribes did not have any student in the post-matric stage.[4] The study further reported that the trend in this regard persisted.

Another study by this Institute on progress of secondary education among the Scheduled Tribes in West Bengal found considerable variation between tribes at this level of education as well. In two tribes more than 35 per cent of the students of secondary school-going age in 1960-61 attended school while in 9 tribes the percentage was less than 10 per cent. Further, eighteen Scheduled Tribes had no school-going students in the secondary stage.[5]

A few other studies indicate the same trend. A study of tribal students getting post-matric scholarships in Maharashtra showed that 17.2 per cent of the post-matric scholarships were availed by Gonds who comprise 11.4 per cent of the tribal population, in the State while no scholarship was availed by the Varli tribe who comprise 10.2 per cent of the tribal population in the State.[6] The study on living conditions of Similipal Hills in Orissa too showed difference in extent of literacy among tribes. Among the Bhumija, for instance, the extent of literacy was only 1.2 per cent while among the Santals it was 16.1 per cent.[7]

Literacy among Females

The extent of literacy among Scheduled Tribe females is only 3.16 per cent as compared to 13.83 per cent among Scheduled Tribe males. The gap at the all-India level between literacy among females and males is 10.67 per cent, but the position varies significantly from State to State as will be evident from the data in Table 8.6. In several States the extent of literacy in the tribal female population is extremely low. In Rajasthan and Madhya Pradesh, for instance, less than 1 per cent of the female tribal population is literate, while in six States, Andhra Pradesh, Madhya Pradesh, Maharashtra, Orissa, Rajasthan and West Bengal, less than 2 per cent of the female tribal population is literate. It is only in Assam and Kerala that more than 10 per cent of the tribal females are literate. In seven

States the gap in literacy between Scheduled Tribe males and females is more than 10 per cent. The coefficient of correlation between the extent of literacy in Scheduled Tribe males and Scheduled Tribe females is +0.935 indicating that States with higher literacy among males tend to have higher literacy among females as well. The coefficient of correlation between percentage of literacy among Scheduled Tribe males and gap in literacy between Scheduled Tribe males and females is +0.839 indicating that States with higher literacy in tribal male population tend to have a larger gap.

TABLE 8.6

Extent of Literacy in Tribal Male and Female Population

State	*Percentage of Literacy in Scheduled Tribe Males*	*Percentage of Literacy in Scheduled Tribe Females*	*Gap in Literacy*
1. Andhra Pradesh	7.26	1.48	5.78
2. Assam	31.09	15.72	15.37
3. Bihar	15.22	3.18	12.04
4. Gujarat	19.06	4.09	14.97
5. Kerala	22.63	11.92	10.71
6. Madhya Pradesh	9.25	0.97	8.28
7. Madras	8.93	2.73	6.20
8. Maharashtra	12.55	1.75	10.80
9. Mysore	13.24	2.81	10.43
10. Orissa	13.04	1.77	11.27
11. Rajasthan	7.39	0.28	7.11
12. West Bengal	11.20	1.76	9.44

Source: Census data.

Table 8.7 gives the number of Scheduled Tribe females per 1,000 Scheduled Tribe males in each educational category. The data show that the number of Scheduled Tribes female per 1,000 Scheduled Tribe males is extremely low in all the educational categories, particularly at the level matric-and-above. Comparatively speaking, Assam and Kerala, which have the highest literacy in the tribal population, have also a larger representation of females at the higher educational levels, while States like Rajasthan and Madhya Pradesh which have low representation of females at the higher educational levels.

Other studies, too, report that female literacy among tribals is lagging behind. A socio-economic survey by the Tribal Research Institute, Udaipur, showed that at the primary level there are 10 tribal girl students for every 100 tribal boy students, while at the middle and secondary level there are 7 tribal girl students for every 100 tribal students.[8] In Chintapalli Tribal Development Block in Visakapatnam district in Andhra Pradesh, the situation was somewhat better, there being 35 tribal girl students for every 100 tribal boy students.[9] A Bihar study reported that 43 girls attended schools for every 100 boys.[10]

Table 8.8 gives the number of Scheduled Tribe females per 1,000 females in each educational category. The data show that, except in Bihar and Assam, the number of Scheduled Tribe females per 1,000 females in the different educational categories is extremely unsatisfactory. In both these States in the category matric-and-above the number of Scheduled tribe females per 1,000 females is about half the number of tribal females per 1,000 females in the total population.

Enrolment Trends

During the last few decades school facilities have expanded in tribal areas and tribal children are increasingly attending educational institutions. Shah, for instance, reported that in Gujarat 1898, 0.63 per cent of the Hindu tribals were literate

TABLE 8.7

Number of Scheduled Tribe Females per 1,000 Scheduled Tribe Males in each Educational Category

State	*Number of Scheduled Tribe Females per 1,000 Scheduled Tribe Males*	*Number of Scheduled Tribe Females per 1,000 Scheduled Tribe Males in each Educational Category*			
		Illiterate	*Literate without Educational Level*	*Primary or Junior Basic*	*Matric and above*
1. Andhra Pradesh	975	1,036	206	181	75
2. Assam	956	1,169	528	318	335
3. Bihar	1,014	1,158	206	231	205
4. Gujarat	969	1,149	186	221	78
5. Kerala	1,006	1,145	540	515	305
6. Madhya Pradesh	1,003	1,094	111	83	67
7. Madras	951	1,015	275	861	177
8. Maharashtra	978	1,099	154	89	55

9. Mysore	953	1,068	204	214	96
10. Orissa	1,016	1,148	142	115	43
11. Rajasthan	926	998	35	29	13
12. West Bengal	969	1,072	162	127	117

Source: Census data.

TABLE 8.8

Number of Scheduled Tribe Females per 1,000 Females in each Educational Category

State	*Number of Scheduled Tribe Females per 1,000*	*Number of Scheduled Tribe Females per 1,000 Females in each Educational Category*			
	Females in the Population	*Illiterate*	*Literate without Educational level*	*Primary or Junior Basic*	*Matric and above*
1. Andhra Pradesh	37	41	5	8	1
2. Assam	182	183	206	99	89
3. Bihar	91	95	36	80	46
4. Gujarat	135	161	29	30	1
5. Kerala	13	18	4	3	1
6. Madhya Pradesh	212	225	33	26	1
7. Madras	7	9	1	1	Neg.
8. Maharashtra	62	73	10	3	Neg.

9. Mysore	8	9	3	Neg.	Neg.
10. Orissa	243	271	49	59	9
11. Rajasthan	116	123	6	5	Neg.
12. West Bengal	68	73	8	4	2

Source: Census data.

TABLE 8.9

Percentage Enrolment of Scheduled Tribe Students to Total Enrolment at Primary/Junior Basic, Middle/Senior Basic, High/Higher Secondary and Higher Education Levels

State	*Percentage of Scheduled Tribe*	*Primary/Junior Basic*		*Percentage enrolment of Scheduled Tribes*					
				Middle/Senior Basic		*High/Higher Secondary*		*Higher educational level*	
		1960-61	*1964-65*	*1960-61*	*1964-65*	*1960-61*	*1964-65*	*1960-61*	*1964-65*
1. Andhra Pradesh	3.7	2.3	2.4	0.7	0.8	0.6	0.6	0.4	0.3
2. Assam	17.4	24.0	25.0	16.2	19.1	9.3	13.0	9.8	11.1
3. Bihar	9.1	8.7	9.7	7.4	7.9	3.7	3.4	2.4	3.2
4. Gujarat	13.3	12.4	15.9	7.5	5.8	1.9	2.4	0.2	2.7
5. Kerala	1.2	0.5	0.6	0.4	0.5	0.2	0.3	—	0.2
6. Madhya Pradesh	20.6	12.3	15.9	6.5	6.0	2.2	4.0	2.2	1.4
7. Madras	6.7	0.5	0.7	0.1	0.3	0.2	0.3	0.8	0.3
8. Maharashtra	6.1	6.6	6.8	0.2	2.3	1.0	1.7	0.6	0.6

9. Mysore	0.8	0.7	0.6	0.7	0.4	0.2	0,4	0.1	Neg.
10. Orissa	24.1	13.6	16.0	12.6	9.8	3.7	4.4	1.3	1.5
11. Rajasthan	11.7	2.3	8.2	0.9	4.0	0.6	3.2	0.5	0.8
12. West Bengal	5.9	3.5	3.5	3.2	3.7	1.4	1.2	0.3	0.3

Source. Ministry of Education, Government of India.

while in 1955-57, the percentage literacy was 14.92 for Dublas, 16.09 for Naikas, 20.69 for Dhankas and 32.64 for Gamit.[11] Similar developments have been reported by other research workers[9, 10, 12, 13, 14].

The Education Ministry collect information from different State governments on the percentage enrolment of Scheduled Tribe students to total enrolment at different levels of education. The data show that, at the primary level, the percentage enrolment of Scheduled Tribes has improved in all the States except Mysore, the percentage of increase being more than 3.5 in Gujarat, Madhya Pradesh and Rajasthan. While in two States, Assam and Maharashtra, the percentage enrolment of tribal children at primary level was higher than the percentage of tribal population in the State; this was so in the case of four States, namely, Assam, Bihar, Gujarat and Maharashtra. In the other States, the gap is reducing and the progress in this direction has been significant in the case of two States with sizeable tribal population, but educationally reported as backward by the 1961 Census, namely, Madhya Pradesh and Rajasthan. In the middle, high/higher secondary and higher educational levels in several States the percentage enrolment is higher; in a few States, however, there is a marginal fall. This could be either because the enrolment in the general population has increased at a faster rate or because there has been a larger incidence of drop-out and wastage in the case of tribal students than in the general population. Four States which have shown improvement in percentage enrolment of Scheduled Tribes at all levels are Assam, Kerala, Maharashtra and Rajasthan.

A study by the Cultural Research Institute, West Bengal, also showed progressive increase in enrolment in the case of students attending the secondary stage of education, though the progress was not uniform in the case of all the tribes. Taking 100 as the base year value of students attending recognized secondary schools the index number in three random later years were 105, 107 and 118 respectively.[15]

Table 8.10 gives the gap at different levels of education between percentage enrolment of tribal children to total enrolment and the percentage of tribal population in the State. The data show that at the primary level in four States the percentage enrolment of tribal children is higher than the percentage of tribal population in the States; in one State, there is no gap while in two States the gap is less then 1 per cent. At the middle/senior basic level, only Assam has a higher percentage of enrolment of tribal children than the percentage of tribal population in the State; in three States the gap is less than 1 per cent. At the high/higher secondary and higher educational levels, in all the States there is a gap. In the States

TABLE 8.10

Difference Between Percentage Enrolment (1964-65) of Scheduled Tribe Children at Different Educational Levels and Percentage Population of Scheduled Tribe

State	*Primary/ Junior Basic*	*Middle/ Senior Basic*	*High/ Higher Secondary*	*Higher Education*
1. Andhra Pradesh	—1.3	— 2.9	— 3.1	— 3.4
2. Assam	+7.6	+ 1.7	— 4.4	— 6.3
3. Bihar	+0.6	— 1.2	— 5.7	— 5.9
4. Gujarat	+2.6	— 7.5	—10.9	—10.6
5. Kerala	—0.6	— 0.7	— 0.9	— 1.0
6. Madhya Pradesh	—4.7	—14.6	—16.6	—19.2
7. Madras	—	— 0.4	— 0.4	— 0.4
8. Maharashtra	+0.7	— 3.8	— 4.4	— 5.5
9. Mysore	—0.2	— 0.4	— 0.4	— 0.8
10. Orissa	—8.1	—14.3	—19.7	—22.6
11. Rajasthan	—8.5	— 7.7	— 8.5	—10.9
12. West Bengal	—2.4	— 2.2	— 4.7	— 5.6

of Gujarat, Madhya Pradesh, Orissa and Rajasthan, which have a sizable tribal population, the gap is more pronounced. In all the States, the gap tends to increase with a rise in the educational level.

The extent of enrolment of Scheduled Tribe students in vocational and technical courses is rather low. A study on Scheduled Tribe students getting post-matric scholarships conducted by the Cultural Research Institute, Government of West Bengal, showed that 78 per cent took courses in Arts and Commerce subjects, about 15 per cent in Science subjects and only about 7 per cent in technical subjects.[16] Data available from two other States, namely, Gujarat and Orissa, show a somewhat better distribution. Information available from the Industrial Training Institutes in different parts of the country show that although in each State, there is reservation of seats for Scheduled Tribes equal to the proportion of Scheduled Tribe population in the State and a stipend of Rs. 45 per month is given to Scheduled Tribe trainees, in all the States the percentage of Scheduled Tribe trainees to total trainees is lower than the percentage of Scheduled Tribe population in the State. Apart from the general preference of all groups for white-collar occupations, the other reasons for this trend are restricted mobility due to which the Scheduled Tribe boys do not go to study at places far away from home, poor economic condition of the family and inability of the family to permit the boy to undergo a fresh period of training instead of supporting the family. Most Scheduled Tribe boys are also not aware of the job opportunities and pay scales after completing a course in the Industrial Training Institute vis-a-vis completing a general course of education.

Stagnation and Wastage

The large extent of stagnation and wastage in Indian education has been pointed out by the Education Commission which stated that stagnation and wastage is highest in class I.[17] The study by the National Council of Educational Research and Training on wastage and stagnation in primary and middle schools in India also showed that the total rate of wastage and stagnation is 65.30 per cent by the time children reach grade V and 78.35 per cent by the time they reach grade VIII.[18] Separate data regarding the tribal population are not available in these reports although reference has been made to the larger incidence of drop-outs among the backward class students, including Scheduled Tribes.

Studies conducted elsewhere point in the same direction. Naik's study of education among Bhils in Madhya Pradesh showed that very few Bhil children attend school after the 5th standard. The study reported only 0.9 per cent tribal students up to 5th standard as compared to 4.9 per cent tribal student up to 5th standard.[19] A study by the Cultural Research Institute of the Government of West Bengal[20] on the extent of stagnation, based on returns from 3.992 secondary schools showed a larger incidence of stagnation among tribal students as will be evident from the following figures:

Percentage of Stagnation in Classes

	V	*VI*	*VII*	*VIII*	*IX*	*X*
Scheduled Castes	24.1	25.5	27.7	31.9	38.6	78.6
Scheduled Tribes	25.4	29.2	34.7	40.5	53.6	78.6
Other communities	21.4	23.4	27.4	29.7	39.8	65.2

The incidence of stagnation among Scheduled Tribes is more than one-third from class VII onwards, whereas for Scheduled Castes this is so from class IX onwards and for other communities this is so in class X.

A study by the Tribal Research and Training Institute, Ahmedabad, draws attention to the large incidence of stagnation and wastage in primary education in tribal areas of Gujarat. It reported that in both Shamlaji Tribal Development Block (Sabarkantha district) and Sukhsar Tribal Development Block (Panchmahal district) there were only 10 and 11 students

TABLE 8.11

Course-wise Award of Post-matric Scholarship to Scheduled Tribe Students

Course	Gujarat		Orissa	
	Number	Percentage	Number	Percentage
1	2	3	4	5
1. Inter Science/B.Sc./M.Sc.	231	17.6	116	22.1
2. Inter Arts/B.A./M.A.	543	41.2	322	61.2
3. Inter Com./B.Com./M.Com.	73	5.5	7	1.3
4. LL.B./Honours/Other Oriental Languages/Fine Arts/Correspondence	14	1.1	5	1.0
5. D.Sc./D.Litt./Ph.D.	—	—	—	—
6. Diploma Certificate Course in Agriculture/Veterinary Science etc.	—	—	—	—
7. Teachers' Training and Physical Education	107	8.1	4	0.8
8. B. Sc. Agriculture/B. V. Sc. Diploma Courses in Rural Science/Civil and Rural Engineering	12	0.9	8	1.5
9. Post-Graduate Courses in Agriculture	—	—	—	—
10. Bachelor of Nursing and Pharmacy	—	—	—	—

1	2	3	4	5
11. Diploma Certificate Course in Engineering/ Architecture etc.	27	2.1	50	9.5
12. Degree Course in Engineering	28	2.1	14	2.7
13. Other Courses	282	21.4	—	—
Total:	1,317	100.0	526	100 0

Source: Report of the Commissioner for Scheduled Castes and Scheduled Tribes, Manager of Publications, Delhi.

TABLE 8.12

State-wise Distribution of the Number of Candidates Undergoing Training in I.T.Is. and the Number of Scheduled Tribe Candidates Among them

State	*Total Number of trainees*	*Number of Scheduled Tribe trainees*	*Percentage of Scheduled Tribe trainees*	*Percentage of Scheduled Tribe Population in State*
1. Andhra Pradesh	7,329	69	0.94	3.64
2. Assam	1,647	82	4.98	17.39
3. Bihar	8,689	378	4.35	9.05
4. Gujarat	3,447	144	4.18	13.35
5. Kerala	5,551	23	0.41	1.26
6. Madhya Pradesh	4,689	709	15.12	20.63
7. Madras	11,013	6	0.05	0.75
8. Maharashtra	12,374	264	2.13	6.06
9. Mysore	3,456	14	0.41	0.81
10. Orissa	1,584	184	11.61	24.07
11. Rajasthan	1,657	18	1.09	11.67
12. West Bengal	5,397	48	0.89	5.86

respectively in standard VII for every 100 children in standard I. The study also reported that nearly 75 per cent of the children in both the Blocks left school before completing standard IV. Further, 84 per cent of the students in Shamlaji Block and 60 per cent of the students in Sukhsar Block who had left their studies dropped out in standard I. Only 31 per cent were able to pass standard I examination in their first attempt, while the rest had to make two, three or even four attempts. The volume of stagnation in subsequent standards was not, however, much.[21]

The survey of Simalwara Tribal Development Block by the Tribal Research Institute, Udaipur, showed that there were less than 2 tribal students in class X for every 100 tribal students in class 1. Further, although half the students up to class V were tribal, the proportion in classes VI to XI was only about one-fourth, indicating greater incidence of discontinuation of studies.[22] Das Gupta, too, in his study of problems of tribal education among Santals reported that in 16 schools out of 60 the extent of wastage was more than 50 per cent.[23]

Programmes of Educational Development

In the past, a large part of the efforts for the educational development of tribal people was initiated by voluntary organizations and missionaries. Since independence, the government has promoted the educational development of these communities to a significant degree. In addition to granting exemption to Scheduled Tribe students from payment of tuition fees, a number of other schemes are being implemented by the state governments for the promotion of education among tribal people. A large number of primary schools have been opened in tribal areas and, apart from some pockets of poor communication and dispersed settlements, primary schools have been set up within fair walking distance. Scholarships/stipends, hostel facilities, boarding grants, midday meals, school uniforms and book grants have been provided to students. During the Plan and a later period Rs. 18.7 crores have been spent by State governments on educational schemes which represents six-tenths of the total expenditure for tribal welfare in the backward classes sector.[24] In the Plan, scholarships and stipends were given to 10.22 lakh students; 876 hostels/boarding houses were set-up/assisted; book and equipment grants were given to 1.14 lakh students and midday meals to 41,282 students; 154 ashram schools were opend. Scholarships/stipends were given to 1,08,922 students.

An important scheme for the education of tribals has been the setting up of ashram schools. These are residential institutions up to primary or middle standard and aim at providing a system of education which is related to tribal life and is also relevant to it. In this system teachers and students live together. The students are given education as well as training in agriculture, crafts, gardening etc. so that, after the students have completed their education, they may be in a position to settle in the community as better citizens and farmers. The schools have agricultural land attached to them along with cattle, sheep, goats, poultry etc. The students are provided with free boarding and lodging. In recent years a few day-scholars and non-tribal students have also been admitted to these institutions. A large number of these institutions are managed by voluntary organizations.

For higher education, post-matric scholarships are being given to Scheduled Tribe students. These scholarships are awarded to all tribal students without any means-or-merit test. The scholarships cover maintenance allowance, compulsory non-refundable fees, study-tour charges in professional courses and thesis-typing charges. The maintenance charges in the scholarships vary from Rs. 40 for hostellers and Rs. 27 for day-scholars for undergraduate and graduate courses to Rs. 75 for hostellers and Rs. 60 for day-scholars in professional degree courses like engineering, medicine etc.

The number of scholarships awarded has shown a phenomenal increase from 84 only in 1948-49 to 576 in 1951-52 (first year of the First Plan), 8,548 in 1961-62 (first year of the Third Plan) and 20,815 in 1967-68, and 33,320 in 1989-90. Table 8.13

TABLE 8.13

State-wise Distribution of Post-matric Scholarships Awarded to Scheduled Tribe Students

State	*Third Plan*		*2nd Decade*		*5th Decade*	
	Number	*Percentage*	*Number*	*Percentage*	*Number*	*Percentage*
1	*2*	*3*	*4*	*5*	*6*	*7*
1. Andhra Pradesh	963	1.8	255	1.6	286	1.5
2. Assam	23,182	42.5	5,813	35.9	6,492	34.6
3. Bihar	16,432	30.1	4,538	28.0	5,881	31.4
4. Gujarat	2,307	4.2	1,317	8.1	1,431	7.6
5. Kerala	430	0.8	214	1.3	214	1.2
6. Madhya Pradesh	3,799	6.9	1,638	10.1	1,477	7.9
7. Madras	194	0.3	86	0.5	98	0.5
8. Maharashtra	1,769	3.2	628	3.9	676	3.6

9. Mysore	197	0.4	68	0.4	80	0.4
10. Orissa	1,777	3.3	536	3.3	667	3.6
11. Rajasthan	1,679	3.1	538	3.3	749	4.0
12. West Bengal	1,848	3.4	583	3.6	696	3.7
Total	54,577	100.0	16,214	100.0	18,750	100.0

gives the state-wise distribution of post-matric scholarships awarded to Scheduled Tribe students in the Third Plan and the two years following it. The data show that more than two-thirds of the scholarships are awarded to students from two states, namely, Assam and Bihar, although they have only one-fifth of the tribal population in these 12 states.

Certain weaknesses and difficulties in the measures for promotion of education among the tribal people have been brought out in several studies. [25], [26], [27], [28], [29] These have indicated that apart from financial constraints, there are deficiencies in the school system and in the socio-economic framework. Establishment of single-teacher schools in many areas, recruitment of teachers unacquainted with tribal language and culture, deficiencies in their training, their weak motivation and unwillingness to stay in tribal areas, difficulties of accommodation and problems arising from staying away from families are important factors which hinder progress. The distance of middle and secondary schools, their timing, absence of adequate hostel facilities, deficiencies in school buildings and equipment, and weaknesses in supervision of schools in tribal areas also impede the development of education. An unattractive school environment, absence of any attempt on the part of teachers to motivate parents, the poverty of the parents, their inability to dispense with the services of their children who assist them in earning a livelihood or in looking after the younger children, late age of admission of children, illiteracy of parents and lack of parental help and encouragement at home in pursuing studies are other factors which often lead to irregularity in attendance or even dropping out.

Even the ashram schools which were conceived as highly suitable for tribal people and have been reported as satisfactory in Orissa and Maharashtra appear to have been found not equally satisfactory in other places like Rajasthan. The strength of this system of education lies in the imparting of education relevant to tribal life and of equipping the students with knowledge and skills which will be of use to them. A further advantage is that irregularity of attendance and the extent of drop-out is much lower, at least, in the case of the better acculturated tribes.[30] Among its weaknesses are the high cost and inadequacies in the crafts and trades taught to students. Das,[31] for instance, reported that 'except a few boys, particularly in Mayurbhanj, who had got sewing machines on loan and were working as tailors, no other student had after passing the Ashram school been settled as craftsman. The first preference of the boys is for higher general education and second; government services; those who could not do either settle down as cultivators.' Although there are a large number of ashram schools in the country, the system has not really been empirically studied. It is worth examining to what extent the education is of a terminal nature. Although, technically, students passing from these institutions can join higher education elsewhere, it is worth empirically investigating how they fare when they come into the general stream of education at the higher levels; also, to what extent this level of craft-training is adequate to enable them to set themselves up independently. It would also be interesting to know how many of them go in for technical education in the I.T.Is. or other technical schools.

The working of the scheme of post-matric scholarship has shown that stagnation and wastage among students continues to be high and a larger share of scholarships goes to tribes or groups within these tribes who are more advanced then others. Hostel facilities, particularly for girls, are inadequate. The rates of scholarship have remained static and tribal students from poor families have to face difficulties on this account. Delay in receiving scholarships put the students to a lot of inconvenience. Educational programmes, like several other development activities, seem to be benefiting the more advanced tribes as well as groups within them. Naik's study of the Bhils in Madhya Pradesh showed that 'children of the upper crust of the Bhill society, Bhilala farmer, big patels and zamindars and other well-to-do Bhils have been able to go to school and take advantage of the scholarships or hostel facilities made available to them by the Government.[32]

Conclusion

While there is no doubt about the progress in education of Scheduled Tribes since independence, there are a number of measures which should be undertaken to accelerate the pace of their educational development. A number of suggestions have been made by research workers, and by committees and commissions set up from time to time.[33, 34, 35, 36, 37, 38] At the pre-matric stage it is necessary not only to bring about larger enrolment of children but also to retain them in school. A great emphasis has to be given to the improvement of the quality of education and to the reduction of stagnation and wastage. School facilities have to be improved and expanded in remote areas and a larger number of students provided with pre-matric scholarships/stipends, book-grants, school uniforms and midday meals. Teaching in the initial stages should be in the mother tongue of the students and the regional language should be introduced gradually to open the door for higher education. Greater care should be exercised in the recruitment and placement of teachers in schools in tribal areas so that not only are they conversant with tribal language and culture but are also able to adapt themselves to the social, economic and physical environment. The school curriculum, school hours, school vocation and the school programme should be consistent with the situation in tribal areas. To the extent resources permit, single-teacher schools should give to appointment of more than one teacher. Their training facilities need to be considerably expanded and improved. At the middle and higher secondary stages, residential facilities need to be expanded and in this regard voluntary organizations have a useful role to play. The weaker students should be provided with coaching facilities while brighter students should be encouraged to enable them to realize their full potentialities of development. The facilities for science education should be expanded in tribal areas and the tribal children encouraged to go in for science and professional courses. Efforts should also be made to bring in more tribal students to the vocational courses. In the cash of ashram schools it is necessary to consolidate and improve the standards of existing ones, particularly in regard to the crafts and trades that are taught. At the post-matric level, the present administrative difficulties leading to delay in the award of scholarships should be removed. Research on various aspects of educational development in tribal areas has to be promoted so that the limited resource are deployed in the best possible manner.

NOTES AND REFERENCES

1. The paper has been written by Dr. A.B. Bose in his personal capacity and reflects his own views. Dr. Bose is Joint Director (Social Planning) in the Planning Commission.
2. A.K. Das and R.N. Saha, Post-Matric Education Among the Scheduled Castes ahd Scheduled Tribes of West Bengal, Bulletin of the Cultural Research Institute, 7
3. A.K. Das and R.N. Saha, Post-Matric Education Among the Scheduled Caste and Scheduled Tribes of West Bengal, Bulletin of the Cultural Research Institute, 7.
4. Under the rules every tribal student at post-matric stage was awarded a scholarship without any means or-merit test.
5. Bidyut K. Roy Chowdhury, Comparative Study of the Progress of Secondary Education Among the Scheduled Castes and Scheduled Tribes of West Bengal, Bulletin of the Cultural Research Institute, 2.
6. Report of the Seminar on Employment of Scheduled Castes and Scheduled Tribes, Planning Commisstor, New Delhi.
7. Tribal Research Bureau, Living Condition of Tribes of Similipal Hills, Adibasi, 10.
8. Needs, Facilities and the People; A Socio-Economic Survey of Simalwara Tribal Development Block, Tribal Research Institute, Udaipur
9. Survey of Tribal Development Block: Chintapalli; Tribal Cultural Research and Training Institute, Hyderabad.
10. Narmadeshwar Prasad, Land and People of Tribal Bihar, Bihar Tribal Research Institute, Ranchi.
11. P.G. Shah, Tribal Life in Gujarat, Gujarat Research Society, Bombay.
12. Charulal Mukherjee, The Santals, A. Mukherjee and Co., Calcutta.
13. Tribals Past and Present, Tribal Research Institute, Udaipur.

14. Survey of Tribal Development Block: Karra, Ranchi, Bihar Tribal Research Institute, Ranchi.

15. Bidyut K. Roy Chowdhury, Comparative Study of the Progress of Secondary Education among the Scheduled Castes and Scheduled Tribes of West Bengal, Bulletin of the Cultural Research Institute, 2.

16. A.K. Das and R.N. Saha, Post-matric Education Among the Scheduled Castes and Scheduled Tribes of West Bengal, Bulletin of the Cultural Research Institute, 7.

17. Report of the Education Commission (1964-66), Manager of Publications, Delhi.

18. Wastage and Stagnation in Primary and Middle Schools in India NCERT, New Delhi.

19. T.B. Naik, Impact of Education on the Bhils, Research Programme Committee, Planning Commission.

20. Bidyut K. Roy Chowdhury and B. Bhattacharya, A Brief Record on Stagnation of Scheduled Tribes and Castes Students, Bulletin of the Cultural Research Institute, 6.

21. Summary of the Report on Stagnation and Wastage in Primary Education in Tribal Areas. Tribal Research and Training Institute, Ahmedabad, (Cyclostyled).

22. Needs, Facilities and People: A Socio-Economic Survey of Simalwara Tribal Development Block II, Tribal Research Institute, Udaipur.

23. N.K. Das Gupta, Problems of Tribal Education and the Santals, Bharatiya Adimjati Sewak Sangh, New Delhi.

24. In addition to the plan expenditure, substantial amounts are spent by state governments under non-plan expenditure as the level of expenditure reached the last year of the plan is treated as committed expenditure and the plan outlay represents the net increase.

25. A Summary of the Report on Stagnation and Wastage in Primary Education in Tribal Areas, Tribal Research and Training Institute, Ahmedabad.

26. Perspective of Tribal Development in Rajasthan, Tribal Research Institute, Udaipur.

27. Needs, Facilities and The People: A Socio-Economic Survey of Simalwara Tribal Development Block II, Tribal Research Institute, Udaipur.

28. T.B. Naik, Impact of Education on the Bhils, Research Programmes Committee, Planning Commission.

29. N.K. Das Gupta, Problems of Tribal Education and the Santals, Bharatiya Adimjati Sewak Sangh, New Delhi.

30. Sachchidananda, The Special Problems of the Education of Scheduled Tribes. In The Sociology of Education in India, Ed. M.S. Gore, I.P. Desai and Suma Chitnis, NCERT, New Delhi.

31. N. Das, Reorientation of Ashram School Education, Adibasi, 14-23, 1963.

32. Naik, T.B., Impact of Education on the Bhils, Research Programmes Committee, Planning Commission, New Delhi.

33. Report of the Education Commission 1964-66, Manager of Publications, Delhi.

34. Report of the Scheduled Areas and Scheduled Tribes Commission (1960-61), Manager of Publications, Delhi.

35. Report of the Seminar on Employment of Scheduled Castes and Scheduled Tribes, Planning Commission, New Delhi.

36. Report of the Commissioner for Scheduled Castes and Scheduled Tribes 1967-68, Manager of Publications, Delhi.

37. N.K. Das Gupta, Problems of Tribal Education and the Santals. Bharatiya Adimjati Sewak Sangh, New Delhi.

38. Sachchidananda, The Special Problems of the Education of Scheduled Tribes. In The Sociology of Education in India, National Council of Educational Research and Training, New Delhi.

9

Dalit Struggle for Liberation: A Prospective

Most of the Dalit struggle for liberation still lies ahead. The road that struggle takes will invariably have important consequences that extend far beyond the Untouchable minority, for in spite of 20th Century changes the Untouchables are still concentrated at the bottom of the two hierarchies caste and class—that define so much of Indian life. The vast bulk of the Untouchable population cannot move without radically restructuring Indian society.

But can they move? And how? There are Dalit proponents of all the prominent strategies for change in India: Gandhian moral reform; orthodox Marxism; Western economic developmentalism, of both the capitalist and socialist varieties. All of these schools of thought are well represented in the Indian and international literature. However, there has also been an expansion and diversification of an indigenous Dalit tradition that has spread to Dalit communities throughout India, and these views are much less well known outside Dalit circles. They do not constitute a cohensive and unified perspective—indeed, there is intense internal dispute—but there is a community of communication within which individuals and organizations argue and evolve.

The following pieces illustrate some of the diverse theories and styles within this movement. The first is an English translation of a manifesto originally written in Marathi in 1973 by some of the early leaders of the Dalit Panther movement in Bombay. The Manifesto became one of several points of controversy within the Panther organization, which has since both fragmented and spread across India. The document does not represent the views of all who identify themselves with the Panthers, while at the same time it represents important themes in the thinking of activists in a variety of Dalit organizations. The second and third articles were originally published in The Outcry, the occasional publication of a Dalit-sponsored organization in Canada. The author of the second, L.R. Balley, is the publisher of Bheem Patrika, a Dalit newspaper in the Punjab. The author of the third is one of Balley's colleagues whose work occasionally appears in Bheem Patrika. The exploration closes with a further sampling of Dalit poetry, which so often captures the diversity and ferment of this movement.

DALIT PANTHERS MANIFESTO

Dalit Panthers (Bombay, 1973)

Revolutionary Stand of the Panthers

Today we, the 'Dalit Panthers', complete one year of our existence. Because of its clear revolutionary position, the 'Panthers' is growing in strength despite the strong resistance faced by it from many sides. It is bound to grow because it has recognized the revolutionary nature and aspirations of the masses with whose smiles and tears it has been bound up since its inception. During last year, motivated attempts have been made, especially in the far corners of Maharashtra, to create misunderstandings about our members and our activities.

Misconceptions about the objectives of the 'Panthers', about its commitment to total revolutionary and democratic struggles and about its policies, are being spread. It has, therefore, become necessary clearly to put forward our position. Because 'Panthers' no longer represent an emotional outburst of the Dalits. Instead its character has changed into that of a political organization. Dr. Babasaheb Ambedkar always taught his followers to base their calculations about their political strategy on deep study of the political situation confronting them. It is necessary and indispensable for us to keep this ideal before us. Otherwise we might mistake the back of the tortoise for a rock, and may be drowned in no time.

The present Congress rule is essentially a continuation of the old Hindu feudalism which kept the Dalits deprived of power, wealth and status for thousands of years. Therefore, this Congress rule cannot bring about social change. Under the pressure of the masses it passed many laws but it cannot implement them. Because the entire state machinery is dominated by the feudal interests, the same hands who, for thousands of years, under religious sanctions, controlled all the wealth and power, today own most of the agricultural land, industry, economic resources and all other instruments of power, therefore, in spite of independence and the democratic set-ups the problems of the Dalit remain unsolved. Untouchability has remained intact. It remains intact because the government did not do anything to eradicate it except passing some laws against it. To eradicate untouchability, all the land will have to be redistributed. Age-old customs and scriptures will have to be destroyed and new ideas inculcated. The village organization, the social organization, peoples' attitudes—all these will have to be restructured to suit true democratic objectives. We must pay attention to the objective process of social development and make an historical analysis of the power that imprisons the Dalit and which has succeeded in making him tie his own hands. The Hindu feudal rule can be a hundred times more ruthless today in oppressing the Dalits than it was in the Muslim period or the British period.

Because this Hindu feudal rule has in its hands all the arteries of production, bureaucracy, judiciary, army and police forces, in the shape of feudals, landlords, capitalists and religious leaders who stand behind and enable these instruments to thrive. Hence the problem of untouchability of the Dalits is no more one of mere mental slavery. Untouchability is the most violent form of exploitation on the surface of the earth, which survives the everchanging forms of the power structure. Today it is necessary to seek its soil, its root causes. If we understand them, we can definitely strike at the heart of this exploitation. The oppression of Dalits still exists despite the lives and work of our two great leaders—Jotiba Phule and Babasaheb Ambedkar. It is not only alive, it is stronger. Hence, unless we understand and give shape to the revolutionary content latent in the downtrodden lives of Untouchables, not a single individual seeking a social revolution would be able to remain alive in India. Truly speaking, the problem of Dalits, or Scheduled Castes and Tribes, has become a broad problem; the Dalit is no longer merely an Untouchable outside the village walls and the scriptures. He is an Untouchable, and he is a Dalit, but he is also a worker, a landless labourer, a proletarian. And unless we strengthen this growing revolutionary unity of the many with all our efforts, our existence has no future. The Dalit must accordingly accept the sections of masses, the other revolutionary forces as part of his own movement. Only then will he be able to fight his enemies effectively. If this does not take place, we shall be condemned to a condition worse than slavery. We must develop and help this consciousness ripen every year, every month, day, hour and every moment. Then alone shall we possess the right to be called human beings at all. It was for this that Doctor Ambedkar made us realize our humanity even in our state of beast-like exploitation. We should, to be successful, accept and understand a thing only after deep study, with a calm mind. We should not fall prey to slogans and outbursts. We must uproot the varna system, caste system that enslaves us in its shares. The soil in which they survive and grow must be made infertile. We must understand that the caste nature of the term Dalit is breaking down.

What has the Government Done for the Dalits?

When India obtained independence in 1947, the face of the administrative class changed. In the place of the king came the President. In the place of the king's prime minister came the 'people's representative'. In the place of the Vedas, Upanishads, Manusmriti and Gita, came the Constitution. On a blank page, independence, equality, brotherhood proliferated. From 1947 to 1974 is a long period of time. In these twenty-seven years the Congress government, turning the electoral process into its own capital, has been ruling with a monopoly. Four five-year plans, five general elections and three wars have gone by in this post-independence 'coming of age'. But the problems and needs of the Dalits, of the entire population, have been kept in a sort of deep freeze by the government. Beyond preserving state power in its hands, the government has done nothing else. On the contrary, by raising slogans of people's rule, of socialism, 'garibi hatao' [eliminate poverty], and green revolution, it has crushed the Dalits, the landless, poor peasants and the working class under its feet. Gambling with their lives, tempting a handful amongst them, the government tried persistently to endanger their very existence. Using divisive tactics that split people along religious, caste and other lines, they endangered the very integrity of democracy. In a democracy where men cannot exercise self-respect, well-being and an importance to their lives, where man cannot develop his individuality and his society, where those who wet with their blood every grain of the country's soil have to starve, where men have to forgo the land under their feet, the roof over their heads, where the upright have to break down and fall, where men have to see their mothers and sisters raped, in such a democracy, independence cannot be called true independence. The struggle for independence was a struggle under the leadership of national capitalists, landlords, feudals, for their own benefit. It was not under the leadership of the people, or of the Dalits. And Dr. Ambedkar had always said that it should be of the latter. That man called Gandhi, in whose hands the leadership of the struggle rested, was deceitful, cunning, an orthodox casteist and one who gave shelter to those who wanted to preserve class rule. Merely to preserve the unity of the Independence struggle, he flirted with problems of the Dalits, of untouchability, of the people. And that is why Babasaheb (Ambedkar) called him, time and again, the enemy of the people, the villain of the nation. Babasaheb used to say, Gandhism means preservation of religious authority, Gandhism means traditionalism, Gandhism means casteism, Gandhism means preservation of traditional divisions of labour, Gandhism means incarnationism. Gandhism means the holy cow, Gandhism means worship of images, Gandhism means an unscientific outlook. The British gave up their rule because of the seamen's mutiny, the emergence of the Azad Hind army, because of the struggles of the peasants, workers and Dalits. Because of these they could no longer remain in power. Giving independence to Gandhi and Gandhians meant that the British wanted their own interests in the country to be looked after. This was the sort of borrowed independence we got. True independence is one that is snatched forcibly out of the hands of the enemy. One that is like bits thrown to a helpless beggar is no independence. In every house and every mind the flame of true independence has to be ignited. This did not happen. That is why the Dalit, the worker, the landless and the poor peasant did not become free, the muck at the bottom of the pond remained where it was and, in fact, the government that retained the status quo kept on telling bigger and bigger lies to the Dalits.

What have other Parties Done for the Dalits?

The Left parties, having fought five elections, have grown bankrupt. They are now interested in moving from elections. In 1967 the Left parties united against the Congress. There was such opportunism in the united front that parties like the Communists joined hands with communalist parties such as Jan Sangh and Muslim League. In some states, Left united fronts came to power. But the absence of a clear-cut programme made the anti-Congress stand useless. In the task of putting some alternatives before the people, of solving the problems of the Dalits, of establishing the rule of the poor in the country, all the Left parties proved powerless. As a result, revolutionary people's groups lost faith in electoral democracy. Uprisings like Naxalbari took place and the spark spread around the country. With the 1972 elections, things came back to square one. The Congress sat like a beast on the head of the Dalits, of the people; famine struck, the very livelihoods of crores [millions] of people were uprooted, animals perished. Factories were shut down, workers faced unemployment, everyone was harassed by the mounting price rise. The full eclipse that Congress rule represents for the life of the country has not yet terminated. But our Left parties, playing the politics of parliamentary seats, are still wasting time trying to get recognition from the Congress. Not one dares to turn revolutionary to take up the problems of the people. All those Left parties who do not possess political power have ignored questions of a social revolution. They have not combined the class struggle with the struggle against untouchability, have not raised a voice against cultural and social domination along with economic exploitation. Untouchability is nothing but an extremely poisonous sort of exploitation. This exploitative system was given birth by Hindu feudalism and thrives for its benefit. The framework of untouchability is simply widening with the help of the army, the prisons, the legal system and the bureaucracy. Under the name of high-flown philosophy and liberation of the soul (moksha, nirvana), Dalits have been deprived of earthly happiness, and have been looted of all they possess. With the industrial revolution, machines came into being. Dalits were harnessed to the machines. But in the minds of the upper castes, feudalism survived. Because the owners of the machines could make a profit only by keeping the social structure intact. Only if a social revolution grips the minds of the Dalits, will there be a political revolution. If this takes place, the upper caste, the upper class, will lose the power it possesses. The stand that is taken by the Left parties prevents the spread of revolutionary ideology amongst the people. Because struggles really and truly meaningful to the Dalits were not conducted, Dalits have grown poorer. They have had to face innumerable atrocities.

The Republican Party and Dalit Panthers

The problems of the Dalits today, be they social, political or ethical, cannot be solved within the framework of religion and caste. This is what Doctor Babasaheb realized after his defeat in the 1952 general elections. A scientific outlook, class consciousness and a completely atheistic and fighting humanism alone could add an edge to the struggles of the Dalits. For this purpose, Doctor Ambedkar wanted to transfer the then-existing Scheduled Caste Federation [SCF] into a broad-based party. This could not happen during his lifetime. After his death, his 'followers' simply renamed SCF as the Republican Party and started to pursue casteist politics. They never united all the Dalits and all the oppressed. Above all, they conducted the politics of a revolutionary community like the Dalits in a legalistic manner. The party got enmeshed in the web of votes, demands, select places for a handful of the Dalits and concessions. So the Dalit population scattered over the country, in many villages, remained politically where they were. The leadership of the party went into the hands of the middle class in the community. Intrigue, selfishness and division became rife. Destroying the revolutionary voice of Doctor Ambedkar, these contemptible leaders made capital out of his name and set up their beggars' bowls. This is Doctor Amedkar's party, they said. This is Doctor Ambedkar's flag, they said, and filled their coffers. And thus, except the satyagraha [civil disobedience campaign] of the landless conducted under Dadasaheb Gaekwad's leadership, the party did not take up any programme worth its name. The atrocities against Dalits grew endemic. In a period of one to one and a half years, 1,117 Dalits were murdered. The land grew barren, not a drop of water was available. Honour was violated, houses gutted, people killed. Along with the very question of living, physical indignities grew sharper. What did the Republican Party do?

The party got caught in the net cast by a cunning ruling-class leader like Yashwantrao Chavan. Its life perished. Unity vanished, impotents filled the party. If we put our future in the hands of such impotent leaders, we will forgo our very lives, and that is why today we have to announce with deep pain that we are no blood relatives of the Republican Party.

The Dalits (Oppressed) of the World and Panthers

Due to the hideous plot of American imperialism, the Third Dalit World, that is, oppressed nations, and Dalit people are suffering. Even in America, a handful of reactionary whites are exploiting Negroes. To meet the force of reaction and remove this exploitation, the Black Panther movement grew. From the Black Panthers, Black Power emerged. The fire of the struggles has thrown out sparks into the country. We claim a close relationship with this struggle. We have before our eyes the examples of Vietnam, Cambodia, Africa and the like.

Who is a Dalit?

Members of Scheduled Castes and Tribes, neo-Buddhists, the working people, the landless and poor peasants, women and all those who are being exploited politically, economically and in the name of religion.

Who are our Friends?

1. Revolutionary parties set to break down the caste system and class rule. Left parties that are left in a true sense.
2. All other sections of society that are suffering due to the economic and political oppression.

Who are our Enemies?

1. Power, wealth, price.
2. Landlords, capitalists, money-lenders and their lackeys.

3. Those parties who indulge in religious or casteist politics, and the government which depends on them.

Burning Questions Before Dalits Today

1. Food, clothing, shelter.
2. Employmeat, land, (removal of) untouchability.
3. Social and physical injustice.

The struggle for the emancipation of the Dalits needs a complete revolution. Partial change is impossible. We do not want it either. We want a complete and total revolutionary change. Even if we want to move out of the present state of social degradation alone, we will have to exercise our power in economic, political, cultural fields as well. We will not be satisfied easily now. We do not want a little place in the Brahman Alley. We want the rule of the whole lane. We are not looking at persons but at a system. Change of heart, liberal education, etc. will not end our state of exploitation. Wnen we gather a revolutionary mass, rouse the people, out of the struggle of this giant mass will come the tidal wave of revolution. Legalistic appeals, requests, demands for concessions, elections, satyagraha—out of these, society will never change. Our ideas of social revolution and rebellion will not be borne by such paper-made vehicles. They will sprout in the soil, flower in the mind and then will come into full being with the help of a steel strong vehicle.

Dalit Panther is not a Mere Slogan

The way we look at our questions is the first step to solving h em. Panthers will paralyzingly attack untouchability, casteism and economic exploitation. This social system and state have taken many a cruel path to convert us into slaves, Turned us long into, shudras'. In the present modern forms of slavery there are mental chains of slavishness. We will try to break th em. In our struggle we will become free.

Our Programme

1. More than 80 per cent of India's population lives in the villages. Of these, landless peasants are 35 per cent, and 33 per cent of all landless agricultural labourers belong to Scheduled Castes. (Those Dalit poor peasants who own pieces of land, own a negligible amount). The question of landlessness of the Dalit peasants must be resolved.
2. Feudal survivals are still to be found in the villages. Due to this, Dalits are cruelly oppressed and exploited. Landlords and rich peasants get social prestige along with wealth. Due to this, the atrocities on the Dalits have grown endemic. This system has clamped itself on the Dalit's chest, affecting every part of his life, from day-to-day living to the deeper economic questions. This system must be destroyed.
3. Landless peasants must immediately get excess land through the application of the land ceiling act. Waste and jungle land must likewise be distributed.
4. The wages of landless labourers must be increased.
5. Dalits must be allowed to draw water from public wells.
6. Dalits must live, not outside the village in a separate settlement, but in the village itself.
7. All means of production must belong to the Dalits.
8. Exploitation by private capital must cease. Foreign capital must be confiscated without compensation.
9. Social, cultural and economic exploitation must be removed and socialism must be built in India. Misleading nationalization must give way to a true introduction of socialism.
10. All Dalits must be assured of daily wages.
11. Unemployed Dalits must be given unemployment benefits.

12. All Dalits must be given free education, medical facilities, housing and good quality cheap grains.
13. When giving employment in educational institutions, the requirement to declare one's caste and religion must be immediately removed.
14. The government must stop giving grants to religious institutions immediately and the wealth of religious places must be used for the benefit of Dalits.
15. Religious and casteist literature must be banned.
16. The division in the army along caste lines must be ended.
17. Black-marketeers, hoarders, money-lenders and all those exploiting the people economically must be destroyed.
18. The prices of essential commodities must be reduced.

We will build the organization of workers, Dalits, landless, poor peasants through all city factories, in all villages. We will hit back against all injustice perpetrated on Dalits. We will well and truly destroy the caste and varna system that thrives on the people's misery, which exploits the people, and liberate the Dalits. The present legal system and state have turned all our dreams to dust. To eradicate all the injustice against Dalits, they must themselves become rulers. This is the people's democracy. Sympathizers and members of Dalit Panthers, be ready for the final struggle of the Dalits.

INDIA NEEDS A CULTURAL REVOLUTION

India is passing through a very critical stage. All norms and moral codes seem to have collapsed. It has been aptly described that there is working anarchy in the country. But how long will it last? If none else is prepared to ponder over it, let the radicals, at least, think over their role and responsibility for the progressive transformation of Indian society.

Dr B. R. Ambedar had said: 'History bears out the proposition that political revolutions have always been preceded by social and religious revolutions'. But since for many centuries no effort has been made to usher in a cultural revolution in India, a vast majority of Indians are still deeply engulfed in acute poverty, supernaturalism, superstitions and a quagmire of rites, rituals and astrological predictions. Priests have a sway over the people and they continue, unchecked and unashamedly, to prey upon them parasitically. Gold and jewellery worth crores of rupees remain deposited in numerous temples and shrines without any productive utility and without contributing anything to the welfare of the needy and the poor. All this without the slightest protest from the so-called high castes, who boast of being the only custodians of the spiritual and philosophical treasure, or even from the so-called low-caste Hindus who are the victims of this system.

The Shankaracharya of Puri [head of a major Hindu temple] openly defies law: he publicly preaches untouchability; he denied entry [to the temple] to the Prime Minister of India, Mrs. Gandhi. But why? Because, according to Shankaracharya, she married Feroze Gandhi who was a Parsi. It is well known that Feroze was converted to Hinduism before marriage and the marriage between Feroze Gandhi and Indira was performed according to Vedic rites. Not only this, after his death he was cremated according to Hindu rites. Despite this, Shankaracharya regards Mrs. Gandhi as a non-Hindu and does not allow her to enter his temple.

Entry in Jagannath Temple at Puri is open to 'orthodox Hindus only'.

This attitude, this behaviour and practice of Shankaracharya, is against the Indian Constitution. Not only this, his act is a criminal offence. But he could not be arrested and prosecuted for fear of Hindu reaction. On the other hand, the followers dragged those who condemned Shankaracharya to the court of law. No Hindu of repute and prominence has criticized the Shankaracharya or demanded action against him.

In this context the following conversation between a Hindu leader and Dr. Ambedkar is very significant.

Dattopant Thengdi. The members of RSS (Rashtirya Swayamsevak Sangh) do not believe in untouchability.

Ambedkar. Whether you handful of people believe it or not, is not of much consequence in the context of solving the problem.

Thengdi. You said this because of the smallness of their numbers.

Ambedkar. Not necessarily because of that. There is an additional reason, which is of greater importance. Suppose on some critical social or religious issue your Golwalkar (the RSS chief) lays down a particular line and the Shankaracharyas give a different verdict. Whose decision will carry weight with the ordinary orthodox caste Hindus?

Thengdi. Of course, Shankaracharya's.

Referring to the above quoted conversation in the Weekly Organiser of 18 March 1984, Mr. Dattopant Thengdi comments thus: 'There are many who would be tempted to flaunt the label of social reformer, but "Guruji" (Golwalkar) preferred a secondary role for himself in the wider interests of society.'

When this same question was put directly to Golwalkar he replied, 'It does not matter whether you or I recognize a Shankaracharya. The point is that the "touchables", whom we want to give up "untouchability", accept their authority. They recognize neither you nor me. For them, the Dharmacharyas' (religious preachers) word is a religious commandment.'

What does the conversation indicate, and where does it lead us to? It once again proves beyond any doubt that to a caste Hindu the commandment of his 'guru', the religious preacher, is supreme. All laws, however revolutionary and beneficial for human dignity, peace and prosperity, are inferior to it.

How was such an imprint made? When did it happen? None among the Hindus has ever endeavoured to answer these questions. But did they not think of answering these questions? This is because the answer to these questions cannot but lead to the conclusion that it is the Hindu religion which is responsible for inculcating the idea of untouchability, practices of social disabilities, hatred and prejudice into their minds.

One may object to this conclusion of mine. Therefore, I want to clear their doubts, real or unreal.

What is Hinduism? 'Hindu religion, as contained in the VEDAS and SMRITIS, is nothing but a mass of sacrificial, social, political and sanitary rules and regulations, all mixed up. What is called religion by the Hindus is nothing but a multitude of commands and prohibitions.'

'What the Hindus call religion is really law or at least legalized class-ethics. Frankly, I refuse to call this code of ordinances religion' (Dr. Ambedkar, Annihilation of Caste, section 23).

Of what kind are the commands and prohibitions laid down in Hinduism? Here are some examples:

1. *Property.* The Shudra [low castes] can have no property. His master takes his possessions; a Brahman confidently seizes the goods of his Shudra (slave). (Manusmriti VIII, 417).
2. *Wealth.* The wealth of the Shudra (shall be) dogs and donkeys. (Ibid. X, 52).
3. *Dress.* The dress of Shudras (of the lower order) shall be the garments of the dead; (they shall eat) their food from broken dishes; black iron (shall be) their

ornaments; and they always wander from place to place. (Ibid. X, 52).

4. *Murder.* A Shudra can be slain at the pleasure of his master, and the same is the penance for killing a Shudra as is prescribed for killing a crow, chameleon, a peacock, a duck, a swan, a vulture, a frog, an iclineumon, a musk rat or a dog. (Apastamba 1, 9, 25, 13).

5. *Education.* If a Shudra listens intentivelv to a recitation of the Veda his ears shall be filled with molten tin or lac. If he recites Vedic texts, his tongue shall be cut out. If he remembers them his body shall be split in twain. (One who tried to educate a Shudra was punishable.) He who tells law to a Shudra and he who enjoins upon him religious observances, he indeed together with that Shudra sinks into the darknass of the hell called Asamvritta. (Dharam Sutra XII 4, 5, 6).

6. A Shudra is denied the right to give evidence.

7. A Shudra is severely punishable for offences of insult of and assualt on the members of the twice born.

8. Some of the important punishments for suppressing and crushing the Shudras were as below:

(i) For using an ironic expression against a Brahman, a Shudra shall suffer corporal punishment.

(ii) A once born man (a Shudra) who insults a twice born with gross invective shall have his tongue cut out, for he is of low origin.

(iii) If a Shudra mentions the name and caste of the twice born with contempt, an iron nail ten fingers long and red hot shall be thrust into his mouth.

(iv) If a Shudra arrogantly teaches the Brahman their duty, the king shall cause hot oil to be poured into his mouth and ears.

(v) A Shudra who raises his hand or a stick, shall have his hand cut off: he who in anger, kicks with his foot, shall have his foot cut off.

(vi) A low-caste man (Shudra) who tries to place himself on the same seat with a man of a high caste, shall be branded on his hip and be banished, or the king shall cause his buttocks to be gashed.

(vii) If out of arrogance he spits (on a superior), the king shall cause both his lips to be cut off: if he passes urine (on him), the penis, if he breaks wind (against him) the anus shall be cut off and gashed in.

(viii) If he lays hold of the hair of a superior let the king unhesitatingly cut off his hands, likewise if he takes him by the feet, the beard, the neck or the scrotum, his hands shall be cut off.

Tons of scriptures were written which contained details and directions of punishments, prohibitions and commandments against the Shudras. Following the dicta of these scriptures a society of discarded people was established by the law of the country:

1. by establishing the institution of slavery;
2. by creating the class of Untouchables;
3. by creating a society of unseeables, unapproachables—a society of enemy classes arising out of hatred, false dignity and the idea of supremacy of the ruling classes called Dwijas ['twiceborn'] and caste Hindus;
4. by creating classes whose water is impure:
5. by making a class of Abhojaniyas, *i.e.* those whose food cannot be taken;
6. by making these people serve perpetually with or without payment;
7. by putting them to menial work of an unclean nature, like sweeping latrines;

8. by making them live in ghettos outside the villages, with an idea of perpetuating untouchability;

9. by denying them proper and adequate education;

10. by denying them access to public institutions and places;

11. by shunning them in private life.

In order to enforce various methods of segregation such heinous institutions as child marriage and sati (burning of the wife at the husband's pyre) were introduced, some of which are still prevalent in the country.

The first evil of such a code of ordinances, misrepresented to the people as religion, is that it tends to deprive moral life of freedom and spontaneity and to reduce it (for the conscientious at any rate) to a more or less anxious and servile conformity to externally imposed rules. Under it there is no loyalty to ideals, there is only conformity to commands. But the worst evil of this code of ordinances is that the law it contains muss be the same yesterday, today and forever. They are iniquitous in that they are not the same for one class as for another. But this iniquity is made perpetual in that they are prescribed to be the same for all generations. The objectionable part of such a scheme is not that they are made by certain persons called prophets or law-givers. The objectionable part is that this code has been invested with the character of finality and fixity. Happiness notoriously varies with the conditions and circumstances of a person, as well as with the conditions of different people and epochs. That being the case how can humanity endure this code of eternal laws, without being cramped and crippled?

It is the Hindu religion that has cramped and crippled a large number of people in India. Commenting on this peculiarity of Hinduism, Dr. Ambedkar remarked on 1 January 1948. . . .

> Besides the Shudras, the Hindu civilization has produced three social classes whose existence has not received the attention it deserves. The three classes are:
>
> (i) The Criminal Tribes, who number 20 millions or so;
>
> (ii) The Aboriginal Tribes, who number about 15 millions; and
>
> (iii) The Untouchables, who number about 50 millions.

The existence of these classes is an abomination. The Hindu civilization, gauged in the light of these social products, could hardly be called civilization. It is a diabolical contrivance to suppress and enslave humanity. Its proper name should be infamy. What else can be said of a civilization which has produced a mass of people who are taught to accept crime as an approved means of earning their livelihood, another mass of people who are left to live in full bloom of their primitive barbarism in the midst of civilization and a third mass of people who are treated as an entity beyond human intercourse and whose mere touch is enough to cause pollution? (The Untouchables, preface, p. i).

Another tall talk about Hinduism is its toleration. What do the massacres, brutalities, uprootings, segregations, discriminations, disabilities and prejudices against the Untouchables in the whole of the country show? Does all this exhibit kindness and compassion? The reality is:

> Hinduism preaches separation instead of union. To be a Hindu means not to mix; to be separate in everything. The language commonly used, that Hinduism upholds Caste and Untouchability, perhaps disguises and conceals its genius. The real genius of Hinduism and social unity are incompatible. By its very genius Hinduism believes in social separation, which is another name for social disunity and even social separation. Hinduism cannot create that longing to belong which is the basis of all social unity. On the

> contrary Hinduism creates an eagerness to separate. (What Congress and Gandhi Have Done to the Untouchables, p. 187).

It is because of Hinduism that India, even after thirty-seven years of Independence, has not become a nation; it is still a warring multitude of castes and communities. Therefore, in order to make India a united country and to make themselves countrymen, Indians first and Indians last—there must be a cultural revolution.

What should be the object of a revolution, and how to achieve it?

The first and foremost object of this revolution should be to free every man and woman 'from the thraldom of the Shastras (Scriptures), cleanse their minds of the pernicious notions founded on the Shastras. It is no use telling people that the 'Shastras do not say what they are believed to say, grammatically read or logically interpreted. What matters is how the Shastras have been understood by the people.' Not only are the Shastras to be discarded, but also their authority has to be totally denied. In short 'you have got to apply dynamite to the Vedas and Shastras, which deny any part to reason, to Vedas and Shastras, which deny any part to morality.'

The cultural revolution must aim at

> a complete change in the fundamental notions of life. It means a complete change in the values of life. It means a complete change in out-look and in attitude towards men and things. It means conversion. It means new life. But a new life cannot enter a body that is dead. New life can enter only a new body. The old body must die before a new body can come into existence and a new life can enter it. To put it simply, the old must cease to be operative before the new can begin to enliven and to pulsate.

Therefore, 'such a religion (as Hinduism) must be destroyed . . . there is nothing irreligious in working for the destruction of such a religion. Indeed I hold that it is your bounden duty to tear the mask, to remove the misepresentation that is caused by misnaming this law as religion. This is an essential step' (Annihilation of Caste, Section 23).

How to bring in this cultural revolution? No doubt, the Indian soil is not congenial to complete change. But change has to be made.

Here are some, only some, preliminary measures that can lay the foundation of such a cultural revolution:

> Priests: In India the priesthood is the only profession where proficiency is not required. The profession of a Hindu priest is the only profession which is not subject to any code. Mentally a priest may be an idiot, physically he may be suffering from a foul disease, such as syphilis or gonorrhoea, morally he may be a wreck. But he is fit to officiate at solemn ceremonies, to enter the sanctum sanctorum of a Hindu temple and worship the Hindu God. All this becomes possible among the Hindus because for a priest it is enough to be born in a priestly caste. The whole thing is abominable and is due to the fact that the priestly class among Hindus is subject neither to law nor to morality. It recognizes no duties. It knows only of rights and privileges. It is a pest which seems to have been let loose on the masses for their mental and moral degradation. The priestly class must be brought under control:
>
> 1. It would be better if priesthood among Hindus is abolished. But as this seems to be impossible at present, the priesthood must at least cease to be hereditary.
> 2. Unless he (the priest) has passed an examination prescribed by the state and holds a sanad (certificate) from the state permitting him to practise.

3. No ceremony performed by a priest who does not hold a sanad shall be deemed to be valid in law and it should be made a penal offence for a person who has no sanad to officiate as a priest.
4. A priest should be the servant of the state and should be subject to disciplinary action by the state in the matter of his morals, beliefs and worship, in addition to his being subject along with other citizens to the ordinary law of the land.
5. The number of priests should be limited by law according to the requirements of the state, as is done in other public services.

Such steps will democratize the priesthood by throwing it open to every class and will certainly help to kill Brahmanism; such steps will also help to kill caste, which is nothing but Brahmanism incarnate.

Shrines. All shrines should be brought under some discipline, if not control. The resources and influence of the shrines should be bridled in such a way that these may not be able to continue poisoning, narrowing and communalizing the minds of Indians. In order to combat communalism, its sources of origin and nourishment must be dried up. Most of the shrines have become centres breeding communalism, ill-will, hatred and even social disabilities. Therefore, all shrines should be open to inspection and be made to conform to the country's laws and secular and social needs.

Secular Morality. What is secularism? It is a doctrine of basing morality solely on considerations of well-being of mankind in the present life, to the exclusion of all considerations drawn from belief in God or in matters of life after death.

Moral values are placed on a firm foundation when they are referred back to the innate rationality of man. They need no other sanction than the good of humanity.

In the words of Dr. Ambedkar, 'Morality does not require the sanction of God. It is for his own good that man has to love man. It is nothing but another name for brotherhood of men.'

Food. Food habits of Indians have become a source of strife, communal disturbance and tension. Indians must stop quarrelling over food. Those who are non-vegetarian must not distinguish and differentiate between beef and pork.

Social Integration. Countrywide plans should be drawn up and executed sincerely to break social stagnation and segregation, and to bring social integration in Indian society. For this purpose, inter-state, inter-community and inter-religious meetings, particularly of young boys and girls, should be regulary arranged at the national level through governmental and non-governmental agencies, so that young people come nearer to each other and cross the caste boundaries in matrimonial ties.

If, in the beginning, only these plans are executed, a good beginning can be made, and they say 'well begun is half done' If we march sincerely the Cultural Revolutions will be completed within no time.

Humanism as a Dalit Perspective

Although humanism as a creed has roots in Protagoras's philosophy, yet the philosophy of humanism is as old as man as a conscious being himself. The philosophy of humanism has been enriched by eminent philosophers, poets, scientists, social crusaders and scores of other scholars and intellectual giants. Humanism, as it has come down to us through centuries, is any system of thought or action which assigns a predominant interest to the affairs of men as compared with the supernatural or the abstract. It is a philosophy of which man is the centre and sanction. Actually, humanism as a philosophy represents a specific and forthwight view of the universe, the nature of man and the treatment of human problems (Corliss Lamont, The Philosophy of Humanism,

p. 10). Humanism is the viewpoint that men have but one life to lead and should make the most of it in terms of creative work and happiness; that human happiness is its own justification and requires no sanction or support from supernatural sources; that in any case the supernatural usually conceived of, in the form of heavenly gods or immortal heaven, does not exist; and that human beings, using their own intelligence and co-operating liberally with one another, can build an enduring citadel of peace and beauty on this earth (Corliss Lamont, The Philosophy of Humanism, p. 12).

Judging by this explanation of humanism, Ambedkar generated a humanistic philosophy rich in content and having various dimensions of its own.

Man and Nature

Like all other humanistic philosophers such as Feuerbach, Marx, Russell and others, Ambedkar held a realistic of man and nature. It is for this reason that Ambedkar accepted the Buddhist view of nature. According to it . . . there is no soul in the highest from that can be said to be governing this universe (Ambedkar, The Buddha and His Dhamma, p. 253) . . . Every change stands in some relation to cause, and that cause in relation to an effect and again that effect in relation to another cause . . . That is why Ambedkar, a true humanist, denied any eternal substance inside the cause which is transferred to the effect. The whole world is always in flux and there is nothing that is eternal in the universe. Thus, Ambedkar, by accepting Buddhism, denied any place to supernatural forces such as Paramatma or Atma, etc.

Ambedkar also rejected the idea of an individual soul which is said to be immortal, eternal and permanent. The doctrine of immortality of soul subordinates body and mind on to this abstract thing . . . Man's personality, according to him, therefore, is the combination of physical and mental elements. Again, for Ambedkar, man's thinking is affected by objective reality, but not absolutely.

It is this view which leaves room for the freedom of man, to which Ambedkar aspired. It is for this reason that he rejected economic determinism or historical materialism, while accepting other aspects of Marxism such as a materialistic outlook on the universe and the economic reconstruction of abolishing capitalism in favour of socialism and communism—an ideal society. (For details see Ambedkar's lecture on 'Buddhism and Marxim', delivered at Kathmandu, 1954). W.N. Kuber rightly speaks of Ambedkar's urge for human freedom and writes:

> 'He stood for human dignity and freedom, for simplicity, integrity, liberality, equality, social and economic justice, material prosperity and spiritual discipline and he was opposed to any social order or institution or any creed or practice, which involved injustice, violence and suppression of human personality' (W.N. Kuber, Ambedkar —A Critical Study, p. 292). Like M.N. Roy, Ambedkar had unshakeable faith in the creativeness of man. Both these humanists agree that men, being creative in nature, posses the capacities to change the world over.

Social Ethics and Morality

Like all great humanists, Ambedkar believed in the necessity of morality for just relations in the society. Rather, his contribution is distinctive and consciouous in this context. Society, says Ambedkar, cannot maintain right relations between man and man or even endure without some standards of sociability. Another name for these standards is morality. And morality, further, is synonymous with Buddhist Dhamma, believes Ambedkar. As he wrote, 'Dhamma is righteousness, which means right relations between man and man in all spheres of life' (The Buddha and His Dhamma, p. 316).

These right relations must be established on the basis of social principles of Liberty, Equality and Fraternity. These three principles, according to him, must serve as basis of any morality.

What is valuable and everlasting in Ambedkar's concept of society and morality, is his rejection of any divine sanction behind moral imperatives.

'Morality arises from the direct necessity for man to love man. It does not require the sanction of God. It is not to please God that man has to be moral. It is for his own good that man has to love man', argues Ambedkar (The Buddha and His Dhamma, p. 316). But morality must be sacred and universal and society must abide by it for the social good. Because, in the absence of any sacred moral code, the best among the citizens cannot be protected; society can't become a harmonious whole and the full growth of the individual cannot be facilitated. Ambedkar as a true democratic humanist—and also like Feuerbach, Russell, M.N. Roy and Sellars—was an ardent believer in atheistic morality, otherwise known as seculer morality or rational morality. W.N. Kuber rightly praises Ambedkar's zest for establishing humane relations in society in the following words:

> Ambedkar's chief concern in life was to meet the challenge of wrongly idealised social relations which threatened the whole of human existence and shook the foundation of a moral and just social order. The aim of his mission was to arouse in men and women the passion for right relations (Kuber, Ambedker—A Critical Study, p. 297).

One thing which is purely humanistic and unique in Ambedkar's concept of morality is that the purpose of following morality is not the attainment of salvation or Moksha, *i.e.* liberation from bondage of Karma. It is rather to create social harmony. Ambedkar, like Marx and Russell, believed in and worked for the establishment of classless society. Ambedkar did this by accepting the Buddhist way of ife, which for him is no different from the Marxist way of life.

Democracy and World Peace

A humanist is he who not only has ardent faith in democracy but he who also defends it and enriches its philosophy with passion. In this respect, then, Ambedkar was a humanist through and through. Democracy, in the political sphere, stands for belief in 'One man one vote', he said. But for him democracy was not this alone. In order to complete the philosophy of democracy, Ambedkar held, social and economic aspects of it must also be realized. In the social sphere democracy requires right but equal social relations among the members of society. He emphatically elaborated and enriched the concept of social democracy: 'Democracy is a mode of associated living. The roots of democracy are to be found in social relationship in terms of the associated life between the people who form the society' (Dhananjay Keer, Ambedkar: Life and Mission, p. 487). What is significant about Ambedkar's view of democracy is that he did not regard democracy as a mere form of government, as was and is the fashion . . . The basis of his democracy is humanistic and is consonant with the idea of human good. Its basis is rational human relations. That is why any sort of curb on the human mind, either in the form of distinctions based on untouchability or caste system or class structure, appear to Ambedkar abominable and inhuman. Therefore, he struggled against these inhuman practices and succeeded in putting 'a good part of mighty Manu upside-down' (H.N. Mukerjee, Gandhi, Ambedkar and the Extripation of Untouchability, p. 23).

Dr. Ambedkar was cosmopolitan in thought and practice. Like Marx, M.N. Roy, Russell and others, he stood for world peace. He thought and preached Buddha's gospel of peace in the world and renounced war. In order to establish peace in the world Ambedkar held that redemption of a world communist society is indispensable. Like a humanist he wanted this stage of communist (casteless, and classless) society [to] usher in peacefully, and more so through a rationalistic way of life, in order to be durable. He yearned for the change of the whole world, a new world in which man would feel a free and creative being in a new culture. In fact, Ambedkar held that man can realize his natural self only in such a society.

10

Dalit Self-Reliance: Two Studies

I

SELF-HELP IN COMMUNITY HEALTH

Just two years ago the world celebrated the thirtieth anniversary of the Charter of Human Rights which, among others, declares that health care is one of the basic rights of every man and woman. However, like so many other clauses of the charter, this one too has remained a dead letter for over 80 per cent of our country's citizens, especially to the rural poor—just the groups that are vulnerable to diseases and have a very high rate of mortality and morbidity and are in the greatest need of these services.

The reasons for this deprivation have to be found in the health system which reflects the inequalities of our society as a whole. Over 90 per cent of our medical care is of the hospital-oriented curative type which depends on costly equipment, expensive medicines and highly qualified professional. In other words, we have blindly copied the medical care system of the West where social security and higher per capita income permit each individual to spend some hundreds of dollors per year on health care. In most rural areas in our country, any system that requires an expense of more then Rs. 5 per capita per year may go beyond the means of those who need health care the most.

Little wonder then, that 85 per cent of our medical facilities are concentrated in the urban areas where the medical practitioner can work efficiently and earn a large income which he may consider a return on the investment he makes on his learning. Even the location of the facilities does not necessarily ensure the flow of benefits equally to all the urban sections. Many health centres have been opened in the rural areas but it is not possible for most villagers to avail of their services, since they are geographically isolated and lack public transport facilities. Hiring a bullock cart to go to the centre may cost Rs. 12 to 15 which very few from the poorest sections can afford.

Initial Perception of Problem

What this means is that the gap between the rich and the poor is widening also in the health field. The structure of effective demand, the highly specialised curative nature of these services and the techniques of the distribution of health services condition the whole system to be limited to those with economic and socio-political power. This convinced us of the need of a new approach in the lines of what Dr. R.S. Arole in Jamkhed, Dr. Dyal Chand in Pachod (Aurangabad) and many others in other parts of India are trying.

The Mobile Orientation and Training Team of the Indian Social Institute (ISI-MOTT) decided to take some initiatives in this direction. It was essential to concentrate on preventive care, spread the benefits of the curative system to a larger section of our population and use it as a tool for building up a village community. This approach would have to move away from the present system which is based on the monopoly of the decision-making power in the hands of a few persons who get all its benefits. It had to be based on the local resources to fix their own priorities and turn it into their common concern. As the recent book on the experiences of the team said:

> When people in India, especially in the rural areas are faced with a problem, they have always been able to find a solution among themselves. This approach has been used traditionally to build houses for individuals, to help with cultivation, during sickness or death, etc. Sad to say, up till now this approach has not been used for health care especially preventive activities such as cleaning wells and drainages.

Realising that the new approach had to base itself on the rural manpower, we decided to start with confidence in what the professionals consider the illiterate and ignorant' rural folk. We felt that the professional approach was good for efficiency but deprived the poor of its services. A choice had to be made between this type of equipment-oriented efficiency that may be going against social justice and another people-oriented approach that may make the services effective by making them accessible to the rural poor.

We also knew that such an approach involved many risks but they were worth taking. With proper care and guidance we can fill the manpower gap by using our real resource, that is, the villagers whose creative talents and capabilities have been ignored. In the absence of proper medical care, they have to depend on the dai, the traditional birth attendant who has not been given any training for decades. Consequently, her techniques are outdated. The new approach had to start by identifying all the local resources and find ways of updating them.

Background of Area

ISI-MOTT was active mostly in Andhra and Orissa and chose Southern Orissa for its community health approach. Berhampur is the main city in the area and it has got a medical college and the towns have got plenty of doctors.

But the rural areas are deplorably neglected. The only health facilities are some government health centres and a few hospitals and dispensaries run by the Christian missionaries. We decided to use these as a base and start a community health programme in which the government centres and the Church-related hospitals/dispensaries would work in co-ordination. Since the voluntary agency we were dealing with was the Catholic Church, we decided to limit the field of work to the three districts that came under the Catholic diocese of Berhampur *viz.* Ganjam, Koraput, and Kalahandi covering an area of 5125.5 sq. km.

Eighty per cent of the area is inaccessible by road, "being covered with high mountains and thick forests. The total population of the three districts amounts to 55,54,103 of whom 45 per cent belong to the scheduled castes and tribes. If we leave aside the plains of Ganjam, the ratio of scheduled tribes and castes is much higher—as high as 49.9 per cent at Kalahandi and 73.7 per cent Koraput. They live in small villages scattered among the mountains. Cultivation that uses outdated technology is the main source of their livelihood. Economically they are poor, educational facilities are meagre and communications very difficult. Literacy among them is only 11.51 per cent and their health situation is deplorable.

Since they do not have any decision-making power in the state and national politics, they are neglected by the government officials. A few governmental and voluntary agencies have attempted to improve their situation. But up to now no satisfactory results are perceived in their living conditions. Poverty and illiteracy have got their repercusions upon the health conditions of the people. Malnutrition and insanitary conditions pave the way for various diseases. Once affected, they have recourse to age old remedies since the other medical facilities are beyond their reach.

Though there are a few mission dispensaries and government centres, people approach them only for serious cases since very few can afford to cover the distance on foot and the other means of transport are too expensive for them. The introduction of mobile clinics by the mission hospital had solved the problem to a certain extent. But the limited number of medical personnel and lack of road communications put limits to their activities. The neglect of these areas by the decision-makers who ignored the needs of the tribal areas while they themselves got good care, put limits even on the efforts of those who wanted these facilities to reach them. Most interior villages still remain closed to medical assistance and are left to their own fate. No wonder then that the villagers fell into a state of passive acceptance of their situation and viewed sickness and death as divine will.

A New Approach

To solve the problems, the first need was to convince those involved in the work of the voluntary agency concerned, of the need of a new approach to health care. A seminar was organised not merely for those running the dispensaries but also for all the priests and Religious Sisters of the diocese of Berhampur, because it was essential to approach the problem as a team. Those not directly involved in the work had to be aware of the situation and had to give their support to those implementing the programme.

In this initial seminar, MOTT offered a fundamental analysis of the present medical system within the socio-economic situation and the decision-making process of the dominating groups. The participants had an opportunity to understand the nature and function of the present health system in contrast to the proposed community-oriented health structure.

However, all this can be called somewhat superficial in the sense that it was aimed at those who would not do the actual work but support them from outside and would often work with the village communities. Though an effort was made at socio-political analysis, the main thrust of the four-day seminar held in July 197 8was to convince them of the need of a new approach to health care. The message at this seminar was that the vested interests were at the basis of inequalities. But the main thrust was on the fact that though we were running dispensaries and caring for a number of patients, we were not reaching out to the people—that the health services would remain outside the reach of the rural poor as long as they were confined to an institution and were curative in nature.

A one-week follow-up seminar was conducted three months later only for those involved in medical work. There was a slight deepening of the socio-political analysis. But even here the main thrust was on the community health approach. This seminar inculcated into the participants the idea that preventive steps are of far greater importance than the curative measures in which they were involved. But if was insisted that prevention is not merely avoiding disease but removal of the causes of these ailments and of the system that deprives the poorest of their right to health care.

Obviously a proper analysis would have involved much greater insistence than what we gave, on the socio-economic causes of inequality and political conditions of their removal. But at this stage we decided on a step by step approach. All the participants were involved in curative care and were not fully convinced of the possibility of using illiterate villagers for health care. Hence at this seminar the team insisted mostly on the approach to the people and on the need of placing confidence and trust in the ordinary villagers and of evolving a system suited to their culture. It was hoped that the process would be analysed slowly as it progressed and the ultimate objective of solving the structural problems would be attained.

Such an approach was important at this stage because most participants were not yet in a postion to place enough trust and confidence in the people and to accept them as co-workers in the medical field. In that sense our task was more difficult than that of persons who start straight away with a community health programme. They can arrange the whole infrastructure to suit the need of this programme. But we were dealing with an already existing curative set up and it is not an easy task to re-orientate it to suit new goals.

After much discussion, the participants realised that if health care has to reach those who need it the most, they have to change their approach to prevention and health education. They were also convinced that they did not have to have highly qualified persons for this work but that the manpower already available in the rural areas could be updated and used for this purpose. This gave rise to the idea of the Village Health Workers who, with some amount of training, could detect common ailments and treat them. This would make curative care much cheaper than it is today. Besides, they would be able to instruct people on certain basic elements of hygiene and sanitation and would prevent many diseases. It was hoped that slowly these workers would grow into village leaders who would be instrumental in building their community.

In spite of all the difficulties, also the diocesan authorities were by now convinced of the need for a new approach. Thus a new community health programme was courageously launched and the Village Health Worker (VHW) project started taking concrete shape. MOTT and the local team worked hand in hand from this moment. They envisaged a three-tier system with the VHWs at the bottom. At the second level there were to be the medical personnel of the existing health centres, supervising the VHW. Finally there was to be a core team co-ordinating the whole work.

Right from the beginning it was clear to us that nothing in the existing medical set up or in the rural culture should be either retained or given up for its own sake. Whenever possible, an existing practice should be used as the starting point. Thus the area already had a CRS-sponsored nutrition education-cum-MCH programme. This worked as the stepping stone for working out the new methodology. The core team of Nutrition

Education is being employed in the training and supervision of the VHWs. All these programmes now work hand in hand in a more effective manner.

Based on the same principle of not duplicating efforts but making the most of the existing resources, we decided to work in close collaboration with the existing government institutions Ultimately, the government alone can make health care accessible to the communities. Voluntary agencies can only create models meant to take it closer to the rural poor. Hence we decided that our work of health care should have official approval and support.

By and large, our experience in collaboration has been very positive. In order to avoid duplication, whenever we have a training programme, we contact the nearest primary health centre and give them the names of the villages from which our new trainees come. The district medical officer is informed of our programme and ordinarily approves the syllabus and countersigns the standing orders and certificates.

Similarly, we decided that what we considered superstitious practices should not be rejected but that a deeper study made of all of them. Take for example, the custom prevalent in many of these villages, of considering the first bath after small-pox sacred. They dig a deep pit, pour into it warm water medicated with neem leaves and close the pit after taking the patient out of the bath water. Though it was given an apparently superstitious form, it was obviously very scientific and meant to prevent the spread of the disease. This custom was analysed somewhat easily, but it was much more difficult to find out the rationale behind many other practices. But once they were studied, many of them were found to be very healthy.

Choice of Village Health Workers

As the motto of the programme 'better health for the people, by the people' shows, right from the beginning we were clear that our efforts should be to try out a system that belongs to the whole community. This had to start with the selection of the VHW. In the traditional rural society, people prefer the health worker to be from the community, for very often she is not just a professional curing diseases but a confidant of the people—women in particular. In fact, villagers often prefer less qualified persons from their own community, the dai for example, to the much better qualified nurse and midwife posted there from outside. Often there is a communication and cultural gap between the villagers and the workers from outside the region.

Consequently, the selection of the health worker is a joint responsibility of the village community and the health team. To be more exact, the village community first discusses with the health team, the qualities required in a VHW and then chooses someone who fits these criteria. By and large we look for persons with qualities such as leadership, acceptability by the community and readiness to serve, Most volunteers selected by the villages are illiterate but they have proved to be successful health workers.

Later in this paper we shall be discussing the use of folklore in training the VHWs and in communicating the health message. This method was worked out at a training course for 40 VHWs 32 of whom were illiterate. Most of it was formulated by the women themselves and this batch is among the most successful VHWs in the entire programme.

Though we also had a few young men as health workers, we feel that women are to be preferred whenever possible. They and the children are more vulnerable than the men who are themselves oppressed by the dominating classes. Hence, motivating women, though very difficult, is extremely beneficial because once they realise that they can be agents of change, they are more effective than men since they suffer the consequences of oppression more than their menfolk.

Moreover, cultural beliefs and taboos are much more deeply

rooted in women than in men. Consequently, once a woman is convinced, she finds it easier to motivate other women from the same cultural background. Besides, she is the one who looks after the sick in the family and can detect illnes faster than anyone else. She has access to every house while not every door is open for men. Besides, there seems to be less fear of malpractices with women than with men.

Above all, we cannot forget that she is the mother and that the child is under her influence at least for the first five years. That is when many values are formed and as such these years are decisive in a child's life. Consequently, if mothers can be motivated to acquire new attitudes, they can have great influence on their society as a whole.

The cooperation of the village community is not limited to the selection of the VHW but continues all along the programme. After the training, the core team, along with the local medical personnel, takes them back to the villages and presents them to the people. There are cases when the village did not accept the VHWs as reliable immediately though they themselves had elected them. In some cases they might have required as much as one year to gain acceptability. But sooner or later the villagers recognise them as persons meant to serve them. Though initially some external aid may have to be got for part of the VHWs' honourariun, the villagers too contribute some funds for the services rendered. Thus health care becomes very much part of the village system instead of being passing charity of some philanthropic organisations or a business enterprise of some professionals.

Training of Village Health Worker

The training programme is conducted in three phases. The first part lasts three or four weeks and is meant to communicate the basics of health and give them the opportunity to learn and live together. After three months in the field, the women come back to the centre once again for about two weeks. The third and final phase comes after four or more months of field experience and lasts three weeks.

The first phase of training can be called a 'live in' experience and is probably the most difficult. It is decisive in forming their leadership qualities. At first the women feel like fish out of water. But after four or five days they mix freely and build up a community spirit to such an extent that many of them weep when they part company. They belong to various castes. But in living and working together they slowly shed caste prejudices, thus removing a major obstacle to the organisation of the villagers. As persons from various castes and creeds cut from the same pot, they also learn to broaden their outlook.

During these days they acquire working knowledge of basic health, nutrition, mother and child care, first aid, home nursing, hygiene and sanitation. They are also instructed in the growth of transmissible disease organism, detection and prevention of common diseases and Natural Family Planning methods. This training which takes eight hours a day, is through lectures, group discussions, song, drama, demonstration and film shows. At the end of these four weeks they have an oral and practical test. Those who are successful are given a simple medical kit containing 8 to 10 simple medicines along with the standing orders and the certificate signed by the government health officer. They are then sent to their village for three months to work under the guidance of the health centre of their area. They have to go to the centre once a week to discuss their problems and exchange ideas.

Knowing full well that illiterate women cannot retain all that they learn in the course of a few days, during the second phase we repeat everything once again in such a way that they are thorough with basic diagnosis and methods of prevention. Then we take them one step ahead.

Finally, the third phase is meant to evaluate the work done by them during the months they have spent in the field and correct any shortcomings. After this they are given further instruction in aspects outside the medical field, in the proper sense of the term. They are helped to be leaders, taught some communication and organisational techniques and the basics of development projects such as saving habits, income generating schemes, etc. This is meant to help them to become leaders of of the community and initiate the procesess of change within their village.

Those who are found fit at the end of this phase are confirmed as VHWs. Out of 100 persons trained so far, we have selected only 67. They attend to over 8,500 families in 71 villages. Twelve health centres are associated with the programme. A total of about 4.000 mothers and over 5,000 children are taken care of.

All of us involved in their training were used to classroom teaching. In the beginning we followed the same system but gradually we learnt that this method is ineffective among the illiterate villagers. We had to take a totally different approach, because anything formal is beyond their reach. Slowly we found that the training programme has to be based on simple dialogue in which the teacher-taught difference disappears and both share knowledge. We had to learn more about rural life from the trainees and give them basic knowledge of health practices.

With this in view, we started visiting the villages methodically in order to know the area and the lifestyle of the places from which the VHWs are chosen. The more we know, the easier it is for us to communicate the message, because our attitudes need to be changed in some aspects and theirs in others. This also helped us to have a simple dialogue with them which, we felt, was the best way of teaching them and us.

Our regular visits also helped us to select simple instances from their life which could be used as examples and analogies in order to lead them from the 'unknown to the known'. Initially we thought of using commercial audio-visual aids. But soon we realised that they were made according to the culture of the artist, not of those to whom they were supposed to communicate a message. In fact, some of these techniques, instead of communicating a message even diverted their attention from it. When, for example, we used a tape recorder, the women were confused. because that was the first time they had seen this apparatus. They could not understand how a box could talk like a human being when it was obvious that it was too small for someone to hide in! But we found charts and posters prepared according to their suggestions and based on ideas gathered from them much more useful for their training than any imported equipment.

One of the elements we found extremely useful was their folkore. The Orissa tribals are fond of song and dance and they express their feelings of joy, gratitude and devotion through these media. When we realised this, we felt that this was the best way of teaching illiterate women who had never got used to class room lectures and abstract reasoning. Hence, with the help of local artists, we composed dramas and songs based on their folklore and popular tunes. We managed to have a song on every disease, explaining their causes, mode of diagnosis and cure.

In the beginning we took the initiative. But soon the trainees themselves took over and started composing dramas, songs and dances of their own. At the end of a training session, the women staged a full length entertainment of health dramas and songs composed by them and put up an exhibition using only locally available material.

The group of 40 trainees mentioned above that took this initiative, has proved to be the best batch of health educators. Their talent for improvising has helped them to react promptly in an emergency. What is obvious from all the training sessions is that the fact of their being illiterate does not create any problem. They are intelligent, creative and hard working. Similarly, our ignorance of the local language did not prove to be a barrier. In fact it was a help because we had to be very accurate in order to make sure that the interpreter understood everything.

Functioning of VHWs

Official statistics present the state of health in terms of the population per doctor or nurse ratio. But like the per capita income which hides glaring inequalities in the country, the health statistics too fail to show the difference between the various classes, sectors and urban and rural areas. In other words, they give the availability of the services, not their accessibility.

Community health on the contrary, proposed to make health services accessible to those who need them. This involves making them available in a geographically accessible manner and putting them financially and functionally within the reach of the community. The methods employed should be acceptable to the group that makes use of them.

That such an approach is possible has been proved by these women who have been rejected by the professionals as being ignorant. They are not given clear instructions on ways of reaching the people. All of them are only part-timers and they find their own way of communicating their new found knowledge to the villagers. Some of them visit families regularly, chat with the women and discuss their problems. Others may bring four or five women or even entire families together, find out their problems and teach them the health songs they have composed or have been taught by others. One of the health workers carries the health kit to the place where she and the whole community go to work. Minor injuries, fevers and similar ailments are treated immediately. During the lunch break she gathers the other members of the community under a tree and teaches them what she has learnt. She needs no health centre to treat the people, no microphone to gather them and no expensive communication equipment to transmit her message.

The village-based approach also involved major changes in

the dispensaries that had been opened as curative centres. Except a few that had a limited nutrition or immunisation outreach programme, all of them were institution-based and their impact was limited. With the decision to start a community health programme, these dispensaries had to become health centres meant to support the VHWs. Many of their curative aspects are still required because less than 40 per cent of the diseases are preventable through health education and another 30-40 per cent can be treated by the VHW. Whenever the village worker found that a case was beyond her capacities, she would inform the health centre which either sent one of its nurses to the village or made arrangements to bring the patient to the centre.

They still have to give pre-natal and post-natal care, help the VHW in her task of health education and early detection and treatment of common diseases. But the result of the new approach is that their services which were extremely limited compared to the needs of the community, have become accessible to a much larger number. The medical personnel that were tied down to the curative dispensary have now got more time to move out to the people since the cases coming to the centre have been reduced drastically. They are thus able to supervise the work of the VHW and guide her in the best way of health delivery.

This involves a certain amount of division of tasks between the VHWs and the centre, with the latter concentrating on the training of the former and supplementing her work. It also requires a clear definition of problems which is not always eassy. Initially, we realised that the VHWs and the health centres functioned as parrallel units and, without their realising it, a gap was formed between them.

That is when we relised that we had to retrain also the staff of the health cenres in order to bridge this gap. A short orientation course enabled the staff off each centre to take full responsibility for the training and suprvision of the VHWs in their zone. They were slowly able to build up a team spirit.

It was also decided to set up a local training team to guide the local health centre staff and to reinforce this team spirit. The coordinator of the whole proramme was in change of this team.

Leadership Building

It should be obvious by now that the ultimate objective of the programme was not merely better health but, above all, transformation of village community by using health as an entry point to people's education and using the VHWs as the leaders to help them to become agents of change. We dare not say that this has been achieved and cannot state with any certainty that the process will attain this end. But a beginning has been made.

By the end of their training, real transformation is visible in the women. It is seen first of all in their dress. They begin to dress well and take pride in it. It does not mean that they use expensive clothes but that they are concious of cleanliness and respectability in their appearance. It is only an external sign of a deeper transformation taking place in them. More than anything else, they become aware of their own dignity.

That also the villagers accepted this new dignity of leadership became clear at times through some external signs. One of the trainees for example, who could not get married because of some physical defect, got an offer after the training and is now a happy housewife. This was a public recognition of her personality and leadership.

The VHWs themselves courageously take up leadership on many occasions—initially in matters concerning health and later on go to other fields. In one of the villages, for example, all the dirt used to be gathered in the centre of the street and left there. Flies flourished and turned it into a health hazard. When the VHW approached the health officer and told him that this dirt should be removed in order to prevent the spread of disease 'what do you know about the disease?' was the arrogant reply of the health officer, a professional medical person. The woman, though illiterate, explained to him the way sickness spreads through flies. He was so wonderstruck that apart from sending a person to clean the area immediately, he praised her and asked her to approach him freely whenever his help was required. This change of attitude both on the part of the government officials and the VHWs helps the villagers to get from the government the services that are theirs by right but have been denied to them. At least a few VHWs have acquired confidence in themselves and their community to demand these rights from the officials who are supposed to facilitiate progress but are oftener than not, an obstruction.

The impact of the VHWs' presence is also felt in the village as a whole. It starts with health conciousness and in many places spreads to other areas. Slowly they begin to build up sanitary habits and through this process become aware of their human dignity that has been denied to them because of the unjust distribution of power. The VHW may start the process of change in her own family as in the case of the one who prepared vegetable soup for her child. In a short time the child put on weight and the other mothers were curious to know what she had done to bring up such a healthy child. She explained to them the method of preparing soup from ordinary vegetable available at their door step and what it does to the human body. The improvement thus effected in the village was noticed by the neighbouring villages who have approached the health centre requesting it to train some of their women as VHWs.

In spite of these positive developments, we are not certain that a process of total transformation will take place. Such a change requires much greater support to the local leaders than the health centre teams have been able to give them so far. Till now, concentration has been primarily on the re-orientotion of the health centres and the training of the staff for the purpose of community health. Not enough attention has been paid to the socio-political aspects of which they are given only the basics. This is not sufficient for sustained action. Much greater depth is required and their training and strategy have to be changed accordingly.

As mentioned above, deeper analysis has begun at the base where both the local team and MOTT spend time with the VHWs, helping them to understand their problems of malnutrition, poverty etc. This understanding helps them to develop further and we hope that ultimately it will lead to a movement of the whole community. They are local leaders and can function much better in the villages. The health centre staff on the contrary, is by and large from outside the state. Many of them have been there only for two or three years and need a much longer time to know the people well enough to give them the support required for a sustained movement.

At this stage we can only hope for such a transformation. We are not certain whether it is realistic to get such a process going, will all its limitations, believing that people grow step by step. What is obvious to us is that the present system has not only not functioned in favour of the poor but has positively worked against them. Hence alternatives have to be found and experiments conducted in this direction. One cannot afford to be dogmatic is such an experiment, but should only be certain that the change introduced will bring them closer to the acquisition of their human rights and will not do them harm as a community.

Finances

One last question that needs to be discussed concerns the finances since the replicability of a programme depends also on this aspect. One thing is obvious is that sooner or later the VHW should be given some remmuneration by the community. We speak of remuneration rather than a salary, because they are only part-time workers. They have to look after their own children, cattle and fields which is full-time occupation. Besides, most villagers are absent from their houses during the day either in the fields or elsewhere. Hence there is no scope for a full-time worker who would be wasting her time during the day.

This is probably one of the reasons why the government-run primary health centres are not accessible to many villagers.

Consequently, the remuneration should be more in the form of appreciation of her services than as salary. The main question is: how is the community to give it? Initially, we too agreed with those who said that it should be paid directly by the community. But now we have changed our mind. The health workers themselves expressed the opinion that if they are paid directly by the community the money has to be collected and paid by the village headman or the panchayat president. This can put the worker under the control of the powerful individuals of the village and would be counterpoductive from the point of view of social change which, among others, involves transfer of power from the dominant groups or individuals to the powerless.

On the other hand, the very purpose of their existence may be defeated if they are paid by the government. The community may tend to look at them as government servants. It should be noted that by and large in India as a whole and the villages in particular, the government is considered a third party. As such, the community will no longer feel responsible for the continuation of these activities.

Finally, as in many other places, we too managed to find a middle way that got the payment from the community but gave it to the worker independently of the existing leaders. The amount is channelled through the health centre and its team.

It may be noted that the programme is less than two years old and the village communities are not yet in a position to to pay the total amount of Rs. 50 given to the health worker and money spent on medicines. Within a year or two we hope that the villagers will have gone through the process sufficiently to see the need of complete maintenance of the programme and of making it totally self-sufficient. At present part of the expenses come from the donour agencies abroad. We view this only as a temporary phase that forms part of the process of education.

At present the medicines are subsidised and this is one of the aspects requiring external aid. Instead of fixing different prices for different drugs got from the pharmaccutical companies, all of them are sold at the same price. Thus some loss is incurred which has to be made up by help from others. But we hope that eventually there will be some sort of a health insurance which should look after this problem.

Moreover, we have now started the process of identifying the local centuries-old remedies that have sustained life of these families for many generations. It they can be updated and integrated into a new system, the expenses on drugs will diminish considerably.

Conclusion

We are still at the beginning of a process and we are not certain about is final outcome though we are trying to take it towards a certain direction. We know our ultimate goal but whether the means we use will be helpful in achieving this purpose has still to be seen. Our training and the rest of our approach need to be evaluated and changed constantly according to the progress of the programme. Whether we can attain our objective within the socio-religious structures within whose constraints we are trying out these new approaches, remains to be seen.

II

HOUSING EXPERIMENT IN SLUMS

When thirty years ago the St. Joseph's School Complex was built on a stretch of land, it was to a certain extent an island amid the slums in the surrounding vacant land. Emigrants from Andhra Pradesh and remote villages of Tamil Nadu would raise a marshy pond to a height of one metre to construct their 'thatched dwelling unit'. These few emigrants became the initial owners of the Poromboke land belonging to the corporation. Letters to their villages mentioning the new 'security' of the city would bring more and more emigrants to settle down in the area, thus resulting in the creation of a huge township which today houses 1024 families in the three slums taken up as a pilot project area by the Don Bosco Social Service Society (DBSSS).

Background

These three namely Dr. Ambedkar Nagar, Nehru Nagar and Sastri Nagar were chosen from among thirty slums because of their proximity to St Joseph's Technical School. Spread over 7 acres of land, they have a population of over 7,000 that is, over 1,000 persons per acre. Each slums has its own identity, economic background, social status and so on.

Dr. Ambedkar Nagar is the oldest of the three slums and shelters 341 families. It is well laid out with 7 main streets and 3 cross streets. Forty three out of the 301 dwelling units are brick-built while the rest are thatched sheds. They are provided with no basic amenities. To be precise, the public conveniences are constructed but hardlay maintained and so they are varely used. For drinking water they have to depend on 3 taps for an hour or two per day. In other words, on an average each tap has to cater to a whole day's need of 100 families in less than 100 minutes.

One can imagine the fights that ensure at the water tap and the occasion provided to the slum 'leaders' to exploit the consequent divisions to their own advantage. Moreover, this artificial scarcity of water results in very poor hygienic conditions, bad health and the dehumanising process that follows. Their socio-economic problem is probably worse than their physical condition. Most of the families are beedi workers or coolies/labourers. Their monthly income is about Rs. 100 which has to feed a family of not less than five persons. Forty eight per cent of them are Muslims. Their literacy level is very low since they have not felt the need to learn, to read and write.

Nehru Nagar has 153 familes in its 109 dwelling units, 28 of them with brick walls and the rest 'thatched-sheds'. The main occupation of those families is pot-making, mostly crude pots and ovents which bring them a monthly income of Rs. 200-250. People of this slum are solely controlled by five individuals who have together formed an association.

Sastri Nagar, the third slum, has 530 families. Their dwelling units are 96 sq. ft. with tiled roofs and mud walls. This slum is divided into two—the better half and the non-better half. The latter consists of low-income families belonging to a 'law caste'. Their man occupation is street-vendors and beedi-making and their monthly income is Rs. 200-250.

The Salesians of the St. Joseph's complex have been working for the Pulianthope slums since 1950. During these years they have been concentrating mostly on their immediate needs through relief measures such as milkpowder, old clothes and reconstruction of huts. However, all their work was not purely relief-oriented Various departments of the domplex have been trying to go beyond relief and take long-term rehabilitation measures.

Though the Technical Institute, industrial skills have been imparted to hundreds of young men from economically weaker sections. This has enabled them to find employment in the various industrial concerns in the city. Mary Help of Christians Parish attached to the Institute was set up in 1953. The parish activities cover almost the entire slums. Apart from purely religious work among Christians, the parish also involves itself with the social and economic problems of the slum and its people irrespective of their religious affiliation. St. Thomas Dispensary is now converted into the Pulianthope Community Health Centre with the parish priest as its director.

The Don Bosco youth Centre (DBYC) started functioning

in 1951. Today it is the centre of cultural activities for over 500 young men and boys of the Pulianthope slums. Besides, it can claim with justifiable pride that nearly a generation of people have passed through its organisation. The formative influence it has had and the loyalties and support it enjoys in the slums are therefore undeniable. Equally important is the fact at present the DBYC is the single and the most effective catalysing factor and focal point of all intervention efforts and development programmes. One can claim with confidence that the DBYC alone can effectively organise the various complex forces that exist in the slums and orientate and divert them towards development since they alone have total success to the people.

One more positive factor about the DBYC in that its ideology and style of functioning have been evolving constantly during the last three decades. Realisation that the youth should go beyond cultural activities and get involved in the development of their community led to the formation of the Don Bosco Social Service Society (DBSSS). Originally thought of as a charitable organisation, the DBSSS has now evolved into a facilitator of community development in the Pulianthope slums. This new role of the society keeps clarifying in the process of the growth of the slum community. The process itself has brought a change in the work of building a new society. The members of the Youth Centre have thus got additional support and have became a force to reckon with and to be oriented to this new thinking make their society a better place to live in by eliminating the exploative situation and by fighting for justice.

The Initial Approach

All of us perceive reality to a very large extent through our prejudices. The way we see things is also a reflection of who we are, what we are, of our culture, of our education, of our value system, of our philosophy of life and our of development model. One's strategy is conditioned by this perception. This is also true about our organisation and many others. We, like many other groups, thought of the slums as a problem to be solved. The govenrnments and the muncipality often tend to view slum eradication and clearance as a solution to what they consider a housing and environmental problem.

Slowly however, we began to realise that slums are, more than anything else, a structural and human problem. They do not just happen but are created by economic, political and social decisions that are the natural consequences of certain development choices which bestow power, prestige, privileges and opportunities on a few and submerge the many into a culure of silence. These marginalised many may have no lives of their own, except what is granted to them by generous concessions of the small decision-making elite. The slum dwellers are defenceless, alone, huddled together in the bustees, frightened by something bigger than themselves.

As our outlook evolved, we realised that we have to start with the basic assumption that the slum is not merely a cluster of hutments but essentially people with a complex number of social, economic, political and cultural factors acting upon them, oppressing and manipulating them, forcing them to be what they are, killing all initiative and stifling all desire for change and improvement.

Slowly, realisation dawned on us that if we accept this position variously we also have to accept its implications. If the entire socio-political and economic structure is responsible for the slum, it is only broad-based economic and political decisions that can finally tackle the problem of slums. By the same logic, slum eradication and clearance are unrealistic solutions to a human problem.

Within the perspective, we like to see the slum not as a problem but as a solution and a very ingenious one at that. To those lonely, frightened and disorganised people daily being thrown mercilessly into the finge-world and marginalised, the slum is a haven of security. Here they find an identity and organised power which can effectively vocalise their demands, protect them from further ruthless exploitation and guarantee them immunity against a nameless and faceless administrative machinery. To this extent the slum is a community, it is a power, it is an indication of the people's power and of people's challenge to injustice.

If this resistance to exploitation becomes inconvenient or smugly, it is because the city is ruthless and intolerant towards them. If the government cannot provide security of tenure, the strongmen of the slum—the slum-dada and his agents will guarantee them security. Of course the strongman himself cannot afford to go by the niceties of laws. The slum world is a tough world. But by and large, the slum is an answer though not the best. More often than not it is the only answer available to those who are marginalised by a society which caters to the dominating groups that enact housing laws and property legislation to suit the needs of their class. If this answer is painful, it is also dangerous, for it is imposed on the marginalised groups. It reduces them to a culture of silence. But they cannot be expected to remain silent forever. We felt that sooner or later their anger of rising expectations was bound to catch up with us and that we could not any more smugly and complacently ignore the fourth world of bustees and cheris for there can be no more peace without justice.

As a result of the evolution of our outlook, it was keenly felt that the DBSSS should make more realistic and comprehensive interventions into the slum community. It cannot be satisfied with just shorterm relief measures. It must work to find lasting solutions, to know the root causes of the social evils that are in the slums and eradicate them. In other words, if there had to be any catalytic effect on the slums, the change had to start in the organisation itself.

The DBYC had to accept a more involving and more responsible role in the community—as an agent of change, through conscientising education, motivational changes, organisation of local leadership for change and constructive action. It would have to act as an interface between the government, the funding agencies and the slum community, while also working to ensure perpetuating self-government, where the role of outsiders would be more and more that of facilitators, resource personnel and not that of doers, thus avoiding the risk of social workers entirely displacing local leadership.

As an agent of social change, it was imperative that the DBYC and its social service wing (DBSSS) bring together educated people and those whose awareness has been aroused, organise them and plan with them a methodology of action that would have a catalysing influence on the community. In this process, the task of the Society was to recognise the problems of the community, vocalise the protests and complaints of the oppressed people and organise them to struggle. As a voluntary agency it should be able to face the issue actively and with a new outlook, constrained by no political or predetermined socio-economic cosiderations, and involve in this action, agencies with greater financial resources and skill.

Initially, DBSSS had viewed the slums as a quantum of houses to be built, drainages and sewages to be constructed, etc. Now it realised that it was to be its task to involve the target groups in the entire process right from the initial thinking and planning to the decision-making and execution. All have to share responsibilities and consequences of their decisions. The agency should not be primarily doers but rather serve as guides, intermediaries, resource personnel. At no time can the Society find short-cuts, sacrifice involvement of people for the sake of efficiency. Slum improvement must be the felt need of the people, their plan and their work. Nobody can do it for them. If anyone does, the slum will remain. Slums are essentially people and therefore slum improvement means investment in people-our main work will be with the people who will carry out the project.

The entire programme demands a partnership with the beneficiaries. There can be no doles. The community is theirs and it is up to them to make the community what they want it to be. We can only guide them, offer the benefits of our experience, knowledge and education.

The DBSSS is trying at present to go through this process and act in such a way that when eventually is withdraws its resources from the slum pocket, it must have a self-governing and self-perpetuating, enlightened and responsible community and leadership, needing no artificial props in the form of external personnel, services or finances. In the whole process of development, stress is not on the quantum of material output but on the education of people—to self-awareness, a sense of identity, community feeling, a sense of responsibility and a vision.

We offer no sectoral, partial or piecemeal solutions. If the forces that operate in a slum are complex, our approach to these problems also should be comprehensive, integrated. What we need is an overall development strategy which will call for programmes of action aimed at involvement in all the sectors—housing, education, employment, upward economic mobility, social amenities, community structures, health and hygiene, sanitation etc.

This programme which we then called the "Environmental Improvement Programme" had begun with a strong organisation consisting of the Salesian priests and Brothers of St. Joseph's Technical School. To this was added an efficient steering committee made up of a chairman, a director, a project director, a doctor, an auditor and two consultants.

This Committee continues even today but it has become only one of the components of a new partnership in which the 'beneficiaries' play the leading role. Besides, a funding agency (CEBEMO, Holland), the Madras Metropolitan Development Authority (MMDA) and the State Bank of India (through their Officers' Association) joined this programme. The new partnership was possible because unlike the 'Slum Improvement Board' that believed only in 'slum clearance', some persons in these bodies viewed slums not as hutments that are a problem but as people who were trying to find a solution. Thus they could become the main decision-makers.

New Objectives and Strategy

After discussion, the partners in this programme fixed fourfold goals and objectives of the project and worked out a strategy accordingly:

(a) To participate meaningfully and constructively in the much delayed and yet most urgently required plans to improve the living conditions of a third of the Madras City whom lop-sided planning has reduced to the situation they are in.

(b) To involve the members of the DBYC constructively and meaningfully in the growth of their own communities and to develop thereby a sense of belonging, community loyalties and awareness in these young men who would become the future leaders of the slum community.

(c) These aims would take their concrete shape in better living conditions, healthy surroundings, decent homes, strong community relations, a new identity as an active social group (not merely the marginalised group that they were reduced to), a sense of their personal and community worth. All these are prerequisites for their education and motivation for their new role as decision-makers and agents of change.

(d) The ultimate and the most important single objective towards which the others are only a means, is the education and conscientisation of the people. It is a humanisation process, whereby the people of the slum communities are able to play adult, responsible and creative roles in their own communities and in the national life and grow up into integrated men and women and families in which lies the future of our country.

It is hoped that our involvement in this project will help

further clarify concepts and make our slum work essentially one of building up people into responsible, aware and informed members of their community and the country.

After detailed discussions involving the steering committee, original programme known as a 'Social Housing Programmes' has undergone radical change in the following direction:

(i) An integrated slum improvement project which takes into consideration the overall needs of the entire slum.

(ii) Low-cost housing would be only one of the project components.

(iii) A well thought-out plan of action involving project planning, implementation and financial contribution by the slum community.

(iv) Involvement and cooperation with the local agencies like MMDA, SBI, voluntary agencies and others.

(v) A plan of action which involves the entire Don Bosco Youth Centre and the Educative Community in an extension service to the slums all around it.

To achieve the objectives and goals of the project, the following organised plan was carried out:

1. Twenty five members of the Don Bosco Youth Centre themselves from the slums, were selected for extension work. They have been divided into cells to work as facilitators and grass-root workers in each community helping local leaders to organise the people, at act as prudent checks on them, to be a liaison between the people and the Society. These members were given community development workers' training for a month.
2. As regards the people's organisation, there are already existing in the slums associations or sangams, some of them fairly representative. But many of them owed allegiance to political parties or some other power

> pockets. It was felt that as far as possible these should not be supplanted but helped to evolve. Only those that worked against the people needed to be replaced.

With this in view, the first task of the DBYC was to identify existing leaders and their loyalities as well as the measure of confidence they enjoy among the people. Where the existing leadership and organisation had been fairly well planned, they were strengthened. When they were viewed as part of the vested interests or 'anti-social elements', efforts were made to replace them. In cases where sangams or associations have inefficient or totally manipulated, new organisations and new leadership were established.

These groups are considered essential for the growth and organisation of the community. However, we consider multiplicity of organisations only a temporary phase. Our principle is: one slum one organisation. Slowly all existing groups will be merged into one society—the slum community—and all families will be encouraged to seek membership in their local sangams.

The committee members were made responsible for the community as a whole and for particular cells as individuals. They were assisted by cell workers from the DBYC. They constitute local leadership, involving themselves directly in project planning, discussion with the people, leading delegations to the government, banks etc. Thus it is hoped that the leaders will acquire self-confidence and that the people will begin to have greater confidence in them.

In the process of community development work the local organisation and its elected leaders, the social action core-group of members of the DBYC and the steering committee of DBSSS were involved. This was given priority since we consider growth of the community more important than physical quantum of improvement turnovers. And yet, also the material component had to be carefully planned. The bulk of office work was assigned to the DBYC members. Besides, they were assigned slums where they were expected to act in conscientising and educating the masses. However, they were not to act as a decision-making body. Their role was one of vitalisation of the community, to put into the community a new life-force and motivational changes. All major decisions were to be with the community as a whole.

Leaders worked along with the DBYC members to get into contact with the people. Informal chats with the people, meetings with the women, the youth groups, between committee members and DBYC members, DBSSS steering committee and leaders of other slum organisations were arranged to discuss problems of the whole area and not merely local issues. Meeting between the State Bank of India (SBI) its Officers' Association (SBIOA), the Madras Metropolitan Development Authority (MMDA) and the people were organised in this context of community-building. The economic inputs and housing became important instruments in this process.

The DBSSS is fully involved in the conscientisation process, but care is taken to see that the local leaders do not become figure-heads. Real authority is given to them. They are responsible for organising the meetings of the people and for identifying the beneficiaries of their area according to definite criteria.

The DBSSS contacts not only the leaders but also the individual families so that a truly integrated educational process can go on. But these direct contacts with the people will never replace the leaders who are involved in this work in order to help them to get to know their people and share with us their experiences and knowledge of the community situation.

Though we had planned the process as above, in actual practice it had to be remodified, certain elements omitted and adjusted according to the changing situation and circumstances in the field.

As noted earlier, the philanthropic attitude of charity and service was replaced with the basic principle of 'help them to help themselves.' The idea of 'giving a fish to the people' was replaced with 'teaching them to fish.' Thus a comprehensive project was worked out. The DBSSS in no way presented themselves as the 'Messiah' but struggled with the people, shared their happiness with them and had a feeling of sympathy. We entered the slums to work with the people and not for the people.

This constant change in approach was possible because, as noted earlier, we entered the slums with no prejudices and bias. We spoke to the people at their level, studied the resources of the community through the rapport established with a handful of families. It was no easy task. The basic question posed by the people was, 'What are you benefitting from it?' 'Nothing' was the answer. This gave us an opportunity to explain the role of the DBSSS in the community. At the suggestion of a few people, a community meeting was organised streetwise. It was found that a majority of the families were at the mercy of a slum data, whose livelihood was the grand collection made from the people through threats and cheating. He was able to buy the MLAs and the ministers and posed himself as the 'Saviour' of the slum-dwellers.

The entrance of the DBSSS was threat to the slum leader. Despite strong opposition from him, the DBYC members went ahead with a socio-economic survey of the families. Since then he has been the 'thorn on the rose plant', for the survey was not an academic exercise but part of the conscientisation process.

After the survey a community meeting was organised in which the elders suggested that each street should elect a representative as their leader. The DBSSS, with the help of DBYC members, conducted streetwise meetings in which their leader was elected. The elected leaders of each street together formed the 'Dr. Ambedkar Nagar Kudiyiruppor (Residents' Sangam' in Ambedkar Nagar. In Sastri Nagar the problem differed slightly. There was a registered sangam dominated by a political party. Yet, considering the principles of Community

Organisation, the DBSSS intervened with the hope of re-organising the sangam and making it more representative of the Sastri Nagar slum dwellers. This never came through. So streetwise meetings were called in which a male and a female leader were elected for every two streets. The elected leaders formed the 'Sastri Nagar Makkal (People's) Podunala (welfare) Mandram' (Association).

Economic Aspect

Today our emphasis and concentration is on a viable and stable organisation in Ambedkarnagar because of the strong social and legal obstacles it poses. The slum-dada and his gang were soon displaced by the elected leaders. Regular sangam meetings and streetwise community meetings instilled hope in the people and also courage to fight against the exploiters. These meetings were the means of communication by which the role of DBSSS, MMDA, SBI, SBIOA and DBYC was defined and the project was discussed at great length, thus turning it into a community enterprise. When economic and other aspects were introduced, they became part of the community's programme. Negotiations with commercialised banks. MMDA, Tamil Nadu Slum Clearance Board (TNSCB) etc., were initiated.

After many rounds of talks with the various organisations, the State Bank of India through its Officers' Association was willing to sponsor Health Service and Income Supplementation Programmes through Differential Rate of Interest (DRI) loans. The MMDA agreed to take up the three slums under the World Bank Slum Improvement programmes. A proposal was sent to CEBEMO Holland, regarding the comprehensive slum rehabilitation programme which was tentatively approved. It was meant only to implement the aspects that were not locally available. Thus, a team with resources was formed consisting of MMDA, SBI, SBIOA, CEBEMO and DBSSS.

Besides conducting a Socio-Economic cum Health Survey, the MMDA engineers conducted a geoditic survey of the area.

Later they worked on a proposed improvement plan which was studied with the people and revised several times.

A Community Health Centre was started in the DBSSS campus which is partly sponsored by the SBIOA. Three para-medical workers attend to the health care of every family with emphasis on the promotive and preventive aspects without neglecting the curative elements. Efforts are made to create a relationship between the doctor and the people through his regular visits to the area. At the time of writing in early 1980, 300 hundred families have registered in the Centre. We hope to have all the 1024 families registered as the Centre progresses. The workers use immunisation and nutrition as part of their educational programme. However, the Centre is still run by the DBSSS. Persons are being trained and the infrastructure constructed and the people expected to take over its running and maintenance in a short time.

As regards the Income Supplementation, Programme, the small scale vendors are assessed by the grass-roots level worker and the DBSSS and then referred to the State Bank of India. The field officer of the bank makes a physical assessment after which they are given a loan under the DRI schemes. To date, about 48 vendors have benefitted through this scheme. The SBI is working on a comprehensive scheme to help beedi workers, post-makers and fruit vendors.

The Madras Sarvodaya Sangh, in collaboration with th MMDA, has come forward with an Employment Generation Programme. About 30 women are employed in the rural Muslin Centre which is at present in the DBSSS campus. They were given a monthly stipend and daily wages depending on the output. We did face a failure in this programme. After the training period, the women were not able to earn as they were expected to. After a careful study it was found that the Charkas were not productive and so the Centre had to be closed down for 2 months. The introduction of the new Model Charkas (NMC) brought the women back to work. They have been on the NMC for 2 months and at present they earn between Rs. 3 and 4 per day. As it progresses we expect their earnings to increase. This Centre too will soon be shifted to the slumn.

Present State

A foundation has been laid for this comprehensive slum rehabilitation project. But why is it that this project has now come to a standstill? In the following paragraphs we wish to bring to light the various problems, obstacles and failures faced by the voluntary group, the people and the collaborating agencies.

As expressed earlier, the slum leader was displaced by the elected leaders of Ambedkar Nagar. His pocket was thinning down. Being a man with no scruples, he encroached upon the adjacent vacant lands which had been reserved for community purposes. He demarcated them into smaller plots and sold them for Rs. 200 or Rs. 250 each. The Madras Corporation, on receiving complaints from the people of Ambedkar, Nagar, dismantled the huts thrice. Fearing further action by the Corporation, a petition was filed by the slum leader against the Corporation. An interim injunction was granted by which the petitioners were prohibited from putting up new huts and the Corporation prevented from removing the existing ones. The case was pending in court for a year with no authority to fight it. The DBSSS got themselves involved and fought the case. The slum-data's petition was dismissed. Yet, there is no one to implement the court order. The Corporation, with their red-tapism, allowed the huts to remain. As a result, more and more huts were put up. From 15 huts, today there are about 80, and a concrete structure too.

When the corporation hesitated to act, the people of Ambedkar Nagar organised themselves into a group of 2,000 and marched to the Secretariate demanding justice in expediting the MMDA programme. The Minister promised to look into the matter and, as usual, no action has been taken. In the meanwhile the slum leader began fortifying his territory by constructing a language school which is today built into a place of worship. Soon the issue was made into a religious one—a slum dweller filed a petition in the court pleading for protection to be granted to the house of worship.

The government had just then passed a Government Order stating that huts constructed after 30-6-77 could be considered as illegal encroachments and removed. The geoditic survey of MMDA proved that the huts constructed on the vacant land fell under this category. But who is to implement this Government Order? No one dared. And the huts remain intact!

During the community meetings, the people were made aware of this injustice. They visited government offices in small groups. Meeting the officials became a regular feature, yet with no results. We were given to understand that it was a DBSSS project and that the Corporation was doing us a favour by removing the huts! Pretexts were found to delay action. The Lok Sabha elections were an excuse, Pongal was an excuse, and the huts remain intact!

The people of Ambedkar Nagar had taken a decision not to allow the government authorities to start physical improvements without evicting the illegal encroachers. It has become a 'prestige issue' for the people. The process of Community Development was centred round this single issue.

When the people realised that the government machinery would not act, they resorted to direct action. They had confrontation with the slum leader's gang, staged demonstration before the secretariate, dharnas before the police station. . . . The huts remain intact but today even a child of eight is aware of the issues and the whole community is united behind this action.

Conclusion

It has been a long and difficult process which still remains incomplete. The problems remain unsolved because many have a vested interest in keeping the slum dwellers under their control. The political history of our country would show that the economically weaker sections are a must for the survival of politicians and of the dominating elite that supports them. Under the guise of slum improvement programme, the slum dwellers are exploited. Given the sense of insecurity and the marginalised state in which they live, they are exposed to exploitation by vested interests, since the protection provided by the anti-social elements is the only security they can find.

They cannot make much progress unless they are helped to become aware of this exploitative situation and take charge of their own society by creating alternative leadership to supplant those who exploit them by posing as their leaders. This new leadership emerges when people are enabled to act on the awareness within themselves. Rallying round a concrete issue like the one mentioned in this paper will help the emergence of leadership.

That is where the voluntary agencies have to play their role. Often such agencies take up a charitable approach because of the long and difficult process involved in developing individual human beings and communities. This can make the people dependent on the charitable organisation. In fact, dependence may be transferred from the exploiter to the voluntary agency and without their realising it, the charitable organisations may take up the slum-data's place. This will only encourage the people to be at the receiving end and never become masters of their own destiny. The role of voluntary agencies in such projects is to be facilitators and not themselves become agents of social change. The facilitators can never replace the people.

Under certain circumstances the voluntary agency may have to coordinate same activities. In this project for example, it was a fourtier coordination CEBEMO, MMDA, SBI and the people. But this has to be a temporary measure and is meant only to facilitate the growth of local leadership and the first step in the process of education.

As agency cannot decide in advance how long it will remain. It depends entirely on how long the local community requires an external agent. In our case, the former 'leaders' controlled by the slum-data have lost their credibility and the people have confidence in the new leaders. However, as should be obvious from the way the G.O. is ignored, the former still remain strong. Hence the people may still need some support from the DBSSS for a year or two till the latter leaders get strong. But already now we have started the process of withdrawal.

In this particular case, the task of DBSSS was rendered relatively easy by the existence of the DBYC. They provided the infrastructure required for the emergence of new leaders. Even this leadership could be easily compromised by governmental inaction. If the governmental machinery is unable to implement its own GO's, it can only encourage those who have a vested interest in exploiting the people. In such a situation the voluntary agency always has the temptation to use its influence with the government officials. Such a posture can only continue its role as a middleman between the people and those who have power—the government, the funding agencies, etc. But this is a short cut. Though the process of education and organisation may be long and tedious, that may be the only way for the marginalised groups to free themselves from their oppressive state.

The supportive role played by the external agent and by the economic content may be some of the replicable aspects of this programme. No project is totally replicable but only a few elements can be followed by others. In our project, the main replicable aspects may be the educational process that used the MMDA housing programme and illegal encroachment as a rallying point for people's organisation. The economics of the project may change, so also the details of the process. But the general approach may be valid in many other cases.

Similarly, the relations between the voluntary agency that acts as facilitator, the government' banks and other funding agencies and the people may be another replicable element. This is so especially because of the process DBSSS itself has gone through. What has happened in our case is not merely the growth of the slum community but the evolution of the DBSSS. From a charitable organisation it has evolved into a group that plays the supportive role of a facilitator. Its consequences are seen in the attitudes of its members.

To conclude, if this project was aimed at a quantum of materials, one would have seen the project through. But since the ultimate aim of the project is to educate and conscientise the people and help the slum community make its own decisions towards a better living, a long time is needed. As Bernard Berenson said, 'Against human nature one cannot legislate. One can only try to educate it, and that is a slow process with only a distant hope of success.'

11

Awakening Dalit Tribals

Exploitation, even in its most oppressive form is part of history both in India and elsewhere. In our own country it has been legitimised more than elsewhere in the name of the caste hierarchy which considers those at the bottom of the social rung inferior beings. Though the tribals do not belong to the caste hierarchy as such, the dominating groups continue considering them inferior. The oppressed groups in their turn have interiorised this low self-image and find it difficult to organise themselves in order to demand their rights. The existence of internal collaborators of the oppressors in the group of the oppressed makes any movement much more difficult.

That is where the role of groups from outside comes in awakening the tribals or other oppressed to the reality of their exploitation and denial of human rights. If not on its guard, such an outside group, while freeing them from their present oppressors, can easily make them dependent on themselves. No community can grow unless animation comes from within. This paper will study the action of one such group that acted as facilitators of a movement. They used health as an entry point but were always clear that it was to be only a tool for education.

Area and People

A mere ten kms. outside Berhampur in Southern Orissa, and you are at the foothills of the Kerandimals. Not many of the townspeople are aware that this hilly region is the home of a few thousand Khond tribals. Long long ago, several small kingdoms flourished in these hills—the Chikiti, the Mahuri, the Khemandi Raj—to whom these tribals owed their allegiance. These kingdoms have long since crumbled and disappeared but the tribals continue to live on in neglect and isolation, on the memories of their past glory.

The Khonds live in small scattered villages on the hill slopes unconnected by roads. They speak Kuri which has no written script. Oriya is used for communicating with outsiders. It is also the medium of formal education.

These tribals depend largely on the forests for their livelihood and theirs is in fact a firewood economy. Most men and women go daily to the jungle to cut firewood which is them dried, cut to equal size, tied into neat bundles and carried down long and winding hill paths to be sold to the firewood sowcars who wait with their bullock carts at the foot of the hills. These merchants usually exchange rice and salt for firewood. The exchange is usually to the advantage of the sowcar —a low price for the wood and a high price for the poorest quality of rice, etc.

Besides cutting firewood, the tribals spend the rainy season in their bogodo cultivation, *i.e.*, hillside shift cultivation of several indigenous grains and vegetables which on an average feed a family for two or three months in the year. Tribals living on the lower hill slopes own small individual tracts of land which they have reclaimed from the jungle. In these tracts they grow ragi and maize. In general, the tribals are poor agiculturists and there is a definite under-utilisation of existing resources of land, water etc.

The forests yield an abundance of fruit. Many of these trees—Mango, Tamarand, Jack fruit, etc.—have either been planted by the tribals or they have been enjoying their fruits from times immemorial. Petty non-tribal traders invade the tribal villages seasonally to purchase the produce of these trees. Paradoxically, while these petty traders in forest produce depend on the tribals for their livelihood, in reality they have become the masters and the tribals, their easy victims.

Despite the existence of several government primary schools in the tribals villages, the level of literacy is as low as 3 per cent. This is because hardly any of the teachers attend the schools. Almost all the other government schemes and infra-structural institutions function in the same way as the education Department. On the block map this area has been outlined in red and noted as 'risky'. This is discreetly understood by all functionaries to mean that no government servant and need risk entering the area.

Unlike the Khonds of Phulbani and Koraput district who have a rich cultural heritage of song and dance, the Kerandimal Khonds are conspicuous by the absence of these cultural forms. Generally speaking, the tribals of Kerandimals reveal a marked dilution of the intrinsic tribal character. This 'acculturation' may be because of the proximity to Berhampur, geographical isolation from the main body of Khonds, ethnic penetration, etc., 'collectivity' and 'co-operative effort' are low key though a limited form of common ownership does exist in most villages in the institution of the 'khoto' which may be in the shape of trees, land or money. The leadership of the village has by and large exercised full control over the 'khoto' with very little accountability to the rest of the village. A few of the tribal leaders are themselves the biggest enemies and exploiters of their people.

In years gone by, the tribals brewed their own mild liquor from 'Mahua'. Today the 'manufacture' of liquor is controlled by a small group of non-tribals called 'Sundis'. The tribals have become their 'wage labourers'. Ammonium Sulphate is used to prepare this illicit poisonous liquor which is then supplied to Berhampur and also sold among the trivals. Today alcoholism is a major problem among the tribals—that being one of the reasons why they cannot break away from the stranglehold of their backwardness and powerlessness.

The role of the woman in the tribal society is important. She is really the backbone of the family. It is she who brings home the day's food while the man often relaxes at home. Tribal women generally enjoy greater freedom of movement and expression than their non-tribal counterparts. But despite these concessions, they receive a poor bargain. They are often subject to the barbaric behaviour of an alcoholic husband who is still the head of the family and the main decision-maker, though not necessarily the bread-winner.

Shaping and controlling the lives of the tribal people is a powerful force, Black Magic. So steeped are they in their superstitious beliefs, that introducing them to a rational system of thinking is often impossible. The tribals of the Kerandimals are doubtless a fascinating combination of simplicity, and complexity of strength and weakness, of selfishness and integrity.

Besides the tribals, we are also in contact with some of the non-tribal villages in the area. These villages which are all on the plains, tend to be large and heterogeneous. Many of them have a very large landless Harijan population.

Gram Vikas

As long back as 1969-70, a group of young students of Madras University became involved in an analysis of the existing educational system as the principal means whereby the social malaise afflicting the country was perpetuated. The group was not native to the reality that the golden age of student life could very well be spent in romanticising about the poor and calling for the overthrow of the existing social order, because these same heralds of change and revolution could, after completing their studies, retrace their steps, make peace with their conscience and find 'each for himself, a comfortable niche in the establishment. Several members of the core group decided to opt out of the usual niche-seeking race and to commit themselves in ways that were as yet not fully unknown, to the challenge of social transformation. 'Young Students Movement for Development' (YSMD) was registered as a society in Madras at this point, as a concretisation of these lofty ideals and thoughts.

A group of YSMD went to Orissa in 1971, in response to a plea for relief volunteers, following the cyclone and tidal wave that devastated its coastal areas. When relief came to an end, a few of these young people remained behind and began an agriculture-based development programme. For several reasons and constraints, the group had to leave the area a few years later after handing over what remained of the programme to local hands.

Gram Vikas has its origins in this group of YSMD which moved to Ganjam District of Orissa in 1977. The experience and process of the years from 1991 to 1977 have left their mark on their thinking and composition. As the group became more localised, the need for more relevant organisation was felt and Gram Vikas was registered in Orissa in January 1979 to facilitate local participation and solidarity. It is a mixed group made up of Oriyas and non-Oriyas and secular in character, having among its members persons of various religious denominations most of them Hindus but also a few Christians and others. They do not have any political party or official religious affiliation.

In the summer of 1977 Gram Vikas first became aware of these tribals who lived in the Kerandimals. As first perceived by us, their main problems seemed to be of 'identity', 'acculturation', 'integration', 'exploitation', and 'lack of 'organisation'. Today, after a period of three years wherein we have had a much closer and more intense involvement with the tribals, we think that our initial perceptions have only been confirmed and strengthened. We began to ask ourselves if there was not something which could be done to revitalise these people, to support them in an effort to take their legitimate place in society—a society which had forgotten their existence. A decision was taken to find out more about these people who lived in obscurity.

Our initial contact was with 11 villages at the foot of the hills. A simple socio-economic survey was made more with the purpose of establishing a friendly rapport than for the efficient collection of cold statistical data. On these visits we carried with us a medical kit for treating minor ailments. The immediate relief that we brought to many, especially those suffering from malaria (and there were many) was the main reason for our quick acceptance among the tribals. However, it took quite some time for us to gain their full confidence.

What struck us early in our contact among the tribals was the complete absence of a functioning health service to meet even their basic curative needs. Malaria and tuberculosis appeared to be rampant and accounted for the loss of many days when in the case of the former just 4 tablets of Chloroquin could have brought great relief. So we decided to begin an awareness building process using 'health' as an entry point until other avenues of need and involvement which were as yet unknown or controversial, could be more carefully explored. After several discussions with the people, we initiated a low-key, simple health programme to meet what we observed, and what the tribals also voiced, as their formost need.

The Technical aspects of our health programme included simple curative services, mother and child health services, chronic disease control and environmental sanitation. Its non-technical aspects centred round community participation and control of the whole programme. With this in view, we concentrated on village health workers training, formation of village communities and a health insurance scheme. Everyone of the 11 villages as a whole participated in the scheme. We visited all the villages daily.

From the outest we were clear that our ultimate goal was

not mere achievement of 'health' which we knew would be very difficult because of the tremendous problems in the field of 'health concerns'. But we knew that these problems could not be separated from the other aspects of the total rural hopelessness complex. So, keeping in mind that 'health' was directly related to the economic and social base of the tribals, we constantly used our involvement through 'health' to build-up awareness in the community on other aspects of their lives.

The basic condition for working in a village was the formation of a 'village committee' that would function as the leadership group. This was done to reinforce the vital aspect of community participation and control and also with the long-sighted intention of developing a grass roots organisation among the tribals. Ultimately, what we had in mind was the unionisation of all the tribals living across the Kerandimals.

People's Initiative

Even in the early days, these committees were never really pure 'health committees' and gradually their scope expanded to include almost all aspects of life. The entire village meets once a month with some of the volunteers of Gram Vikas. Besides the village level meeting, all committee members come together every month to determine the needs of each village and to work out a plan of action with the resources available within and without the community. In village Nunighore, for example, all the children were having scabies. The reason was ascribed to lack of a water source for bathing. A well was needed. Where were they to get money for that? So an application was written by the committee to the BDO asking him to provide a drinking water well in the village.

We see instances like these as the first faltering steps the people take on a road that is new and unknown. It is the beginning of their effort to acquire their rights that have been denied to them. Perhaps the people had so far viewed the sarcar (government) as the benevolent sowcar who bestowed a few favours on them such as an occasional sanctioning of a well. They had, also in the past, put in many applications for the 'favour'. But now they began to see themselves as human beings and realised that their humanity gave them a natural right to clean drinking water and that such a right did not have to be bestowed on them by a benefactor. Consequently, this new application, though following the same old format at the previous ones, was of a totally different nature. This time they were acting as human beings and demanding it as a right from those who had deprived them of what belonged to them.

By this time we knew almost every man and woman in the villages by name. As the rapport between the people and the group grew, the people began to voice spontaneously their problems and constraints in other spheres of their lives. More important, the tribals began to identify us as their friends, as persons who stood for certain principles of integrity and service.

Thus, within about 8 months, what had begun as a health programme grew into an integrated development programme, with the people taking the initiative in specific issues with the support and encouragement of the group.

Though agriculture as practised by the tribals is in a primitive stage, it is still an important function. We took our time to study and collect facts on the entire agricultural system of the tribals. As specific agriculture-related activities. we organised several workshops for men and women in collaboration with AFPRO and the block in 1978 and early 1979. Besides the opportunity to come together, share ideas, etc., these were important occasions for the people to meet and voice their problems to various officers and functionaries of the district—BDO, AEO, VLW, SFDA Director, Banks, Co-op. Institutions, etc.

Historically, credit and government subsidies have always been appropriated by the rich and the powerful. We found this to be the case in our area as well. Except for a few who had taken loans from an almost defunct, corrupt co-op. society, the majority of the people had no access to fair credit.

Most tribals did not own a pair of bullocks and were unable to buy one since they could not get loans. One of the reasons for under-utilisation of existing land and water resources was the lack of viable credit facilities for agricultural development. We recognised economic development as a support and as a foundation for democracy itself. We further recognised the need for adequate agricultural credit inputs as a stimulus for increased agricultural activity. So we decided to act as catalytic agents in bringing credit facilities to the marginalised sections of society.

The United Commercial Bank, Berhampur, came forward to finance the tribals at 4 per cent interest under the DRI scheme, with a 50 per cent subsidy on loans from the SFDA. Almost all families in the villages where we operate have by now received loans for various agricultural development and related purposes.

At about this time, we tried to introduce the concept of Young Farmers' Clubs in the villages. 8-10 such clubs were formed but the idea never really took root and these clubs have more or less fizzled out. Today, while analysing the causes of the failure of our efforts in this direction, we see more clearly why we failed to get our 'Young Farmers' Clubs' going. Besides being our idea, we ourselves were apparently not fully clear on why we wanted to start them, what would be the activities of these groups, what kind of initial support these would require, who among us would give this support etc. Lacking the basic clarity of purpose and definition of its objective—wanting to be a leadership group or a mere farmers' group or of integrating the two—we generally failed to sustain even the few groups that did get formed.

The tribal philosophy is to five from day to day and there is seldom a question of surplus money to meet unexpected expenditures—illness, death or even anticipated expenditure like marriage, social feasts, festivals etc. The tribals therefore contact loans from the money lenders too meet these consumptional needs. Interest usually ranges between 60 per cent and 15 per cent. Since these loans contribute nothing to production, it becomes impossible to provide for their repayment and the tribal is further entrapped in an ever-widening circle of exploitation. A small savings scheme was started around February 1978 as a possible solution to the problem of indebtedness in collaboration with the Punjab National Bank.

It was linked to the availability of institutional loans for consumptional needs, the idea being that common savings would be used to finance later needs. Though the whole concept was completely new to the tribals, the small savings scheme has caught on in every family and today there are nearly Rs. 60,000.00 in the savings accounts. However, from the beginning it was clear to us that a bank account was an end in itself but only a means to help the people free themselves from the money lender and get from the commercial institutions loans that are their right.

Emergence of People's Power

Something has already been written about the exploitative system whereby a non-tribal group called the Sundis manufacture illicit liquor in the depths of the jungles using tribal labourers. Working for the Sundis is apparently a good job—Rs. 4 per day plus a free meal and liquor. But this seemingly rosy job carries with it several hidden risks and evils which are not immediately perceived by the tribals. Illness, addiction to alcohol, police cases, mounting debt to the Sundis gradually sap every drop of the man's mental, physical and economic strength.

Despite our awareness of the problems of alcoholism and Sundi exploitation, we reasoned that time was not ripe for any direct action. But around December 1978 we were more or less forced into confrontation with the Sundis.

On December 11th 1978, a tribal of village Banyamari was assaulted by the Sundis because he had dared to ask his Sundi sowcar for the wages that were long due to him. The day following this incident, the Sundis further beat up his mother and wife and took away his goats. This incident was reported to us by the people of Banyamari who asked our support in action that they would take against the Sundis. At first we were very sceptical about interfering in what we felt was a temporary skirmish between the Sundis and the tribals. Moreover, almost all the people of this village were employed by the Sundis and were entirely in their grip. It could be bad strategy to start action so soon.

In any case we went to the village that night and to our great surprise found every adult member of the village gathered for the meeting and not one was drunk. It is difficult to recapture on paper the fire and spirit of that meeting which continued late into the night. For the first time, the people began to unravel the intricacies of their exploitation by the Sundis. The mystifying vial of tribal exploitation through liquor was demystified. A unanimous decision was taken to drive all the Sundis out of the village. Besides this, no member of the village was to be allowed to harbour materials or equipment of the Suudis in their homes nor would the Sundis be allowed to distil alcohol anywhere within the boundaries of tribal land or to sell it in the village. Wisely, a decision against police action was taken, the tribals knowing better than us the futility of such recourse.

The young men of the village further reasoned that merely throwing out the Sundis from their village would not check the entire system of Sundi exploitation of tribals. They decided that time had come for a well organised total liberation of all the tribals from alcoholism and exploitation. They took it upon themselves to spread the news of the Banyamari incident to all the other villages and ask for the support and co-operation of every tribal, for what had happened in Banyamari could well happen elsewhere.

One week later, an area meeting was called. All the villages except one adopted the resolution of village Banyamari. This village was also finally made to the line by a group of young, newly awakened tribal men of that village.

All during this time, we in YSMD had to take some hard decisions. In the period preceeding the Banyamari incident, we had concentrated only on awakening the tribals to the evils of excessive alcohol and the exploitative relations of production that existed between Tribals and Sundis. Now, for the first time, we were on a course of open confrontation with the Sundis, without fully knowing the strength of the tribals to stand by their resolution and decision. But during the initial period of the boycott we were continually amazed and humbled by the strength and leadership of some young and old leaders who were the rallying force behind the tribal struggle for liberation.

During the initial period of the boycott, various meetings took place to strengthen the tribals in understanding the process that was taking place, of their strength in unity and determination to end what was being newly understood by several tribals as an exploitative system. It was a busy period. Alternative work had to be found for those who had been working for the Sundis. The Orissa Forest Corporation which was cutting down trees in the area was contacted for giving employment to the tribals.

The Corporation was only too willing to absorb the tribals in their felling operations because they needed people to work for them. The more work that got done, probably the greater the profits to the Corporation or rather to the immediate employers of the tribals. The supervisors of the OFC were probably more interested in their immediate profit than in the battle of the Sundis against the tribals. Today, perhaps, given an opportunity, the Sundis, OFC, Forest Dept., the functionaries of various other government departments such as Health, the Block, Education and money lenders would more consciously unify their forces against our group, the tribals.

Underneath the apparent calm prevailing was a smouldering tension, especially in village Purunapatna—the hornet's nest as it were. The Sundi of this village who was also running a commodities shop refused to stop selling liquor in it. One evening, some young men of the village seized his liquor and deposited it with the local sarpanch. That night the Sundi's elder brother made an apology to the sarpanch in writing and promised not to sell liquor again in the village. But the very next morning, the Sundis were back in the village. They daringly beat up one of the young men before the stunned village.

Following this incident in village Purunapatna, another big meeting was held at which nearly 200 people were present. It was decided at this meeting to give Gopi Sahu 24 hours to make a public apology and should he refuse to apologise, the people proposed to go on a mass protest to Berhampur to make known to the authorities the violence prepared against the tribals and to ask for protection and redress. Gopi Sahu refused to apologise.

On 8th February 1979, the tribal leaders called on every tribal family of the area to be represented in a procession that the Adivasis would take in silent protest to Berhampur. On the 9th morning, near about 600 people collected at Narasinghpur from where they marched two by two 15 kms to Berhampur. They presented a memorandum to the Revenue Divisional Officer and to the Sub-divisional Officer (S.D.O.). In the memorandum they alleged that Gopi Sahu and his brother Paramananda Sahu virtually kept the tribals under perennial bondage. They remained the officials that the road linking the tribal lands with Berhampur and other cities was in such a state of disrepair that not even jeeps could pass through it. Wild elephants causing depredation in the area. But all their representations had been unless.

The S.D.O. at first refused to appear before the people to hear their complaints. So the people decided to sit in the courtryard of the S.D.O. Finally, the Additional District

Magistrate came out to meet them. She promised an official enquiry into the harassment of tribals and legal action against those Sundis involved in illicit distillation of liquor.

The walk back to the village was hard and exhausting. Most reached their villages around midnight. But the tribals were triumphant. For the first time they saw proof of their hidden strength through collective action. Never before had the town of Berhampur witnessed such a well organised mass of protesting people and tribals at that! Many local newspapers carried news of the unusual procession of tribal men and women whose proximity to Berhampur was hitherto unknown to most. The All India Radio also carried a broadcast of the event.

The official action that followed is another story. What was significant was the emergence of people's power among the tribals—the emrgence of a new consciousness—precisely what the tribals were supposed to lack. For those of us who had been working with the people, the explicit understanding of what they were already but confusedly aware of before the march to Berhampur, this was a triumphant moment!

Movement to Redeem Mortgaged Tribal Property

Land and trees are the instruments of production and gainful economic activity among the tribals. An outsider who can take over the ownership of these means of production can slowly take total control over the life of the tribals, using the commonest method of exploitation. As in many other parts of India, prevalent also in this region was an outrageous system of mortgage, whereby the ownership of the best tribal property has been slowly but steadily passing out of tribal hands.

Around the summer of 1978, faced with this glaring injustice of usurious exploitation; the team decided to take this up as an issue of education and liberation through collective action by the tribals. Not one of the tribals know of the existence of the moratorium on rural indebtedness. This ignorance speaks for itself of the effectiveness of so many government policies and the state of their implementation. This one was a highly published policy to free rural people from indebtedness and human bondage. A campaign to mass educate and conscientize the people on the existing and flourishing system of usury was begun sometime around September-October 1978.

This was the core issue of every meeting—big, small, personal, causal—with the people. And gradually they began to understand the dynamics of the social and economic order that exists on the exploitation of man by man, that nourishes and sustains social oppression and injustice. Initially, the people's response was weak: "What can we do to free ourselves? We are after all only tribals". This was a genuine challenge. They had come to think of themselves as 'only tribals'. They had internalised the low self-image that had been imposed on them by their exploiters and had come to consider themselves as a group that cannot do much.

This self-image had to be changed if they had to become agents of change and not merely passive sufferers of events imposed on them by others. They had to be helped to get out of this attitude and to acquire self-confidence and trust in their group as a community that can act. This took time and finally the People's Council decided to take this up as an issue somewhere near December 1978 and accordingly plans were made. Right from the initial stages, the tribals insisted that justice and fairness should weigh in their approach to this issue. This is because of the inherent tribal quality to honour all debts and obligations. The movement was to take the following shape:

1. Survey of the amount of indebtedness in each village.
2. Preparation of the people and leaders to face the sowcars.
3. Areawise meetings with the sowcars—something like a "People's Court" where the tribals themselves would

arbitrate each and every case of mortgage. Judgement would be just and impartial, *i.e.*, if the sowcar had taken more than his due through interest and use of land and trees, he would be paid nothing. But where he had taken less than the capital amount borrowed, he would be compensated as per the rate of interest at which tribals were receiving loans from banks.

4. Utilization of collective strength of the people to physically protect the property of tribals in cases where the sowcars refused to acknowledge the judgement.

5. In those cases wherein the sowcars had to be compensated monetarily, a loan would be made to the individual tribals if he himself could not pay this amount.

6. Every tribal whose case was arbitrated by the Court would have to give in writing to the village Committee that henceforth he would strive not to remortage his property and if in times of dire need for money this could not be avoided, the committee would first be consulted. This clause had been added because of an attempt to strengthen the village 'khoto' or common property, whereby is is hoped that non-productive credit needs can be met within the village at fairer terms.

7. Those tribals who received monetary assistance to compensate their sowcars would declare in writing that the village had control over the land until such time as the loan was repaid. Repayment of the loan would be made by giving half the value of every crop received from the property that had been released, until such time as the loan was repaid.

8. No tribal whose land had been released, would be allowed to keep his land fallow. If in season he could not cultivate any part of his land, the committee would have the right to lease his land out for the season to

the landless families of the village on a share--cropping basis.

With this as the matrix of the strategy for releasing mortgaged land and trees, the movement took off. At every stage the sowcars worked out a new strategy to sabotage the movement. They tried their best to tempt key leaders and witnesses with bribes, other inducements and with persuasive arguments aimed at touching the intrinsic tribal loyalty. Several of them threatened the tribals with dire consequences if they persisted in their pursuit for liberty from bondage. Knowing that a few of us in the group were Christians, they circulated a rumour that we were in fact Christian missionaries in the garb of social workers and that the ulterior motive of YSMD was mass conversion of the tribals and appropriation of their property at the most appropriate time. These rumours were meant to produce confusion in the minds of the tribals who trusted us as their friends.

The money lenders could not succeed because the relations of power had changed. Our years together had produced a broad-based organisational structure and alliance between Gram Vikas and the people on the one hand and the people among themselves on the other. A new People's organisation had grown with its 'cadre' of 'workers' at every level, among women and men of every village. Of the greatest importance was the existence of some strong and determined leaders whose presence was crucial in resisting the exploiters and preventing them from penetrating the collectivity and breaking it up.

Besides, we discussed the issues openly with the people without any hesitation. The 'issue of conversion' came up for discussion in many places. When it was raised at one of the meetings in village Singabadi, we made our stand very clear to all those present there. We stated that we were not in the area to coerce people into adopting alien religious, but we insisted that as educated. enlightened people we did not subcribe to the caste feelings and divisions among them. We accepted only two castes or groups of people: the rich and the poor. But we also told them that we were in a vulnerable position because of the past tradition of missionary activities in the area. That there was such an effort at 'conversion' was part of history and could not be denied. But we insisted that we had 'Time' as our only ally—'Time' would prove our intentions.

Briefly, the confidence which the people had acquired in their own 'collectivity' and the open dialogue which we had maintained with them had changed the relations of power in the area. The people were closer to Gram Vikas than to the sowcars and our alliance proved stronger than the threats of the money lenders who were forced to capitulate. Those sowcars who refused to accept the arbitration of the people were asked to take their cases to a count of law. Several of them actually approached their lawyers who seemed to have counselled them against such a step and told them that their case was hopeless and could even boomerang on the complainants. This forced them to come to terms with the People's courts. They attempted not to bring their written documents, to exaggerate loan claims and under-estimate the amount of interest enjoyed by them in the form of cash or use of land and trees. But these were harshly dealt with.

Initially, cases pertaining to mango, jack fruit and tamarind trees were taken up because of their approaching fruit-bearing season. After they were declared released without compensation, the most important period was in physically protecting them from the vengeful and angry sowcars. And this, the people have done thoroughly. With the exception of a few cases, no sowcar has enjoyed the fruits of tribal trees in the area since then.

Following the release of trees came the release of land. This in fact is still going on. Today nearly 60 villages have been covered by this movement. We are in the process of compiling and analysing the individual cases of release and hope to prepare a documentation of the same. This has been one concrete issue and struggle with the greatest learning value for us and the people. It has given the tribals tremendous confidence in themselves.

One more interesting aspect has been discovery of the same form of indebtedness to a limited extent among the tribals themselves, *i.e.*, some tribals lending money to others and keeping them under their control. As a strategy, we decided to initially ignore the existence of the same system within the tribals themselves, because we did not want to risk upsetting the broader aims of the movement. We reasoned that the second step should be directed against the internal contradictions. And true enough this is what happened. Spontaneously, people began to question the money lenders within their own committee and to exercise the same forms of judgement as was done in the case of external exploitation.

This has not met with total success. But exploitation within the community has to be tackled and internal collaboration with the exploiter abolished if a community of the exploited has to grow. Internal collaboration with the exploiter is seen much more clearly in the marketing sector where they get easily exploited because of their lack of bargaining power for a better price and the links of the traders if with some tribals. The bulk of tribal produce: tamarined, mangoes, jackfruit, vegetables, maize, firewood, eating leaves, tooth sticks etc, is now purchased through middlemen whose margin of profit is probably greater than that of the tribals. These middlemen, because of their long acquaintance with the tribals, have an indirect hold over other aspects of the tribal life as well. Any attempt to get a better price is settled by the middlemen with the help of tribals with whom they keep in contact.

We have often discussed whether an alternative system of marketing could be worked out to stop the existing exploitation by the petty traders. But this has never materialised because of the scattered nature of the villages, the lack of entrepreneurial skills among the tribals, the strong personal ties that several traders have with the tribals and the petty nature of this exploitation. We have always rejected the idea of introducing a government tribal marketing society in the area, because objective studies reveal that such societies, by the own internal dynamics, become bigger exploiters of the people than the existing petty traders.

The above problems connected with marketing and indebtedness among the tribals raise a very important issue of internal collaboration with the exploiters. No colonialism is possible without internal collaborators. So also, no exploitation is possible for a long time unless the economic, organisational, cultural and other power of the oppressed is broken and collaborators from among the oppressed are found. Apart from the fact that the existence of informers of the dominators in the group of the dominated renders the task of their organisation extremely difficult, the oppressed themselves become oppressors—and this is the worst form of oppression.

Today this is our greatest problem. Existing among the tribals is a small band of men who have been their traditional leaders: the ward members, the dealers for sugar and kerosene, the 'friends' of the local petty politicians, who are now becoming petty government contractors and achieving new economic positions for themselves. We have the example of a tribal Sarpanch who is playing his role as Sarpanch almost as perfectly, if not better than, the non-tribal Sarpanches. This problem will soon have to be tackled and brought more directly into the open at every forum of the people.

Strategy for Uniting the Poor

Around mid-1979 we realised that our involvement was largely with tribal communities and that this was being 'used' against us by external vested interests such as money lenders, land owners, Sundis, traders etc., who had an axe to grind with us due to our direct participation in tribal emancipation from years of exploitative usury and official neglect. They bring up the issue of 'conversion' again and again but do not succeed with the people who do not trust them any more.

Another more dangerous trend was to play upon the existing tribal fear of the 'Bauris' and 'Dandasis' as the scheduled castes of the surrounding villages are known. The socio-economic situation of the Harijans who are mostly landless labourers, is no better than that of the tribals. But while the tribals are fairly timid; peace-loving people, the Harijans are more fiery and impulsively violent by temperament. Their loyalties are shifting in nature. So the vested interests began inciting them to steal tribal produce, destroy tribal crops and even to assault tribals.

In its analysis, Gram Vikas recognised that in order to unify the poor in a common struggle against injustice, discrimination, exploitation and poverty, time was ripe for making wider contacts than those existing with some of the non-tribal villages within the area with a large Harijan population. Rather than initiating contacts with the scheduled caste group alone, we decided upon the strategy of establishing links with the entire village community. The argument in favour of this approach was that the initial relationship that Gram Vikas might forge with the scheduled castes would be fragile and if perceived as a threat by the landlords and rich upper caste groups, in might invite immediate counter-pressure from them. Greater strength was required to resist these counter attacks. Moreover, there were likely to be non-scheduled caste groups also caught in the same throes of poverty and who might be interested in becoming partners in a process of self-liberation.

So Gram Vikas initiated contacts in several non-tribal villages. Recently, meetings have been held in village Medinipur, Sahala, Judugi and Singabadi. In January, 1979, the tribals registered a local organisation called Kerandimal Gana Sanghatan to give legality and strength to the people's movement which was taking shape in the area. This organisation is still in the process of becoming a well-knit, cohesive body, truly representative of the aspirations and hopes of the people. To date, nearly 60 villages are active participants in this organisation.

All along these years the committee members were aware that they were working mostly in the less inaccessible villages. Exploitation was much greater in the more interior areas where entire villages had sometimes succumbed to the usurious influence of the money lenders and Sundis. Besides, Kerandimal Gana Snaghatan and Gram Vikas continue to be approached by tribals from these villages with requests to extend our support to them in fighting their sowcars. So we realised that to be effective, we had to cover a much bigger area. We felt that any attempt at eradicating existing social evils cannot be confined to a small oasis, that such attempts must necessarily take the shape of a people's movement over a definite geographical area. Otherwise it is impossible to attack the very roots of a well-knit system of oppression.

So, towards the end of 1978, we had to make a difficult decision to extend our involvement to interior tribal villages. Despite the inaccessibility of the area and our own limited strength, we extended our work to another 30 villages in the hills. Today we are directly involved in about 70 villages and have indirect influence on another 30—a long way from our initial contact with 11 villages in 1977.

Education for Unity and Organisation

All the recent happenings—direct struggle against Sundi exploitation, attempt to reduce alcoholism, struggle against money lenders and various meetings that had been held, have been the richest education that the people could have. Yet we were convinced that unless action led to reflection and became a conscious, deliberate and continuing process, no amount of action and struggle would be truly liberating. So, in order to ensure this continuity of reflection-action-reflection, adult education was formally introduced into the programme around October 1978.

We opted to use young men from outside the region to play the vital role of 'social animators'. They would be fulltime workers with the dual function of adult education and social animation. Originally, we planned to have one animator per village and to develop our own teaching materials and syllabus based on the Paulo Freire method of creative dialogue and alphabetization.

However, we are now realising that there are several shortcomings in our original programme, because education of this type cannot be tightly time-tabled and programmed and requires 'facilitators' who are themselves 'concious' and aware. In fact, our biggest shortcoming was the 'animators', all of whom were outsiders and most had came more for the 'job' and the 'salary' than out of any deep committment to a qualitative transformation of society. So, how was the animator to get involved in a process of sensitising education when he himself was a prisoner of the same society and bound by its social, cultural, religious and economic frills? The first programme of education had to start with the animators—and it is still continuing.

Apart from the question of sensitised animators, another problem concerns 'programming'—organising into a time-table and compiling into a syllabus the volatile, dynamic and delicate aspects of human life. Thus, for example, while we go prepared for a discussion on money lending and its consequences, the immediate problem in a village might be the changing nature of man-woman relationship or the challenge of the younger generation to the old. Hence while we may be stuck with our 'target-oriented' approach to the money lending problem, the people may have no interest in it. This convinced us further, that despite the failure of the Young Formers' Club, we should make a renewed attemt to prepare leader among the tribal youth. No community can grow unless animation comes from within. And to have a future, it has to be through its youth.

Around February 1979, the first attempt at organising the

young men of the villages was made. However, it is only since September 1979 that something concrete has got off the ground. We now have a regular group of 60 young men who meet thrice a month for a day and who are gradually being initiated into an awareness of the situation in which tribals and other backward groups live in relation to the socio-economic-political realities of the Indian situation. Many of these young men show great promise in carrying on the awareness creation process that has begun and a lot of our energy at this stage is being directed into supporting this group.

The regular contact through an average of three meetings a month and work together that we now have with this group of 60 has grown out of a much greater analysis of non-tribal education than we did in our earlier programmes, especially the Young Farmers' Club. Now we realise that 'literacy' is not a priority for the people, nor is it one for us any more. Hence, if literacy is not an immediate priority, the role which the 'animators' were to play can very well be played by the tribal themselves and more effectively and realistically too.

We do not see this 'group of 60 becoming the 'animators' that we have today. We see them as the very beginning of some type of a 'cadre' or 'core group' belonging to the future of the tribals. Whether this 'future' is there or not or when it will come is deovolente. But it is part of our 'hope'—what we see as part of our 'task' to help these men glimpse what could be the future of the tribals of all mankind.

Unlike the 'Young Farmers' Clubs' where there was a basic confusion regarding 'purpose', at present we think that we are clearer on the 'why' and 'how'. This gives us greater hope in the success of the enterprise.

We had realised equally well right from the srart, that the education of the tribals can never be complete unless the women are organised. From the very beginning of the programme, we trained women to act as health educators' in their communities. We began with a batch of 8. We now have 20 women in the first batch and 40 more in two subsequent batches of animators. Each of them maintains a regular contact with the women of their villages and through them we are in contact with the entire female population of the area.

Initially, our health workers, chosen one from each village, worked only towards giving simple curative treatment and preventive health education. Gradually, however, we changed the pattern of training so as to equip them with broader leadership and organisational skills, for we were clear in our minds that health care and education could only be a tool for more important things.

Since August 1979, we have been holding monthly women's camps where all the women of a geographical unit come together. We have 8 such zonal groups. Usually, at these meetings local issues are raised to stimulate the awareness-building process and news happenings across the Kerandimals are shared and discussed. These meetings give women the opportunity to realise their rights and responsibilities. We still have a long way to go with them but we know that our work can never be complete untill more awareness and leadership emerges out of this group.

Factors to be Changed

As the educational process progressed, we realised that we should abandon some factors to which we had till then attached some importance—the dairy project being the first. When we first came to Narasinghpur, we had begun a small dairy farm with the intention of promoting animal husbandry as a subsidiary occupation among the tribal and non-tribal marginal farmers. We tried in village Narasinghpur itself by giving 10 families a cross-bred jersey cow each on loan basis. Despite allowing them the use of a common cow shed, arranging for veterinary care, purchase of feed, sale of milk, etc., this scheme was more or less a failure.

We were soon forced to realise that we should no longer

waste our time and resources on implementing a scheme which could hold no real hope for the category of people we wanted to reach. We felt that we ourselves were more concerned about the animals, the repayment of the loan, the sale of milk etc., than about the people, their acceptance of a new way of keeping cows. We perhaps over-managed the scheme for the people, with the result that they never really got sufficiently involved and soon most of them opted to sell their cows.

Besides, at that stage we had a predominantly development orientation, and continuation of the scheme could have confirmed us in it. Even now we still operate within this framework largely dependent on funding agencies. But we realise that people have to come first that we cannot be prisoners of a target-oriented approach, especially physical targets. We have to live in the tension between people's education and the economic aspect. On the one hand, many experiences of the past have clearly indicated that 'economics' alone will not solve the problems of the 'people'. And yet the group still believes that unless a man has certain basic natural conditions as part of his environment, he cannot give of his best. This basic tension is what perhaps gives a certain balance of approach favouring the material, social and political dimensions of our work. At the same time, it might also be an impediment for adopting a more radical fundamental approach.

We also had to give of our plan to start an agricultural cooperative. Many of the people we worked with had received agricultural waste land from the government without receiving the necessary financial assistance for its development. We wondered if these farmers could not be formed into co-operative groups for developing it. Accordingly, after several discussions with the people, we more or less cajoled them into accepting a scheme for co-op. land development. This scheme never really took off the ground because of the strongly individualistic mentality and private.interest of the people.

As already mentioned above, we also to give up our

attempts at creating alternative systems of marketing because of the close ties many tribals had with the merchants.

Evaluation of the Project Today

It is hardly three years since we got involeved in the Kerandimals and it is perhaps too early for an objective evaluation of the process that has been set in motion among the people in the area. However, we are able to pinpoint the reactions of the various groups and some specific options we had made, which today we see as positive or negative points in our approach.

There is certainly a marked change among the tribals in their level of awareness of their exploitation and their rights. With this increase in awareness, there has also grown an increase in the vocalization of their problems. The tribals have begun to experience the power of united action through a series of struggles against the Sundis, money lenders, school teachers, local health functionaries etc. The local power structures and functionaries of vested interested groups (like the Block, Health, Education and Tourist Departments) have begun to feel the backlash of tribal awakening. The tribals have now gained access to fair credit minus the bureaucratic red tape and corruption—a blow to the Agricultural Extension Officer (AEO) and the village level worker to whom credit disbursement was a source of extorting bribes. Many villages are demanding from the BDO more efficient and honest implementation of block development schemes. A spate of written complaints have been sent to the Education and Health Departments against absentee teachers, auxiliary nurse mid-wives, malaria workers etc. The Forest Department functionaries—the kings of the jungle—are now being challenged in their blantantly corrupt practices. The money lenders have been put in their place. Their so called legal documents have been proved to be worthless pieces of paper.

The above actions against age-old institutions of exploitation and injustice have certainly disturbed the existing relations of power and invited the wrath of local vested interests on the people and on us. The working relationship we had with the local Primary health Centre and the Health Department has gradually eroded. Our supply of free government drugs for malaria was stopped without a plausible explanation. One of our village animators was assaulted by a forest guard and later, a police complaint was loaged with the connivance of his superior on a trumped up charge of stealing forest produce, when actually the reverse was the case.

The most interesting reaction has been that of spreading a rumour among the local population that we are a Christian group with covert purpose of converting innocent tribals to Christianity. Another rumour that is circulating is that we have appropriated large amounts of money meant as subsidy on loans given to the tribals.

Besides these external vested interest groups, there is another group while the people we work with—a group of corrupt, reactionary leaders—who would have like the old laws to continue. These people, however, have not come out at yet in the open, and we assess that they cannot do any real harm. They will have to be gradually re-educated.

Besides, we notice many positive and negative points in our approach. On the positive side are:

1. our strategy to adopt a 'safe entry point' (health), gradually working towards a wider awareness building process;
2. gaining the full confidence of the people, building up some sort of a progressive leadership organisation before becoming involved in certain specific issues and the collective struggle for the redress of these grievances;
3. the early emphasis on training of cadres—women as 'health educators and animators', men as leaders of

grass root democracy, youth as the final hope for a deeper transformation of existing structures;

4. the co-ordination of all local leadership—women, committee members etc.—on a regional level;
5. decentralised pattern of our own organisation, we have as many volunteers as possible living in the villages where the people are; helping people to see not only their rights but also responsibilities as individuals and groups;
6. Involving the people's organisation, 'the K.G.S.' as much as possible in the decision-making process and facilitating educational and organisational processes to develop from the start, rather than being mere managers in development.

On the negative side we are faced with the eternal question "which came first—The chicken or the egg?' Today we analyse that many of the issues that were pin-pointed for stimulation of the awareness building process, perhaps followed too fast into programmes of action and struggle, the result being that "true consciousness' had not really developed among the people. Take for example, the struggle against the liquor manufactures culminating in the march to Berhampur. How many of the people who participated in this really understood the exploitative relation of the Sundis, the dynamics of a government that thrives on the exploitation of man by man? We are not sure. And yet at the same time, we analyse that the initiation of action against the Sundis, money lenders etc., was needed as a practical experience to sharpen the growth of a new conciousness among the people. Perhaps, we may need another epoch to really build up a qualitative change in our values, ideas, beliefs and hopes and for the time being must be content with the staggered development of our people from powerlessness etc., to a new unionisation and awareness.

Another such 'necessary evil' as it were, is our decision to use outsiders as 'agents of change'. Today we see more sharply that our original expectations of the 'animator' may never be realised because of the contradictions implicit in such a person who is an outsider, motivated by the 'salary' etc., and whose avowed interest is not the 'people'. The animators can only play a limited role. The real animators will be the young people who are now glimpsing new perspectives of thought and action about the future of their society.

Conclusion

We can see from the above that we have been partially successful in our work and have set a process in motion. We were successful with the initial group because of the choice of the entry points and our work could spread to a bigger area because of the proper choice of issues. With replicability in mind,we shall study the elements that led to this success and the role played by ourselves *i.e.*, outsiders.

Our point of entry in to the tribal society of the Kerandimals 3 years ago was 'health' in a very modest, subduned manner. We were not highly target and programme-oriented at all. Today we feel that we succeeded with the entry point because it was:

1. broad-based and brought us into close contact with all sections of the village community;
2. met immediate needs of people;
3. It was slow, steady, non-aggressive and kept pace with the people's acceptance of us as strangers.

The reason why our involvement spread so rapidly *i.e.*, to 100 villages in a span of 2 years in mainly because of certain definite issues that we got into:

1. release of mortgaged property;
2. implementation of institutional credit schemes for tribals;

3. support to individuals and groupes of tribals in various cases of naked exploitation and injustice.

In these issues we took a clear stand whereby we apparently gained the confidence of the tribals. Consequently, we were effective though we are outsiders.

In our particular case we are 'outsiders' in more than one sense. Firstly, we are not ourselves tribals. Secondly, some of us (5 in a group of 30) are not even Oriyas and this places us in an even more vulnerable, undesirable position. We continuously face so many obstacles—new culture, language, local politics . . . that one often wonders if one should not be working in one's home state. We cannot be the leaders of the movement—these leaders must be from among the people. The most we can do is to be 'midwives' who assist in the birth of these men and women who begin to find their identity and demand their legitimate place in society.

We do not think that our people have reached the stage when we could be called a 'people's movement'. And not having reached that stage we cannot really discuss out of praxis what elements of support a people's movement would require.

However, even at this rudimentary stage we realise that we are still more 'powerless' than 'powerful'. We do not have the support of a group outside the area, within the state. We need wider linkages, but with whom—a political party, tribal movements elsewhere, a support group of likeminded friends and supporters? We do not know. But all that we know is that movement for social changes cannot survive in isolation.

APPENDIX I

Eighth Plan Approach to Welfare and Development of SCs and STs

Background

In 1981, India had 105 million people belonging to Scheduled Castes, which constituted 15.75 per cent of the total population of the country. To this number should be added about 4.1 million neo-Buddhists specified as Scheduled Castes during 1990. The projected figure for 1991, assuming the same decadal increase as for the general population. Would be 134.74 million. More than twenty per cent of the population in Punjab (26.87 per cent), Himachal Pradesh (24.62 per cent), West Bengal (21.99 per cent) and Uttar Pradesh (21.16 per cent) belonged to the Scheduled Castes. Eight states, *viz.*, Uttar Pradesh, West Bengal, Bihar, Tamil Nadu, Andhra Pradesh, Madhya Pradesh, Rajasthan and Karnataka, accounted for 77.5 per cent of the total Scheduled Caste population of the country in 1981.

The population of Scheduled Tribals was 53.8 million in 1981, Constituting 7.8 per cent of the total population of the

Excerpt from Eighth Five Year Plan document, Government of India, Planning Commission, Reproduced with due acknowledgement.

country. In Jammu & Kashmir, Scheduled Tribes were notified in October. 1989, their estimated population being about 0.8 million. The projected figure for 1991, assuming the same decadal increase as for the general population, would be 67.4 million. Majority of the population of Arunachal Pradesh, Meghalaya, Mizoram, Nagaland, Dadra and Nagar Haveli and Lakshadweep are tribals. Madhya Pradesh (11.99 m). Orissa (5.92 m) and Bihar (5.81 m) accounted for about 46 per cent of the total tribal population of the country in 1981.

A number of Constitutional provisions of the interests of these weaker sections. In conformity with the Directive Principles of State Policy, social justice has been an avowed goal of development. During the four decades of planning, a variety of programmes were launched with the objective of improving the socio-economic condition of Scheduled Castes and Scheduled Tribes. These measures have, no doubt, yielded results but not commonsurate with the efforts or the needs of the target groups.

A specific sector of Backward Classes was included from the First Plan to cater to the special needs of Scheduled Castes/ Scheduled Tribes/Other Backward Classes. It was visualised that the general development programmes should be so designed as to take care of the needs of Backward Classed as well and the special provisions in the Backward Classes Sector would be additive, to be used, as far as possible, for meeting the special developmental needs of these groups. Unfortunately, this expectation was belied in most cases and the Backward Classes Sector provisions, instead of supplementing the general sectors of development, tended to supplant the general sector provisions. It was, in this context, that the concept of Tribal Sub-Plan was introduced during the Fifth Plan and Special Component Plan for Scheduled Caste during the Sixth Plan to facilitate monitoring of development programmes for the benefit of Scheduled Castes and Scheduldled Tribes.

Review of Seventh Plan and 1990-92 Plans

In the Seventh Plan, Special Component Plans for Scheduled

Castes, Tribal Sub-Plans for Scheduled Tribes and specific schemes for the welfare and development of Scheduled Castes and Scheduled Tribes were implemented. At the end of the the Plan, the Tribal Sub-Plan strategy was being implemented through 191 Integrated Tribal Development Projects, 268 pockets of tribal concentration (Modified Area Development Approach—MADA), 74 clusters and 74 primitive tribal group projects. There was substantial increase in the flow of funds for the development of Scheduled Castes and Scheduled Tribes, resulting in expansion of infrastructural facilities and enlargement of coverage. There was limited involvement of Scheduled Castes/Scheduled Tribes in the formulation and execution of programmes resulting in non-adaptability of schemes/policies to cater to their specific needs.

Emphasis was laid in the Seventh Plan on the educational development of Scheduled Castes and Scheduled Tribes. Prematric stipends and scholarships were gives by the State Governments to 190 lakhs, Scheduled Caste/Scheduled Tribe/ Other Backward Class students. Other educational incentives included free supply of uniform, stationery and text-books to about 100 lakh students. Post-matric scholarships were given to about 15 lakh Scheduled Caste and Scheduled Tribe students in 1991-92 as against 9.75 lakh scholarships in 1985-86 and only 1.56 lakh scholarships in 1968-69. These scholarships were given for study of post-matriculation/post secondary courses of study in arts, science, commerce, as well as professional and technical degree/diploma and certificate courses on the basis of a graded means test. For Scheduled Caste and Scheduled Tribe students studying in medical and engineering colleges, a scheme of book banks was started in 1978-79 which benifited about 21,000 students in 1990-91. Hostel facilities for Scheduled Cast and Scheduled Tribe students were considerably expanded.

For the enconomic development of Scheduled Castes and Scheduled Tribes, two national level institutions were set up:

(i) Tribal Cooperative Marketing Development Federation

in 1987 as an apex body for State Tribal Development Cooperative employment Corporations; and

(ii) National Scheduled Castes and Scheduled Tribes Finance and Development Corporation, primarily to act as a catalytic agent in developing schemes for employment generation and financing piloy projects.

The Scheduled Caste and the Scheduled Tribe Development Corporations in the States continued to provide economic assistance for self-employment projects. Economic assistance was given to 118.82 lakh Scheduled Caste families and 52.76 lakh Scheduled Tribe families under various programmes including IRDP. Margin money loan was disbursed to 22.56 lakh Scheduled Caste families through 21 State Scheduled Caste Development Corporations.

Special consideration was accorded to Scheduled Caste and Scheduled Tribe families in the Integrated Rural Development Programme (IRDP), the most important poverty alleviation programme in the country. The target of coverage of Scheduled Caste/Scheduled Tribe beneficiaries in the Seventh Plan was 30 per cent of the total number of beneficiaries. However, the actual coverage was 32.05 per cent in the case of Scheduled Castes and 13.04 per cent in the case of Scheduled Tribe beneficiaries. A target of 50 per cent has been fixed for Scheduled Caste and Scheduled Tribe beneficiaries with effect from April 1990. Since 1990-91, Scheduled Caste beneficiaries are being treated at par with Scheduled Tribe beneficiaries for subsidy purposes, both getting 50 per cent subsidy subject upto a ceiling of Rs. 5,000. Prior to 1990-91, the subsidy admissible to Scheduled Cast families was only 33 $^{1}/_{3}$ per cent. In the wage employment programme of Jawahar Rozgar Yojana, preference is given to Scheduled Castes/Scheduled Tribes and freed bonded labourers. It has also been provided that at the village panchayat level, 15 per cent of the annual allocation must be spent on items of work which directly benefit the Scheduled Castes and the Scheduled Tribes. Diversion of funds meant for Scheduled Castes and Scheduled Tribes is not permitted.

TABLE 1

Percentage of Scheduled Caste/Scheduled Tribe representation in Central Government Services

Category	Scheduled Castes		Scheduled Tribes	
	1-1-71	*1-1-91*	*1-1-71*	*1-1-91*
Class I	2.58	9.09	0.41	2.53
Class II	4.06	11.82	0.43	2.35
Class III	9.59	15.65	1.70	4.98
Class IV	18.37	21.24	3.65	6.82
	(excluding Sweepers)			

Percentage of Scheduled Caste/Scheduled Tribe Representation in Public Sector Undertakings

Category	Scheduled Castes		Scheduled Tribes	
	1971	*1989*	*1971*	*1989*
Class I	0.52	5.76	0.17	1.29
Class II	1.54	8.41	0.16	2.31
All categories	8.17	20.36	2.24	9.68

(Separately for Cl. III & IV not available)

To enhance the competitive ability of Scheduled Caste and Scheduled Tribe students, about 8,000 seats were created in 101 pre-examination training centres where coaching was given to candidates appearing in competitive examinations for entry into public services. The Scheduled Caste and Scheduled Tribe candidates have been able to increase their representation in Central Government Services and Public Sector Undertakings over the years, as seen from the Table 1, due mainly to implementation of reservation policy coupled with educational and coaching facilities.

For elimination of scavenging, about 10 lakh service latrines in 490 towns in 19 States were taken up for conversion into pour flush latrines. Reports indicate that by the end of the Seventh Plan, 9.63 lakh dry latrines were converted, 14,529 seavengers rehabliitated and scavenging was eliminated from 40 towns.

The Protection of Civil Rights Act, 1955 and the Scheduled Castes and the Scheduled Tribes (Prevention of Atrocities) Act, 1989 are the two important legislations to deal with untouchability offences and check commission of crimes on Scheduled Castes and Scheduled Tribes. Fiftyseven special courts for trial of offences under the Protection of Civil Rights Act have been set up in eight States. Similarly, for implementation of the Scheduled Castes and Scheduled Tribes (Prevention of Atrocities) Act, State Government and Union Territory Administrations have specified existing District and Session's Courts as special courts for trial of offences under this Act. Exclusive special courts have also been set up in Rajasthan and Andhra Pradesh. Monetary relief and rehabilitation assistance were given to the victims of atrocities. Schemes to encourage inter-caste marriages and legal aid were implemented. Programmes were developed through the media, both formal and non-formal, against the evil practice of untouchability.

Details of outlays and expediture for Special Component Plan/Tribal Sub-Plan and Backward Classes Sector during the Seventh Plan are given in Table 2.

Current Status

A very large number of Scheduled Castes and Scheduled tribes continue to be socially and educationally backward and are languishing at the bottom of the social and economic pyramid. In rural areas, in 1987-88,the percentage of Scheduled Caste population below the poverty line was 44.7 and of Scheduled Tribe population 52.6, as compared to the All-India percentage of 33.4. The

TABLE 2

(*Rs. in crores*)

Sl. No.	Item	Seventh Plan Quality	Seventh Plan Expenditure
A.	Scheduled Castes		
1.	Flow from States Plan to SCP*	7385.42	6916.92
2.	Special Central Assistance	930.00	876.00
B.	Scheduled Tribes		
1.	Flow from States Plan to TSP*	6216.76	7074.50
2.	Special Central Assistance	756.00	847.00
C.	Backward Classes Sector—SCs/STs/OBCs		
1.	Centre/CSS	281.22	388.42**
2.	States Sector	1239.33	1456.13

*Include outlay/expnd. under backward classes sector. Excluding share capital contribution of Rs. 50 crores to National Scheduled Castes and Scheduled Tribes Finance and Development Corporation.

**Includes grant-in-aid of Rs. 10 crores to Tribal Cooperative Marketing Development Federation.

comparative picture in the incidence of poverty during the period 1977-78 to 1987-88 is given below:

TABLE 3

(*in percentage*)

Year	*Total Population*	*Sch. Castes*	*Sch. Tribes*
1977-78	51.2	64.6	72.4
1983-84	40.4	53.1	58.4
1987-88	33.4	44.7	52.6

Thus, while there has been a reduction in the percentage of population below the poverty line in the case of both Scheduled Castes and Scheduled Tribes, the incidence of poverty is still very high. Most of the Scheduled Caste and Scheduled Tribe families do not land or other productive assets. The constitute bulk of agricultural landless workers, construction workers and workers in the unorganised sector. They suffer from long periods of unemployment and under-employment. They are also handicapped due to non-enforcement of protective laws such as the Minimum Wages Act and Prevention of Land Alienation Acts. Inequality and exploitation of Scheduled Castes and Scheduled Tribes, particularly in the rural areas, whether in the form of bonded labour or in other forms, both latent and manifest, still continue. Poverty, ignorance, lack of options in employment opportunities and non-existance of organisations which can fight for their rights, facilitate the continuance of age old exploitation. Scheduled Caste and Scheduled Tribe families have often not been able to derive the full benefit of development programmes. Wrong identification of beneficiaries, poor selection of projects, unrealistic and simplistic assumptions in regard to their viability, administrative costs, and leakages have been other problems which have been further problems which have been further compounded by a largely unresponsive administrative structure.

The dwindling resource base of the tribal people in the shape of loss of land, restriction on access to forest produce, and lack of opportunities for reasonable ways employment and usurious money lending have caused hardships to tribal people. Consequently, developmental inputs for the benefit of these people have had little impact. Significantly, development processes have interfered in many cases with traditional tribal institutional structure and ethos and have produce negative results. These were the contributory factors for dissatisfaction amongst tribal people and simmering unrest in some tribal areas.

The literacy rate amongst Scheduled Castes and Scheduled Tribes has no doubt increased over the years but the levels are still very low. The gap in literacy between Scheduled Castes, Scheduled Tribes and the rest of the population has been increasing, as is evident from Table 4.

TABLE 4

All India Literacy Rate of Scheduled Castes and Scheduled Tribes

(*Percentage*)

Year	*Scheduled Castes*	*Scheduled Tribes*	*Rest of the Population*	*Gap between rest of the population and*	
				Scheduled Castes	*Scheduled Tribes*
1961	10.27	8.53	27.86	17.59	19.33
1971	14.67	11.30	33.80	19.13	22.50
1981	21.38	16.35	41.22	19.84	24.87

Variation in literacy rates among the different castes and the different tribes is also family pronounced. Among certain Scheduled Caste and Scheduled Tribe communities, the percentage of literacy in 1981 was below five per cent. There is also wide inter-State variation in literacy levels of Scheduled Castes and Scheduled Tribes. For instance, in the case of Scheduled Castes, Kerala, according to the 1981 Census, had a literacy rate of 55.96 per cent, while Bihar had only 10.40 per cent. Likewise, in the case of Scheduled Tribes, Manipur had a literacy rate of 39.74 per cent while Andhra Pradesh had only 7.82 per cent. Among females, in both the categories, literacy rate is very low. In the case of Scheduled Castes it was 10.93 per cent and for Scheduled Tribes 8.04 per cent, in 1981.

A large number of Scheduled Caste and Scheduled Tribe children discontinue their studies prematurely before completing the level for which they were enrolled. The dropout rate in 1986-87 for classes I-V was 50.79 in the case of Scheduled Castes and 66.12 in the case of Scheduled Tribes. In classes I to VIII, the dropout rates were as high as 69.15 per cent and 80.19 per cent respectively.

Untouchability stands abolished by virtue of Article 17 of the Constitution and its practice in any form is punishable. But Social discrimination against Scheduled Castes still linger in many parts of the country. It is a matter of concern that inspite of legal measures in the form of Protection of Civil Rights Act 1955 and the Scheduled Castes and the Scheduled Tribes (Prevention of Atrocities) Act, 1989, 76,748 cases of atrocities against persons belonging to Scheduled Castes and 17,101 cases of atrocities against Scheduled Tribes were reported between 1986 and 1990. Of these, 3,328 cases were of murder, 5,339 of rape and 4,325 of arson.

The development process in many tribal araes, instead of providing succour, has been instrumental in causing numerous disadvantages, prominent among them being displacement and loss of land, the tribal's main resource base. Notwithstanding the fact that the State Governments have enacted law/regulations to control/prohibit transfer of land to non-tribals, land alienation still continues.

While educational development programmes have widened the opportunities for Scheduled Castes and Scheduled Tribes, the number of job seekers among Scheduled Castes and Scheduled Tribes has also increased. At the end of 1990, there were 44.53 lakh Scheduled Caste and 11.48 lakh Scheduled Tribe job seekers on the live register of Employment Exchanges as compared to 19.69 lakh and 5.54 lakh respectively in 1981. The number of placements during 1989 was only 0.47 lakh in the case of Scheduled Caste job seekers and 0.27 lakh in the case of Scheduled Tribe job seekers.

Strategy for the Eighth Plan

In the nineties there has to be an intensification of efforts to bridge the gap in the levels of development of the Scheduled Castes, Scheduled Tribes, Backward Classes and other sections of the population so that by turn of the century those disadvantaged sections of population are brought on par with the rest of the society in all spheres of national endeavour. Problems of access for Scheduled Castes and Scheduled Tribes of programmes and services have to be identified and removed Elimination of exploitation of Scheduled Castes and Scheduled Tribes and removal of all forms of oppression of Scheduled Castes and Scheduled Tribes must receive high priority. Untouchability, suppression of rights, usurious money lending, land alienation, non-payment of minimum wages, and restrictions on right to collect minor forest produce have to be removed to enable these people to avail of the benefits of development efforts.

Problems of Scheduled Castes and Scheduled Tribes have to be tackled by suitable streamlining of the mechanism of planning and implementation of programmes of special Component Plan, Tribal Sub-Plan, and the schemes specifically targetted for the welfare and development of Scheduled Castes and scheduled Tribes. The strategy of Special Component Plan for Scheduled Castes and Tribal Sub-Plan will be reviewed *inter-alia* to make them effective instruments of planning to ensure real and tangible flow of benefits to the target, group, both individuals and families.

Re-orientation of administrative structure at all levels for functional coordination, integration and effective delivery of services will be necesary. There is considerable inter-caste and inter-tribe variation in the levels of socio-economic development of Scheduled Castes and Scheduled Tribes and in the social and economic organisation of their life. It is essential that planning gives full cognizance to these variations and responds to their specific problems and needs and the socio-cultural values of the community through decentralised participatory planning.

Alleviation of poverty through sustained employment and generation of incomes is vital so that at least the basic needs are met. National poverty alleviation programmes will have to ensure that the Scheduled Castes and Scheduled Tribes are able to derive adequate benefit. Skill development programmes will be necessary to improve their earnings and help them to diversify into trades and occupations. It will also be necessary to provide assistance to Scheduled Castes and Tribes in the matter of choice of projects, marketing, procurement of raw materials, and introduction of new technologies.

Elimination of scavenging and rehabilitation of scavengers will be an important programme in the Eighth Plan. Education, training and other incentives will be provided to children of parents engaged in unclean occupations so that they can prepare themselves for occupations, which provide better incomes and a higher social status. Occupations like tanning and leather work would be modernised with improved technology to remove the stigma attached to these professions and to produce goods which have a better market.

A national policy on rehabilitation of people displaced by large-development projects will need to be evolved. It is important that project authorities give as much attention to this aspect as to the projects themselves and ensure that full rehabiliation is completed before or by the time the projects become operational. Rights and concessions of the tribals in forests should be codified and the Forest Policy implemented in letter and spirit to maintain the symbiotic relationship between the tribals and the forests.

When belonging to the Scheduled Castes and Scheduled Tribes are in a far worse situation by all development indicators. Poverty and deprivation affect them more adversely. Although they work along with men, they are not recognised as producers in their own right. The strategy for the development of Scheduled Castes and Scheduled Tribes will have to include a major thrust for the benefit of women folk.

Voluntary organisations will need to be promoted and assisted to play a partnership role in the designing and implementation of programmes. Their role in advocacy and acceleration of the process of change and development and in playing a constructive role of intermediaries in general and in innovating new programme structures, in organising and preparing the people and in giving them as take in the success of their endeavours, in particular has to be recognised. Voluntary organisations can also help in the training of grass-root level workers and in mobilising community resources.

Facilities like schools, hostels and institutional structures for health care, nutrition, drinking water supply, road linkages and housing will be made availage in such a manner that these promote integration of Scheduled Castes and Scheduled Tribes with the rest of the society. Agencies and institutions excelling in promotion of integration and removal of all discriminatory practices will be suitably encouraged through appropriate incentives.

Programmes

While both Scheduled Castes and Scheduled Tribes lag behind the general population on most of the social and economic development indicators and in several areas the developmental needs are common, there are some important aspects in which the problems of Scheduled Castes and Scheduled Tribes differ. For instance, the Scheduled Castes suffer not only from economic backwardness but also from social disabilities. The Scheduled Tribes problems arise from geographical isolation characterised by low level of techno-economic development and wide varation in the levels of living between different areas and different tribal groups but all the same assiduously retaining their distinct socio-cultural identity in a large measure. The programmes for these groups during the Eighth Plan will, therefore, need to be attuned to meet specific needs of these communities.

Educational Development of Scheduled Castes

For the educational development of Scheduled Castes and Scheduled Tribes, steps will be taken to ensure that at both pre-matric and post-matric stages, the problems such as high dropout rate, stagnation, non-enrolment of girl students and uneven growth amongst specified communities are effectively tackled. While the general sector would take care of the institutional arrangements for locating the necessary infrastructure, the programmes under the Backward Classes Sector would continue to pay special attention in supplementing these through incentives and support services.

At the pre-matric stage, programmes covering scholarships, boarding grants, hostel facilities, free supply of books, stationery and uniform and mid-day meals will be expanded. An appropriate package of services will be worked out to promote literacy and raise the level of education of communities where the current level is very low. Special attention will be paid to the retention of the girl child in school.

The post-matric scholarship scheme for Scheduled Castes and Scheduled Tribes in operation since 1944-45 has helped students from these communities to pursue higher education. Although the rates of scholarship under the scheme have been increased from time to time, no structural changes aimed at increasing employment opportunities have been made. The attempt during the Eighth Plan would be to rationalise the scheme to:

(i) provide guidance with reference to employment opportunities and offering appropriate incentives for courses which have a larger market demand;

(ii) improve the performance, if necessary by prescribing minimum standards; and

(iii) identify causes for inter-caste/tribe variation in availing benefits under the scheme and chalk out appropriate remed ial action.

Economic Development of Scheduled Castes

The economic development of Scheduled Caste families will be given high priority. The Scheduled Caste and Scheduled Tribe Development Corporations will strengthen their activities to enable proper identification of beneficiaries; selection of projects in non-traditional as well as traditional areas and matching them with the capabilities of the beneficiaries; provide financial assistance in the form of margin money or direct loan on concessional rate of interest in order to lessen the burden of repayment liability; facilitate the flow of credit through financial institutions for these projects; ensure tie-up with poverty alleviation programmes like IRDP; provide infra-structure support where necessary to enable the group of beneficiaries to take up their own ventures in a common work place; organise training in different skills to the target group; arrange for inputs such as supply of raw-material, marketing of finished goods, etc.; and monitor the implementation of the projects.

A time-bound programme, to be completed within the period of Eighth Plan, will be launched to achieve complete elimination of scavenging. The objective will be achieved by:

(i) making provisions of flush latrines mandatory in every house in urban areas and

(ii) providing alternative work opportunities to those presently engaged in scavenging.

For this purpose, necessary training facilities will be provided and rehabilitation undertaken.

The National Scheduled Castes and Scheduled Tribes Finance and Development Corporation would take up projects for the benefit of Scheduled Castes and Scheduled Tribes. In addition, the Federation would organise training courses to provide skills.

Other Programmes

Under the provisions of the Protection of Civil Rights Acts, most of the State Governments have taken measures for effective implementation of the Act including appointment of officers for initiating or exercising supervision over prosecutions, setting up of Special/Mobile Courts, appointment of Committees at the appropriate levels, periodic surveys on the working of the provisions of the Act and identification of areas where persons are under any disabilities arising from 'untouchability'. Later, in 1989, the Scheduled Castes and the Scheduled Tribes (Prevention of Atrocities) Act was promulgated to prevent commission of offences and atrocities against the members of the Scheduled Castes and the, Scheduled Tribes involving their person, dignity and property. The measures taken for implementation of the Act include strengthening of existing police cells, mobile squads, increasing the number of special and mobile courts for trying atrocities cases, survey of untouchability prone areas, provision of legal aid and relief, encouraging inter-caste mrrriages, monitoring, publicity and propaganda. The endeavour during the Eighth Plan will be to strengthen the enforcement of Protection of Civil Rights Act, 1955 and Scheduled Castes and Scheduled Tribes (Prevention of Atrocities) Act 1989 and undertake programmes for mass awakening leading to attitudinal changes.

Educational Development of Scheduled Tribes

For the educational development of scheduled tribes, existing programmes for prematric and post-matric educotion of Scheduled Tribes will be continued. Residential schools, including ashram schools, will be expanded. As envisaged in the National Policy on Education, 1986, priority will be accorded to the opening of primary schools in tribal areas. The socio-cultural milieu of the Scheduled. Tribes will be taken into consideration in developing the curricula and devising the instructional materials in tribal languages at the initial stages with arrangements for switching over to the regional language. Anganwadis, non-formal and adult education centres will be established in tribal areas on a priority basis. Further, the curriculum at all stages of education will be so designed as to create an awareness of the rich cultural identity of the tribal people as also of their enormous creative talent.

Economic Development of Scheduled Tribes

The Tribal Cooperative Marketing Development Federation through the State Tribal Development Cooperative Corporations would organise collection and marketing of minor forest produce in such a way as to ensure reasonable returns to tribals. A new policy on Minor Forest Produce in relation to the Scheduled Tribes will be formulated. The cooperative structure in the field for this purpose will be suitably reoriented and restructured.

The functioning of cooperative institutions including Large Multipurpose Cooperative Societies (LAMPS) in tribal areas will be reviewed with a view to meeting the genuine needs of tribal people in forests, credit, marketing of minor forest produce and supply of essential commodities. In addition, cooperatives for different occupational groups amongst the Scheduled Tribes will be formed. Essential productive and managerial skills would be developed in them through training and entrepreneurial development programmes so that they may seek self-employment. Measures aimed at greater participation of tribal people in conservation and development of forests and preservation of ecology, in a manner that their traditional rights relating to forest produce are not adversely affected, would be undertaken. Also, rights and concessions of the tribals in forests would need to be codified to ensure unhindered access to minor forest produce and use of forest resources by the tribals.

Limited access to credit for consumption and production purposes has resulted in increased dependence of Scheduled Tribes on money lenders/traders leading to:

(a) siphoning of developmental benefits in order to

discharge loan liabilities to money lenders and traders; and

(b) loss of resource base in the form of land or other assets.

An important objective during the Eighth Plan will, therefore, be to provide increased access to credit from banks and cooperative institutions.

For the primitive tribal groups, detailed plans will be prepared for their economic development, as far as possible, with the family as the unit. Infra-structure and other developmental needs will be specifically identified so that an integrated plan is developed. Schemes will be developed which take into account the social and economic organisation of life of these communities, their interests, aptitudes and abilities.

A viable and lasting solution to the problem of shifting cultivation, involving an area of about 10 million hectares affecting 6 lakh tribal families, is yet to the found. Even though special programmes under the Central Plan including a Centrally Sponsored Scheme with an outlay of 75 crores, have been operating and these have been supplemented by the States own schemes, many of them have been unable to make any real impact. During the Eighth Plan, schemes on water-shed basis, in which sectoral programmes like agriculture, forestry, horticulture, infrastructural and social services facilities will be interwoven in an integrated and viable manner to enable the shifting cultivators to take to settled cultivation.

Originally created for meeting the manpower requirements for exploitation and regeneration of forest resources, the forest villages numbering about 5000, wherein more than 2 lakh tribal people live, have remained largely deprived of normal developmental benefits. In March 1984, the Ministry of Agriculture had advised the State Governments to confer long-term heritable but inalienable rights, say for 15-20 years, in respect of lands in occupation of tribals for more than 20 years. But this suggestion does not seem to have been fully implemented. In September 1990, the Ministry of Environment and Forests advised the State Governments to convert the forests villages into Revenue villages after denotifying requisite land as forest. It was further suggested that administration of these and other Revenue villages in forest areas should be entrusted to the State Forest Departments. While details of conversion are not readily forthcoming, the progress does not seem to be encouraging.

During the Eighth Plan an attempt will be made to reach developmental benefits to forest villages in a manner suited to the situation. Arrangements for review, on a regular basis, of the functioning of developmental schemes in forest villages for their all-round development, keeping in tune with environmental requirements, will be made.

Other Programmes

Legal and administrative measures and programmes aimed at elimination of exploitation in matters relating to land, forest, money lending, trade and labour will receive priority attention. These will be so implemented as to ensure for the Scheduled Tribes, the retention of basic resources like land, access to minor forest produce especially items for food, fuel and fodder and self and wage employment opportunities.

Peoples' initiative and participation would be made a key element in the process of development of Scheduled Castes and Scheduled Tribes and protecting their interests. Towards achieving this end, peoples' initiative and participation would be enlisted through continued assistance to non-governmental organisations working amongst Scheduled Castes and Scheduled Tribes. Research will be carried out to help identify the problems of Scheduled Castes and Scheduled Tribes. Tribal Research Institutes in the States will be activated to undertake concurrent evaluation of programmes under implementation. A bench-mark survey was undertaken in 1978 in tribal areas. It would be useful to undertake a similar survey in respect of the Tribal areas during the Eighth Plan.

Most of the State Governments have drawn up their own lists of socially and educationally backward classes and are implementing developmental schemes for them, mainly in the field of education. For the denotified communities, nomadic and semi-nomadic groups, rehabilitation measures have been taken up. Some State Governments like Andhra Pradesh. Assam, Gujarat, Haryana, Jammu and Kashmir, Karnataka and Maharashtra have also set up Development Corporations for other Backward Classes and Denotified Tribes. Efforts during the Eighth Plan will be to critically examine the ongoing schemes and modify them to more effectively cater to the needs of different groups amongst these communities.

The National Backward Classes Finance and Development Corporation will promote the economic and other developmental activities for the benefit of the backward classes. Assistance will be given to promote self-employment and other ventures subject to such income and/or economic criteria as may be prescribed from time to time.

An outlay of Rs. 2548 crores in the Central Sector, including Rs. 1125 crores as Special Central Assistance for Special Component Plan for Scheduled Castes and Rs. 3086.06 crores for the State Plan under Backward Classes Sector have been provided. In addition, a provision of Rs. 12·0 crores has been made for Special Central Assistance to Tribal sub-plan.